THE LIBERAL
MIDDLE CLASS:
MAKER OF RADICALS

THE LIBERAL
MIDDLE CLASS:
MAKER OF RADICALS

Richard L. Cutler

ARLINGTON HOUSE　　　　*New Rochelle, New York*

Library of Congress Catalog Card Number 73-76193

ISBN 0-87000-210-4

MANUFACTURED IN THE UNITED STATES OF AMERICA

To
a sane America
and
her children's future

CONTENTS

PREFACE

Though the title and much of the content of this book deal with the radical minority of young people in America, it is in addition a work about the general condition of our country: about where we are, and how we got that way. When I began to write it, I had in mind a more limited purpose—merely to try to add to our understanding of the radicalism of some young Americans; its origins, its various expressions, and its possible future course. In attempting to do this I soon perceived that radicalism was not something that stood apart from the rest of American life in the 1960s and 1970s; rather, it was the result of some basic and pervasive conditions in American society as a whole. An understanding of these conditions became necessary to an understanding of the young radicals.

It also became necessary to ask and to attempt to answer some questions that have occurred to all of us at one time or another, questions about our country and our children: How, in the midst of affluence, technological progress, and great promise for the future, could a small but important group of our children become turned off on the system, alienated from the mainstream of society, embittered about our prospects, and desolate about our mutual future? How could our system, which seems to the majority to have delivered so much and to promise so much more, seem to the minority to represent an utter, immoral, despicable failure? How could rancor and distrust have come to replace good faith and belief in one another? How could the promise of the "great society" of 1964 have been translated into the cries and ugliness of the "sick society," as some came to characterize us short years later? In short, how could there have developed among us, in less than a decade, such a remarkable set of schisms that we were no longer a vital, confident, and united people, but instead were rent by strife, violence, unhappiness, crime, and suspicion?

Many easy answers have been proposed to these questions. Most involve matters that represent the momentary political hobbyhorse of the respondent, and have the simplistic appeal the demagogue needs to rouse his following. Depending on the tide of the moment and the potential popularity of the issue, the mess we are in has variously been the fault of the Vietnam War, the racial crisis, the repressive nature of the system, poverty, the pollution of the environment, the failure of the educational system, materialism, imperialism, or one or another kind of immoral exploitation. The imaginative demagogue with a truly cosmic flair will even suggest that all of these are of a piece, interrelated in some highly complex but unstated way, and representing different faces of the totally evil system. Fortunately, there are few among us sufficiently gullible or paranoid to swallow that, but the appeal of simple explanations, oft repeated, is great. In fact, America's troubles are much deeper than any of these simple explanations or any combination thereof would suggest. To understand fully where we are and how we came to our present condition, we must examine closely how changes in our society over the past few decades have slowly but surely altered our national attitudes, subverted many of our traditional institutions and approaches, and now threaten in a fundamental way to lose for us not only a highly successful system of government, but also the basic personal freedoms on which our way of life has been based. How this has come about, and how it relates to the emergence of radicalism among some of our youth, is one of my main themes.

Throughout this book you will find two sometimes conflicting attitudes expressed. One of these is concern: about the damage already done to our country, about our country's future course and strength, and about the loss of a decent future for many of our youth, which has already resulted from their dabbling in various forms of the new radicalism. The other is faith: in the ability of the nation finally to solve its problems, and to find a new strength and pride with which to reverse the trend to mediocrity and decadence; and in the resiliency and common sense of the vast majority of our young people, who may ultimately be trusted to rise to the challenges of their time, and, in the context of a free society, to deal with these challenges with energy and responsibility.

I have spent my entire adult life working closely with young people. For more than ten years I taught at a major university, and for another seven I was an administrator at the same institution. More recently, as a psychologist in private practice, I have worked almost exclusively with the problems and frustrations of children and young adults. In almost every case, I have found reason to respect their energy and idealism, to sympathize with their difficulties, and to share in their aspirations. I have also found reason to worry about the stress to which they are exposed, the temptation offered them by the easy answer and the demagogue, the damage many of them have already suffered, and the poor job we are doing in preparing them to deal with the very difficult problems they will have to solve. But it is rare to find a young person so disturbed, dulled by drugs, embittered by radicalism, or corrupted by indulgence that one cannot reach to the core of common sense, reason, and responsibility within him and help him to recover the prospect of a satisfying and productive future. Thus, when I engage in occasional critical commentary of the radical minority, the reader should keep in mind that such criticism is not intended for the majority of our young people, and that my faith in them and their ability to take responsible custody of the future is not impaired. Even though the destructive and self-defeating nature of the spreading radicalism represents a grim and occasionally discouraging panorama, I believe that the reader will find, as I have, that the steadfast purpose of most young Americans justifies a long-run optimism.

My concern about and faith in our nation and its system of government is in many ways similar to my feelings about our young people. I see many of its deficiencies and am occasionally frustrated by the absence of quick solutions to our national problems. Personal experience and observation have convinced me, however, that none of the alternatives offers equal hope of success without a destructive sacrifice of personal freedom, economic stability, or social order. I am concerned about our present condition not only because of the well-recognized prob-

11

lems we face but also because certain other factors, most of which are not even recognized as problems, have endangered our will to stand up to our responsibilities and make the tough decisions and sacrifices necessary to the solution of the recognized problems. But even here, my faith dominates my concern. I have been most fortunate in the breadth of exposure I have had to American life. From the crossroads hamlet in which I grew up and the one-room country school I attended as a child, through World War II service in the navy and periods of study at the regional teachers' college and the state university graduate school, to struggling with the problems of individuals, universities, and cities, I have had a fair sample of what America and its people are like. In every case, however desperate the moment, however trying the challenge, I have always found a basic commitment among the people to do what had to be done to make things better, and an inspiring willingness to have reason dominate impulse and future override present. Out of this experience has grown an unabashed pride in our country and our heritage, and a fundamental patriotism that transcends the fashion of making light of such virtues as country, family, and apple pie. Once again, when I am critical of our self-indulgence, or of our tendency sometimes to drift away from the tough decisions and to be taken in by slogans and glitter, the criticism is intended as a statement of concern rather than as a destructive assault on our national character. Only out of such candid facing of some of our weaknesses, I believe, can come a rebirth of strength, purpose, and unity.

One final comment about the scope of this book is in order. Much of its focus is on the liberal middle class in America, and the attitudes and behavior this subgroup communicates to its children. While this group has been influential on American society out of proportion to its numbers, it is neither very representative of nor importantly influential among black Americans. Most middle-class blacks in America have generally middle-of-the-road to conservative attitudes toward child rearing, and cannot be considered liberal on most political matters, with the obvious exception of the race issue. Thus I do not provide an explanation of the sources of radicalism among middle-class black youth—not because such an understanding is less important than what I have tried to do in this book, but because the causes and expression, as well as the goals, of middle-class—and non-middle-class—black radicalism are so significantly different from those of our liberal middle-class white children as to require a separate and equally extensive treatment. Also, while I believe that one does not have to be able to lay an egg to tell a good one from a bad one, I think it is inappropriate at this time for a middle-class white man to try, however earnestly, to explain why middle-class—or poor—black people, radical or not, behave as they do. The most sincere and objective effort possible would not remove questions about credibility and racism in a white author. Therefore I have made no attempt to explain radicalism among young blacks, although I do believe that my conclusions have a validity for middle-class young people, regardless of race.

Finally, as in every other undertaking of my life, I owe a series of debts, for several people have been part of the creation of this book. First, to my children, Patrice and Scott, whose steadfastness and decency secure my faith in our future. Next, to those who have provided intellectual stimulation, technical suggestions, and tangible support, including Stephen Tonsor, Alex Sherriffs, James Lee and his colleagues, and W. Glen Campbell and the staff of the Hoover Institution, of which particular gratitude is due Edward Boccaccio, whose dissertation served as a basis for needed improvements in Chapter II. Next, to my secretaries, Debbie Huffman and Marilyn Kisly, who have stood up under great pressure and tolerated my changing too many passages too many times. Next, to the thousands of students and hundreds of patients I have known well, who have given me the opportunity to share in their lives, sharpening my thinking and moving me to the writing of a book that I hope will assist in making their nation stronger and their lives more fulfilling. And finally, to Polly, who represents every decent and tender instinct of the human spirit and who has been the ideal wife to me and the perfect mother to our children. To all of these, my deepest thanks.

RICHARD L. CUTLER

Ann Arbor, Michigan
November 1972

13

I
THE SYSTEM

Considered against the vast span of the earth's history, man's tenure on this little planet has been brief indeed. Throughout most of his existence, man has been almost entirely occupied with the matter of survival in a setting that by no means guarantees survival. For only a few thousand years has he been able to devote himself to anything more than keeping himself fed, warm, and safe from the many threats of the natural environment. The instances in man's history when the light of civilized society has been raised above him are few, and it is not an exaggeration to say that mortal struggle, chaos, and threat represent the ordinary condition of man, rather than peace, order, and safety. All the civilizations of the world through all of time can be counted on a few fingers. In the cultures of the Fertile Crescent, Egypt, and ancient China, the light was raised for a moment. In Greece and Rome it burned even more briefly. In every case the light dimmed or was snuffed out, and man fell again into the mist and darkness.

Our most recent rise from the darkness has only been in process for a few hundred years. Even in America, this most secure and materially blessed of societies, where most of us rarely think about the threat of a hostile environment or the deadly competition with other species, the margin of survival is exceedingly thin. We are removed from famine by only a few extra spoonfuls, from darkness by a few metal strings, from pestilence by a few quarts of inoculant, and from the jungle by a modicum of reason. The maintenance of a civilized society is not automatically assured, particularly when we recognize that the total period of ordered, reasonably secure life has occupied only a few centuries of history. Genetically and physically, we are not recognizably different from the barbarians of Northern Europe of fifteen hundred years ago, nor from the peoples of Africa, South America, and New Guinea, who until very recently lived in stone-age cultures.

What separates us from the jungle is no deeply ingrained altruism or commitment to peace and brotherhood. We are different from our uncivilized ancestors, who killed, raped, and plundered as an accepted way of life, only in that we have been able to profit from the experience of the past, and have accepted, superficially at least, the idea that an ordered society, based on reason rather than emotion and on persuasion rather than force, offers us a somewhat improved chance for individual and group survival and satisfaction. One thing that distinguishes man from the other species with which he competes is the ability to walk upright, thus freeing his hands to develop the tools that have become our technology; another is the special development of the frontal lobes of his brain, which enables him to anticipate and foresee the possible consequences of his actions before he takes them. Out of these two unique possessions has come man's civilization, so that we are now separated from the jungle by three things: the rule of law, which limits the exercise of individual freedom on behalf of the common good; our aspiration and ability to be reasoning creatures, factors which cause us to take the future into consideration and to limit the expression of emotion and impulse; and our technology, which provides us with a degree of material security and control over the fundamentally hostile environment around us. Man's instincts, left to operate freely, without the control of his reason and judgment, would quickly move us back to a primitive level of individual survival, procreation, territorial possession, and force. The essence of civilization is man's reason, which allows him to view things in other than purely selfish, short-range terms, and his technology, which makes possible a degree of mastery of his surroundings, and thus makes survival a more likely possibility.

In one sense, man's struggle to establish an ordered and civilized society may be seen as a struggle between two sets of forces within him. On the one hand, man possesses a set of instinctual drives, which demand immediate satisfaction.

Several of these basic drives have long been recognized as motives shaping his behavior; among them are sex, the need for nourishment, and needs relating to the maintenance of physiological equilibrium. Without the ability to satisfy these drives, the individual, or the species, would not long survive. They are pressing urges, deeply patterned into our genetic constitution, and they operate almost universally among us. More recently, there has been growing scientific evidence that at least one other basic instinct operates within man, namely a drive to obtain and defend territory. Some scientists consider this an even more basic force than sex, although the evidence at present is insufficient to support such an interpretation. Additionally, some postulate the existence of a basic drive toward aggressive behavior, either as a corollary of survival urges, or as something that stands alone. In any case, there is no question that man is possessed of a good many genetically determined urges, which demand quick gratification, and which, if left unbalanced by other forces within him, would soon carry us back to a very primitive level of existence. The balancing force is represented by man's ability to think and reason. Unlike most other species, he is capable of visualizing the consequences of actions before he takes them. He is also unusually capable of profiting from his past experience, through his unparalleled ability to learn. Since he has developed a written language, he is able to learn not only from his own immediate experience and communication from his contemporaries, but also from the accumulated experience of the past. While man is not the only species with a history, he is certainly the only one with a *sense* of history, and this unique grasp of the dimension of time is a central force in his movement toward and maintenance of a civilized society. Thus, man alone has managed to transcend the immediate pressures from his gut and his gonads, to deny the central importance of the now, and to take into account the experience of the past and the anticipation of the future. When this sense of the importance of the time dimension is lost, or gives way to a preoccupation with the immediate, the instant gratification of impulses, or the self-indulgent expression of basic needs, a very vital aspect of man's hold on civilization also is lost. Thus, the power of man's intellect—characterized by reason, judgment, anticipation, logical and abstracting ability—is the major civilizing force in an organism that would otherwise be no more than a reflection of impulses demanding immediate satisfaction, victimizing others, and living at the level of mere survival in a primitive jungle.

As men have gradually learned to band together into larger and larger groups in order to enhance the possibility of survival, and to secure certain other benefits that arise from mutual effort, they have developed systems designed to regulate the behavior of individuals in the interests of the group. In a general way, these arrangements and understandings can be seen as evolving into various forms of governments. The quest for an ideal form of group arrangement, or government, has been a major preoccupation of all civilized groups, and in one form or another this quest has certainly existed since men first joined together in the smallest groups with very limited mutual goals. For a long time, the nature of the governmental form was determined almost entirely by the exertion of direct physical force: a strong man would impose his ideas on the tribe or community, or a small group would pool their strength in order to dominate the other members. From a very early time, however, there came to be an awareness of the danger to the group when force alone was the basis for the governmental form. Thus, even though force implicitly remains as the final basis on which systems of social organization stand or fall, there was interjected very early in man's history some element of appeal to reason and consent. In a way, the development of more and more sophisticated forms of government has shown a swinging back and forth between systems established and maintained on the direct and frank use of force, and others in which reason and consent play a greater role.

Throughout the evolutionary development of systems of government, there has been an underlying question as to the basic nature of man. Some governmental forms are based on the assumption that man is basically evil, that wisdom and virtue are the possession of the few, and that the proper role of government is to control man and prevent him from destroying himself and society by the exercise of his basically evil character. Such governments tend to rely more on force, to concentrate power in the hands of a few, and to be repressive and controlling. Other governmental forms, most notably those proposed by the utopian philosophers, take it as a given that man's basic nature is essentially good, and that he will, lacking the destructive effects of social and governmental influence, naturally express this

18

good in the form of charitable, compassionate, cooperative impulses and behavior of benefit to himself and to the group. Evidence of both aspects of man's character is plainly seen in the flow of historical events as well as in his day-to-day behavior. Although the basic question of man's ultimate good or evil is best left to social philosophers and theologians, there is a strong suggestion that man is neither perfectly good nor perfectly evil, and that a system of government based on the assumption that he is either, is likely to be inappropriate both to his needs and to the realities of his existence.

During the eighteenth century there began to be recognized the fact that man's intellectual equipment gave him certain unique abilities not only for developing a technology, but also for dealing with other men in the context of social groups and governmental forms. These intellectual qualities, which have already been mentioned, include the ability to make logical and systematic judgments, to anticipate consequences, to deal with abstractions, and to exercise reasoned control over his behavior, which would otherwise be largely dominated by impulses and emotions. The making of reasoned decisions serving both one's own interests and the general good, came to be seen as a virtue and a basis on which an effective system of government could be based. This concept of rationalism, which had a profound influence on the men who conceived and shaped the initial form of the American system of government, implicitly placed great value on the individual. To the extent that considerations of the basic good or evil of man are involved in the system, reason is seen as the overriding virtue and the forces that oppose reason as an evil.

The experience of the Founding Fathers with the government of Great Britain also sensitized them to the dangers of power concentrated in the hands of a few. Their commitment to the value of the individual was insulted by the notion that somebody else knew better what was right for an individual than the individual did himself. Accordingly, they developed a government dedicated to the idea that power should be spread out and the abuses of power carefully guarded against. Seeing an extreme danger in the possibility that a strong central government might eventually dominate individuals against their collective will and judgment, they carefully provided for a system of checks and balances within government, and for the ultimate accountability of the government to the governed. Their essential notion was that the central government should perform those and only those tasks that the people or the states could not manage for themselves. If the Preamble to the Constitution may be taken as a statement of values and goals, it is clear that the intention was that the central government should have only a narrow set of functions, including insuring justice and the internal peace of the nation, providing for national defense, and promoting the general welfare. In theory and in early practice, extreme reliance was placed upon the individual's interest and competence in managing things for himself.

In displaying such tremendous faith in the individual, the American system of government also makes certain assumptions about his basic qualities as a human being and a citizen, and about the conditions necessary for him to fu ction effectively in society. We have already mentioned our system's great emphasis on man's essential rationality, and the value set on him as an individual. Closely related to these is the belief that the free citizen will recognize the need for productive effort, not only in his own behalf, but also in pursuit of the general prosperity, security, and welfare. As a corollary, it is assumed that he will be willing to be judged on the merits of his performance, not only as a matter of personal pride but also as a testimony to his basii competence and energy, which are respected by his fellow citizens for the contribution they make to the general welfare. It is also assumed that he will, on the basis of his rational conviction, pursue a life of honesty and integrity, and that he will adhere to the truth as a fundamental virtue in his life and in society. The character of the free and self-respecting citizen is also assumed to include the ability to recognize and respond to similar qualities in his compatriots, so that dealings among citizens are marked by an essential trust and a profound sense of good faith. Finally, the architects of the system perceived clearly that the functioning of citizens in a free society had to be balanced by a commensurate sense of responsibility, and were convinced that such responsible participation would be largely assured again by the reasoned conviction among the citizenry that licentious expression was not in the interest of the common good.

However, the ideas underlying our system are not limited to the idealistic notion of man as a totally rational being. There is also a clear recognition of man's basic instincts toward per-

20

sonal survival and gratification. The system makes ample provision for the acquisition and protection of territory and property, and for the right of the individual to defend himself. There is an implicit suggestion that the person whose quickness of mind or storehouse of energy is greater than that of his fellows will gain a commensurate level of reward and satisfaction. Thus the system takes into account man's potential for what the philosophers have considered to be good, but also gives significant recognition to qualities generally viewed as selfish.

But the real genius of the system, as it has been developed and refined, lies in the fact that even qualities that are less than perfectly altruistic are channeled in such a way as to serve the general good. Two examples will illustrate this. Consider a man who fails to perform his share of society's work. He is first subjected to social pressure and general disapproval, which we know to be powerful incentives. His implicit dependence on society is brought home to him in this way, and the fact that his immediate selfishness or sloth is not a social benefit is underlined. Second, he may ultimately be denied some of society's important benefits, not only in the material sense, but even more importantly, in the form of the acceptance and approval of his fellow citizens. Thus, even though he may be totally without altruistic commitment to his fellow citizens, the consequences of his lack of social responsibility come home to him in the very area of his selfish, personal motivation, namely, by eventually denying him the indulgence he sought through his original inaction. Or consider a man who is unusually productive and gathers therefrom the benefits offered by the system. By two basic means, such a man is strongly encouraged to feed the gains of his efforts back into society: first, he is promised by the general value system that if he harbors his resources and lays in his stock against the future, he will gain added satisfaction and pleasure from having denied himself the immediate indulgence; and second, if he invests his reserve in job-producing enterprises, he will have the promise of even greater security at a later time. In this fashion, the free enterprise system turns what would ordinarily be a destructive selfishness into a remarkable potential for social benefit.

The system also recognizes that not everyone is able to manage himself with a total sense of responsibility. While the general incentive system and the informal pressures of group disapproval are the major impediments to irresponsibility, the recognition that such procedures do not always work is clearly implied in the provision of a system of law. Once again, the law is seen not as something imposed from above, without consideration of the wishes of the people, but as a set of constraints imposed by the people themselves, in order to insure an orderly framework within which personal freedom can be fostered. As its basic approach to law-making, the American system assumes that the constraints of the law are only imposed when the individual's internal constraints on himself have broken down. Here again, the great faith in the individual's ability to manage himself on the basis of reason and judgment is underlined. It is recognized that the operation of the law is a collective function, and that the development of masses of legal constraints threatens the freedom of the individual both directly and by encouraging the development of a powerful central government. Later in this book, we shall look at some of the consequences to the individual of the extent to which we have already developed a group of laws and a powerful central government. Even so, our legal system is designed and has generally functioned with strict attention to the rights of the individual, as opposed to the collective power of the state. A whole series of protections are guaranteed the individual against the possible injustice of laws and procedures enacted by the majority. The individual is assured a speedy, public trial by a jury of his peers. He is assumed innocent until otherwise proven; he has a right to be represented, to remain silent, not to incriminate himself, and to appeal. In no other system is such care taken to justify a basic faith in the individual's honesty, integrity, and commitment to the responsible use of his freedom on behalf of the general good.

The distrust of governmental power and the desire to secure the strength of the responsible individual in society are seen in another aspect of the American system. Not only are the rights of individuals protected in the way described above, but the danger of an untoward concentration of power in an individual or a small group is guarded against by the doctrine of separation of power. In the process of designing the system, the Founding Fathers were so suspicious of government that they carefully divided its powers among three co-equal, and formally independent, branches. They then designed a carefully arranged system of checks and balances to insure that no one branch could gain superior advantage over the others. Both the legislative and executive branches are directly responsible to the people through the election process, and the judicial system, which is supposed to serve as the ultimate dispassionate arbiter of disputes, was theoretically removed from the immediate shifting tides of politics through lifetime tenure and selection based on the consensual judgment of the President and the Senate. In practice, this system of checks and balances has worked very well, and while the pendulum of power and influence may periodically swing from the legislative to the executive branch, there has always been a compensating movement in the other direction. In the only major conflict between the executive and the judicial branch, which occurred when Franklin D. Roosevelt attempted to pack the Supreme Court with justices who favored his New Deal policies, no change was made and the basic integrity of the system was preserved. While there are sharp disputes among the branches from time to time, for the most part this arrangement has prevailed and it has repeatedly been validated. Finally, the writers of the Constitution intended that the power of the central government be confined to matters specifically designated as its responsibility, with all other powers carefully reserved to the states and ultimately to the people. No system of government has ever provided such assurance of freedom and individual power. At the same time, no system makes greater demands for individual responsibility and competence.

The inspired genius of the men who framed the basic documents of our government was not limited to their insights into the nature of man as a free citizen or the necessity of guarding against concentration and abuses of power. Perhaps equally important was their recognition that an effective system of government must make explicit provisions for its own modification. Without such provisions, a system becomes rigid, poorly attuned to the evolving wishes of the people, and, eventually, subject to revolutionary overthrow. At the same time, the founders saw equally well that a system that could be expediently or whimsically modified would be so subject to momentary tides of opinion and political ferment that it would not provide sufficient stability to insure reasoned consideration of issues and orderly change. Thus, the American system is designed to lend itself to slow and deliberate modification, and this aspect of it again reflects the faith that majority opinion among intelligent and rational citizens will operate on behalf of the long-run general good. Change is eminently possible, and changes have been gradually made, but these are changes with safety and order based on persuasion and reason rather than force and emotion. Underlying the entire process is a commitment to the maintenance of an orderly system within which the free, rational, and responsible majority can and will come to decisions in support of the general good. Change based on sudden tides of events or immediate emotional responses is inconsistent with this pervasive faith in man's reason.

The democratic process, thus defined in operational terms, has certain consequences that may cause dissatisfaction among those who seek instant solutions to problems. It does not always appear to be efficient, since it is based on the premise that time and deliberation are required for citizens to reach a proper consensus. It is not by any means guaranteed to satisfy everyone all of the time, so that minorities may feel their interests are not being quickly enough responded to, and persons who cannot tolerate temporary frustration are likely to resent its deliberate pace. It does not provide a guarantee of security, for it recognizes that absolute security is not possible in a society that depends on the efforts and competence of individuals, and expects them to take final responsibility for their own decisions and actions. But these disadvantages, if they be such, are carefully weighed against the alternatives of sacrifice of individual freedom, centralized concentrations of power, social instability, and efficiency purchased at the price of oppression. It is much easier to solve certain kinds of pressing social problems if a people are willing to turn over their power to a dictatorship, but the price ultimately paid for such efficiency is a sacrifice of individual choice. Considering the delicate balances between the people and their government, our system has been unique in its ability to deal with problems while still maintaining the freedom of the individual citizen.

So great was the preoccupation of the Founding Fathers with the danger of power concentrations and with the central importance of individual freedom that the system hardly contains sufficient provision to protect itself from being subverted internally. Beyond the proscription that no one is allowed to overthrow the government by force and violence, there are virtually no built-in limits on what citizens may do to alter it in any direction they choose. So great is the faith that rational men will protect their individual freedom by maintaining the democratic processes, which enable them to control their government rather than be controlled by it, that there is practically no formal protection against the citizens giving away the very system which offers them the free choice of doing so. Thus it is quite possible for free men, acting under conditions of immediate emotional pressure, internal threat, or vague visions of quicker solutions, to destroy the very system that guarantees their right to modify it according to reasoned decisions. No other system, once established by force or by the expedient choice of its citizens, offers the chance to reverse the trend and to reestablish free choice as the basis for determining its form or evolution. Thus the American system, if its form and guarantees are to be protected, requires a much more vigilant participation by citizens.

In a system placing so little emphasis on formal structures and centrally determined processes, a great responsibility falls on the people to develop their own informal methods of dealing with their lives and their problems. American society is absolutely unique in the number and variety of informal and voluntary activities emerging from the efforts of the people to deal with their own problems and to pursue the general social benefit. Voluntary associations and organizations of every imaginable kind flourish. There are tens of thousands of ad hoc, loosely organized, often transient associations arising out of the free choice of the people and intended to deal with one or another perceived need. A good many of these become permanent and self-sustaining, simply because they are successful in providing effective approaches to problems or in some other way meet the desires of their members and the larger society. No governmental initiative is present in their formation, few of them are dependent in any way on public financing, and virtually all of them are initially formed with a social benefit in view or soon take up a social program in which the members have, or are encouraged to develop, an interest. These voluntary associations exist in every imaginable form, at every level of society, and are concerned with every possible issue and concern. They include block clubs, fraternal organizations, parent-teacher groups, service clubs, YMCA and YWCA associations, children's activity and recreational programs, unions, nationality groups, business associations, cultural and historical societies, hobby clubs, and a myriad of special-interest support groups. There is literally not a single day when such groups are not being formed and no moment when millions of people are not occupied with them and their activities. So many "Citizens for . . . " and "Citizens against . . . " operations pop up, engage in a concerted effort to deal with a pressing problem, and then subside that it would be impossible to catalog them or to assess reliably what their impact on our lives and the solutions of our problems has been. It is manifest, however, that the voluntary actions of American citizens, expressed in these forms, represent billions of dollars and trillions of hours expended in freely chosen efforts to bring the reason and competence of the individual to bear in the solution of social problems. They develop out of free choice, they are self-supporting, they are meaningful to the individuals involved, and they play a vital part in dealing with issues that would otherwise depend for their handling on an impersonal, remote, and perhaps oppressive governmental structure. They represent one of the better evidences that free men, left to their own devices, will make rational choices on behalf of the common good, and gain a sense of satisfaction and personal competence in the process, just as was envisioned by the founders of the system.

If a system based on free choice rather than governmental dictate, force, or detailed legal constraint offers the individual the broadest possible latitude in voluntary action for the common good, it also raises the possibility that the unscrupulous, irresponsible, or criminal few may express their freedom to the detriment of society. It opens the additional danger that people with little understanding of and less commitment to the requirements of a free society may easily become a threat to the entire process. In the past, deliberate efforts at political subversion were few, partly because of the system's success, partly because the mass of Americans understood the precious benefits of their freedom, and partly because a broad-based patriotism brought effective social and legal sanctions to bear on anyone who proposed to subvert our free system. As we shall see in succeeding chapters, this situation has so changed that, to our great misfortune and danger, we are no longer assured that internal subversion is no threat to our national system. Even without that, however, we have had ample evidences of how freedom can be abused and the general good diminished. Just as voluntary associations can give rise to great social benefit, so they can be turned into vehicles for exploitation, conspiracy, deceit, and selfishness. The informality of the system allows persons who are so inclined to develop arrangements which, while not illegal, do have the effect of betraying the fundamental tenets of good faith, honesty, and integrity. The most well-publicized of these are in the fields of business and industry, where conspiratorial schemes of various degrees sometimes take advantage of the public. Monopolistic setups, under-the-table agreements to limit competition, and the marketing of inferior products are all examples of how commercial charlatans try to turn a free system to selfish purposes. Gradually, legislation has been enacted to make such abuses more difficult, although evidence of them still occasionally appears. Much more frequent, and much less easy to deal with through legislative action, are instances of individuals simply failing to demonstrate the level of responsible action necessary to maintain a free system. Shading the truth, doing as little as possible, deceiving one's colleagues, abusing the reputation or rights of others, allowing emotion to dominate reason in the process of making important decisions, putting immediate satisfaction ahead of long-run implications, and treating with others in the absence of trust and good faith are all inconsistent with the image of the free citizen held by the architects of our system. These items of personal failure are, in their way, as damaging to the operation of a decent society of free men as the most flagrant dishonesty of the commercial operator. Fundamentally, the success of a free system rests on mass acceptance of a very high standard of personal responsibility, integrity, and rationality, and the failure of even a relatively small minority to adhere to these standards attacks the foundations of the system by destroying the basic sense of mutual trust and good faith among the citizens.

The men who established the American system had a strong antipathy toward collectivist approaches to the solution of social problems, at least those that required the giving up of individual power to the government. Voluntary collective action was of course recognized as legitimate, so long as it did not impose uniform requirements or societywide constraints. In the Jeffersonian conception of democracy, however, and very early in the evolution of the American system, the value of education was strongly emphasized as a means of preparing citizens for responsible citizenship. The basic faith in man's reason was considerable, but neither unconditional nor blind. For man's rational potential to flower, it was necessary that it be cultivated, and education was the means to its growth and development. Thus, from very early in the nation's history, the insuring of a basic education to all citizens became a consideration of such great import that the general avoidance of public involvement in private affairs was laid aside, and education became a general responsibility of government paralleling the collective responsibility of national defense in importance. For the most part, however, the responsibility for developing and maintaining the educational system was left to the states and the local communities. Even so, education was clearly seen as a necessary preparation for responsible citizenship, not only in terms of giving the citizen the tools of personal competence, but even more importantly as an assurance against uninformed, undisciplined, or irrational actions. If collective arrangements for the national defense were a requirement for protection against external threat, collective arrangements for education were a prime requirement for the maintenance of a citizenry that would be responsible in its use of freedom, effective in its productive efforts, and capable of reaching informed decisions on the basis of facts and reason.

A further indication of faith in the judgment of individuals is found in the Bill of Rights. The proscription against the imposition of a state religion assumes that the free citizen can make his own decisions in matters of spiritual faith. The guarantee of a free press assumes that, given complete access to the facts and to all interpretations and views of the facts, the educated free citizen will be able to come to sensible and logical conclusions and to act on those conclusions in his own behalf and in support of the general good. The guarantee of the right to bear arms is much more than a design to keep the nation prepared to defend itself; it is also a recognition of the free citizen's right to protect his person and his property, and of his ability to exercise responsible control of himself in so doing. The guarantee of free speech is another instance of basic commitment to reasoned discussion, without limit on the nature of the matters discussed, and assumes again that the free citizen will think and act responsibly, and be able to come to reasoned decisions if he has free access to facts and ideas. The balance of the Bill of Rights is essentially a guarantee to the citizen of his freedom from unreasonable and oppressive acts of government, and repeatedly reflects the fundamental belief that the citizen is honest, responsible, rational, and therefore capable of conducting himself within a society of men, and of doing so with good faith, mutual trust, and decency.

Subsequent amendments to the Constitution have represented an evolution toward more specifically stated guarantees of individual rights. Virtually all the amendments, except those concerned with housekeeping and technical aspects of our national government, are statements of what people may not be prevented from doing, or of limitations that government may not impose on individuals. These include the Thirteenth, Fourteenth, and Fifteenth Amendments, which dealt with the abolition of slavery and the rights of former slaves as citizens; the Nineteenth, which guaranteed the vote to women; the Twenty-third, which extended the right of representation in national elections to citizens of the District of Columbia; and the most recent, which extended the same right to persons eighteen years of age or older. The sole exceptions are the Sixteenth, which granted the federal government the power to levy a tax on incomes, and the Eighteenth, which prohibited the use of alcoholic beverages. The Eighteenth Amendment has, of course, long since been repealed; thus, only one amendment to the Constitution has the effect of taking power away from the citizens and bestowing it on the central government. In light of the central government's use of that one amendment as a means to gather power, authority, and the control of individual citizens' lives unto itself, we may well be cautious about any more such amendments if we cherish our free system based on individual choice and self-determination.

There is much talk these days about the evils of the system, the failures of the society, the immorality and hypocrisy of our way of life, and the repressiveness of the law. Some of this talk arises from the radical minority, but some of it is evident in popular discourse; the negativism of certain social critics, newspaper columnists, and television commentators; and increasingly as a kind of naive attempt at cleverness and popularity among younger and younger children. To those who

29

are eager to condemn the system, a humble suggestion or two may be in order. First, acquaint yourself with its basic documents, such as the Declaration of Independence, the United States Constitution, the Bill of Rights and the fourteen other amendments. As a simple exercise, read them through, and observe whether they are expressions of the rights of free men or the outline for a system of governmental control of individual lives. Second, obtain similar fundamental documents from a system you believe to be superior, and read them with the same view, comparing the two in terms of their guarantees to the individual as opposed to the powers of government. Third, examine the governmental systems you admire most in terms of the extent to which they are capable of being modified in their basic form by the actions and initiatives of the people. Fourth, compare with our system the style of life, the level of personal satisfaction, the opportunity for reward of individual effort, and the ability to solve social problems without infringing the rights of individuals. Fifth, try to imagine (or better yet, go and give it a brief try) what your personal opportunities for realizing your potential as a human being, your aspirations as to a standard of living, and your urges toward a general life style would be in the system you think superior to ours. Sixth, if it passes your examination on all, or even most of the items suggested above, return to our society, provide as many of our citizens as possible with your critique and evaluation, and work through the persuasive process to change our system to the form you have come to believe is superior. And, oh yes, in the process, be sure, if you please, that you do not sacrifice our right to change the system back to what we now have in case we don't like your solution. Finally, give Americans the same credit for reason and responsibility as is given by our system's basic documents, and do not credit yourself with the right to deceive us, or with an intelligence or insight superior to our collective reason.

One of the favorite targets of critics of our system is something vaguely known as the "Establishment." The Establishment, at least as pictured by the radical minority, is a mysterious, conspiratorial, exploitative, power-mad group who manage to keep the people chained, economically enslaved, and politically repressed totally against their will and largely without their even realizing it. In its most limited definition, the Establishment is supposed to consist of a small group of military leaders and powerful corporation heads, who desire perpetual war, the irresponsible consumption of our natural resources for their own personal profit and power, and the oppressive tyranny of a powerful centralized government, which they manipulate through economic pressure, personal graft and corruption, and the threat of power coups. Under this definition, the people are seen as victims or fools, without the intelligence to understand what is going on, the wit to penetrate the grand conspiracy, or the power to alter it. If this conception be accurate, most of us are indeed fools, our elected representatives at the various levels of government are parties to the conspiracy, the managers of business and industry are irresponsible idiots with no devotion to the nation's future welfare, our military leaders are more concerned with the establishment of a totalitarian state than with our national defense, and the radical minority has an inspired, objective view of the true state of affairs. This rather paranoid conception of the state of the nation also requires, if it is to be believed, that the leaders of our unions, the members of the opposition political party, most of the writers, newsmen, TV personalities, professional entertainers and sports figures, persons in positions of responsibility in major institutions of the society such as the universities, etc., etc., are also either dupes or co-conspirators. Worst of all, if this view of our society and the distribution of power within it is accurate, it indicates that the original faith of the founders of the system was totally misplaced—that the mass of the citizenry, albeit well educated, productive, and responsible in their own right, cannot manage to maintain a system that perpetuates their freedom, cannot through reason make decisions for their own general good, and are not sufficiently intelligent even to recognize when they are being oppressed. If this be an accurate characterization of a people who have had nearly two hundred years of experience with a free society, we may as well give up the myth of individual power and responsibility, and simply wait until the Establishment decides to make our slavery a matter of formal declaration rather than informal arrangement.

In reality, what is the Establishment? It is a group of persons who have risen to leadership and influence within a system that allows every individual the opportunity to obtain such positions on the basis of his own energies and talents. It is a collection of individuals who temporarily occupy positions of power through informal associations and consensus rather than governmental dictate, and through the freely taken decisions of the citizens rather than force or conspiracy—who have, through their effort and competence, their demonstrated ability to serve the general good, their responsible use of freedom, and their intelligence and reason, temporarily come to positions of influence and decision-making responsibility. The Establishment is not a closed, limited, self-seeking elite group. It is open to everyone, and so long as we maintain a free system in which the performance of our leaders is a reflection of the wishes of the mass of citizens, it is eminently within our power to control the Establishment and to be members of it. In fact, when the case is examined carefully, the vast majority of American citizens are themselves members of the Establishment, for scarcely a single person is prevented from taking an active part in decisions affecting the national life and his own welfare. And to the extent that we, the people, do not approve of what the Establishment does, it is in our power to change it.

The matter comes down to the fact that virtually everyone in the nation is in one way or another a part of the Establishment. We all have a piece of the total action, a part in the decision-making process, and a stake in the maintenance of the system. Whenever we vote, not only in our national elections, but in our unions, our clubs, our school districts, or our neighborhood organizations, we are reflecting our free and reasoned decisions on issues of personal concern. If we have an insurance policy, own a share of stock, open a savings account, participate in a group retirement plan, contribute to or draw benefits from Social Security, exercise our free choice to purchase something, or even pay taxes, we are in and of the system. The benefits of these largely voluntary actions to each of us as individuals are a reflection of the productive capacity of our farms and industries, the collective judgments of all of us, and the total operation of the system we have devised for ourselves. The Establishment is the sum total of those who gain personal reward, satisfaction, power, or influence from the operation of a national system that is ultimately a result of the actions and decisions of the mass of individual citizens. The system is not a mysterious, closed, conspiratorial club whose membership is limited by class, race, sex, or even political viewpoint, and the

32

destruction of it, as advocated by the radical minority, would have dire consequences for most Americans.

The men who founded the American system had a great vision of freedom. It rested on some basic assumptions about the qualities of the individual citizen. He was seen most importantly as capable of managing his affairs on the basis of reason, rather than emotion and impulse. Education was emphasized as a means of developing this rational potential, and was early assured to all citizens. While man was also seen as capable of selfish actions, due to his urge to survive, his reason could enable him to lay aside immediate satisfaction of his personal urges in the interest of the future and the general good. As the system developed, it was able to turn even these more selfish motives into actions that had a general social benefit. The belief in man's essential rationality was also revealed in the provision of an ordered society, operating under the rule of law, within which the process of rational discussion and deliberate consideration of decisions could go forward without danger of disruption by the tides of the moment. Thus the system allowed for gradual and orderly change in its basic nature, depending on consensus and allowing for an evolution to meet changing conditions and needs among its citizens. The citizen was seen as devoted to honesty, integrity, and productive effort, and capable of operating in good faith, with trust in his fellow men. He was self-reliant, proud, and independent, but he was also believed capable of exercising his freedom with responsible restraint. Out of these articles of faith in the individual citizen grew a system that emphasized the rights of individuals rather than the powers of government, and the pursuit of social goals on a voluntary rather than a mandatory basis, carefully avoiding the concentration of power in the hands of a few. The American system has indeed been a government of the people, by the people, and for the people, and in spite of its inefficiency and weaknesses, it has largely validated the faith of its founders in the spirit of the free citizen.

In later sections of this book, close attention is given to certain failings of the American system and the American people. Before undertaking that critique, however, it is appropriate to take note of America's successes and its potential. Every nation and civilization in history has had problems and failings, and no system can ever be more than the men and women who make it up. But we have existed as a nation for slightly less than two hundred years, and in that time we have become the most powerful and economically blessed people in history. We have fashioned a civilization out of a wilderness, developed a technology of unbelievable sophistication and promise, fed and clothed a large number of people for whom we have no responsibility other than humane interest, and given freely of ourselves and our resources in pursuit of a better world for all. We have taken up the challenge of racial equality and are making progress at it. We are devoting ourselves to the elimination of poverty and the extension of personal freedom. We have made ourselves healthy and our living conditions decent if not yet perfect. We have committed ourselves voluntarily to changes necessary for the further improvement of the individual condition. And we have done all of this by our own free choice, without being told, guided by a commitment to conscience rather than selfishness, and without a sacrifice of individual freedom and self-determination. We have no concentration camps, no secret police, and few restrictions, except what we choose to impose on ourselves in the responsible exercise of freedom. This is not a bad record for a people most of whom had nothing but what they wore on their backs and many of whom could not even speak the national language when they arrived, and some of whom were slaves three or four generations ago. Certainly we must be cognizant of what remains to be done, but we may take some measure of pride in what we have already accomplished.

One final comment is in order before closing this discussion of the American system. Our government is based on the free choice of its citizens and does not provide for detailed legal constraints on the actions of individuals. In offering the opportunity for men to exercise their personal freedom and rational judgment, our system depends for its survival on its citizens' ability to live up to the faith that is put in them. The expectation is that people will be honest, productive, reasonable, and responsible in their behavior, and mutually supportive in maintaining for themselves the limits on conduct necessary to prevent abuse and perpetuate the system. The good faith believed to characterize the free citizen's approach to his fellows must also be present in abundance in his relationships to the system, which assumes that he can be trusted and believed. Breaches of personal honesty and integrity are quite literally breaches of faith with the free society, which takes it for granted that the general faith of men in one another will be reflected in loyalty and trust in their relationships to the system.

It is easy to cheat in a system where no one really checks up on you, where you are assumed to be honest, and where you are supposed to recognize the relationship between personal integrity and the general integrity of the society and conduct yourself accordingly. When only a few violate the basic trust placed in them, it is possible to maintain the processes of a free society through social disapproval, economic pressure, and legal action specifically aimed at the untrustworthy individual. But when the number of such offenders increases to the point where, even though they are still a tiny minority, they provide subcultural support and mutual justification to one another, the problem becomes extremely difficult to handle. When a determined minority comes to the conclusion that the system is evil, and on that basis decides not to abide by even the most rudimentary rules of honesty and integrity, they can have an effect far out of proportion to their numbers. And when their program is based on an appeal to freedom itself, without any consideration of the responsibilities connected with it, it becomes possible to turn the very benefits the system provides against the system itself, and thus to create conditions in which a very subtle, but nevertheless fundamental, subversion of our ideals occurs. Herein, rather than in force, persuasion, or an ideological system of greater attraction to the people, lies the danger of the radical minority to the American system.

II

A HANDFUL OF REBELS

Radicalism and rebellion are nothing new to American life. As the present-day radicals are fond of telling us, in an effort to elevate and dignify their own maudlin pursuit of revolution, our country was conceived in rebellion and established through violent protest against repression. Though we are a people whose system of government and basic way of life are predicated on deliberate and reasoned decisions, we are also periodically capable of direct and violent action. Many movements that have since become an accepted part of our system, and many men who were later respected for their idealism, were originally viewed as radical. In a free system, it is natural for many new and challenging ideas to be proposed and even experimented with at the level of action, so it is not surprising that various challenges to the system will arise. Nor is it dangerous to believe that further changes may become necessary and gradually evolve in the system. But it is a dangerous mistake to assume that change is valuable for its own sake, that anything advocated in the name of radicalism and supposed freedom is a constructive improvement over what now exists, and it is a disastrous travesty to equate the ideas, goals, and methods of today's young radicals with those of the men who fought to establish the American system of government.

Who is raising this self-proclaimed radical challenge to the American system? It is ironic that most of the early leaders and many of the present devotees of left-wing radicalism are individuals who have been highly favored by the system. They come

36

mostly from liberal upper-middle-class backgrounds, have had the benefit of good educational programs, attend creditable colleges or universities, and would seem to have a guarantee of success in their futures. Yet a few of these products of the American middle class are engaged in a rampage of mindless disruption of our social institutions, with the destruction of the system as their intended goal. Just who comprises this tiny minority will be considered later, through the presentation of a few illustrative cases and by a detailed examination of their social and psychological origins. For the moment, it is only necessary to identify them in a general way, by examining their organizations, their ideas, and their tactics.

It is most difficult to develop a coherent picture of the recent radical movement in America, because the phenomenon itself is highly fragmented, poorly organized, and ever changing in its detail. It has gone by various names, sometimes being referred to as the "New Left," sometimes as "student activism," and it is often termed by its affiliates simply the "movement." It has been characterized by the formation of numbers of transient, ad hoc organizations, which have sprung up in response to various local issues on college campuses, or have been initiated by very small groups of radicals seeking uniqueness, publicity, or a totally local and highly autistic version of the revolution. The political tenor of the movement is neither fascistic nor Communistic; while certain subgroups seem to have a fascination with the teachings of Chairman Mao, others would appear to maintain a working liaison with revolutionary groups in Cuba, Algeria, or North Vietnam, and some few seem to have a definite affiliation with domestic Communistic groups such as the Progressive Labor Party, which is close to the Chinese Communists in its ideology, tactics, and goals. To the extent that any coherent ideological statement has come out of organized groups of new radicals, or even from articulate individuals among them, they would appear to seek collectivist, socialistic approaches to social problems. Even here, however, conventional labels are not very useful, because running heavily through their public statements, and clearly evident in their actions, is a strong flavor of anarchism or even nihilism. The rebellion, whenever it takes coherent form, seems to be mainly against organization and discipline. Attending a meeting of the Students for a Democratic Society is an experience unlike anything else in political life. There is little semblance of a party line, unless a few dogmatic traditional leftists happen to be present. Leadership, if present at all, is transient and only vaguely identified, and argument is interminable. One is led to believe that if such a group has a program at all, it is not to have a program. Having a program implies having made at least a temporary determination on some position or action, perhaps demands a commitment from the participants, and further implies an organization and a process for implementation. Going this far puts the group dangerously close to a process like that of the system, a stance, apparently, that must be avoided at all costs. Thus, what seems to be advocated is a revolution, without a program other than to destroy the existing order, in the hope that some magical process will cause a new and better system to rise from the ashes.

However foolish or irrational the idea of a revolution without a program, it contains certain manifest dangers. First, such a scattered activity is extremely difficult to pin down, and thus impossible to discuss in the logical terms of traditional political analysis. It is more an appeal to frustration and emotion than to logic and rational persuasion. It is filled with terms that have an instant appeal, like "freedom" and "the rights of the individual," which are nowhere further defined or pursued in the light of their implications for other matters or for what they really mean in operational terms within a system. Second, if such a program were ever to succeed, it would be easily seized by a more disciplined group with a clear ideology, which would very likely be antagonistic both to the vague ideas of the revolutionaries and to our existing system of individual freedom in an ordered society. The success of such a revolution would, at the least, betray the faith we have traditionally put in the citizen's ability to make reasoned decisions for the general good.

The young radicals with whom we deal in this book must be distinguished from certain other leftist, radical, and/or revolutionary movements. First, the application of the term "New Left" to them is quite incorrect. The term "New Left" had its origins in a movement that took shape in England and to some degree on the Continent in the middle and late fifties. It was largely an effort by liberal intellectuals to revitalize the principles of a broadly based democracy within the framework of a bureaucratized, technological society. While certain early advocates of the new radicalism in America were influenced by the original New Left, and to a degree borrowed certain of their notions from it, the form the movement has now taken in this country bears little resemblance to its European namesake. Nor is the movement closely related to the radicalism of certain black revolutionary groups, such as the Black Panthers and the Republic of New Africa. Even though there was an early effort by young white radicals to involve themselves in the radical activities of blacks, and even though there has been some interchanging of rhetoric and tactics, the two groups have found little common ground. The black radicals are too clear about what they want to be much impressed by the vague programs and pretended determination of the white-liberal middle-class children who occupy our attention in this book, and they are too tough in rhetoric and tactics to be comfortable associates for the whites, who want the revolution to be conducted with due consideration to their personal comfort and safety. The early political emphasis of the movement, which has been pursued by those who were initially involved and has been taken up by certain of their psychological descendants, also must be distinguished from the forms of rebellion evident among groups like the hippies and other advocates of the so-called counterculture. The hippies are essentially in social rebellion: those among them who seriously pursue the hippie life style are seeking to set themselves off from the system and to establish once more a simple, pastoral, and basically spiritual existence. Again, certain phenomena are common to the two groups—a distaste for the system, a rebellion against organization, a difficulty in dealing with authority, and a superficial similarity in style of dress, personal habits, and so on. But the original hippies were political only in the broadest sense of the term, while the "movement radicals" were flagrantly and deliberately political, albeit in a disorganized and chaotic way. If the movement radicals were political activists, the hippies were political passivists. If the former in their frustration were determined to destroy the system through violent revolution, the latter were resigned to withdrawing from it, dropping out, and fashioning their own subculture within it. These differences arise from some fascinating psychological contrasts between the two groups, which will be dealt with more explicitly in a subsequent chapter. More recently, there has been some coalescing of interests and membership between those committed to political

39

revolution, and those whose drop-out instincts might once have made them devotees of the hippie movement. These groups, also loosely organized and without any ideology beyond hate and nihilism, have come to be termed the "counterculture" and, as I will show, they pose at least as great a threat to a rational and ordered society of free men as do the radical political activists.

One early impetus to the development of the activist movement came from the civil rights activities of the late fifties and early sixties. A good many idealistic young people were sincerely interested in the cause of racial justice, and some of these became actively involved in the programs of the Southern Christian Leadership Conference (SCLC), led by Dr. Martin Luther King, Jr., and of the Student Non-Violent Coordinating Committee (SNCC), with which Stokely Carmichael was then associated. Numbers of liberal college students, mostly from the major universities of the East and Midwest, went south for one or more summers to work in voter registration drives, in peaceful protests of various kinds, and in educational centers sponsored by SCLC and SNCC. Out of that experience came several results. Many of these students were exposed for the first time to the existence of real injustice in our society, and came away with the impression that some immediate, urgent, and direct action was necessary to remove it. The practical situation being what it was, however, they saw little possibility that their efforts would have much effect, and in their impatience and arrogance, decided to try to remove the injustices by changing the system that allowed them to exist. They found little in common with either the oppressed southern black or the leadership of the civil rights movement. Lacking the basis to identify with a cause that was not in fact theirs, they rapidly came to the conclusion that they must develop a cause of their own. The psychological basis for this development will be discussed in detail in the body of this work, but certain aspects of it should be noted here. The early activists were in search of something of vital consequence to be involved in. Failing to find a personally satisfying outlet in an activity of vital importance, from which they were excluded or within which they labored unrecognized, they turned their energies to doing something that could offer them a sense of personal power, importance as individuals, and public recognition.

In late 1962, under the combined influence of their direct involvement in the SNCC movement in the South, and of the exposure of some of them to the original New Left, with its emphasis on liberal-intellectual reform designed to reinvolve masses of the poor and the powerless directly in the democratic process, a group of northern liberal college students met in Port Huron, Michigan. There, with Tom Hayden as the principal draftsman, they developed the so-called Port Huron Statement, which provided an ideological basis for later attempts to unite blacks, poor whites, and other "powerless" groups into a broad base for political action. This program, which was to be initiated and directed by the framers of the document and like-minded college students, rested on a set of tactics borrowed from the original New Left, including the notion of participatory democracy, in which all members of a community participated as equals in making every decision. Also present was the seed of the idea that somehow students, workers, and other groups could be welded together into a kind of combined political party, medieval craftsman's syndicate, and scholar's guild.

Some scholars credit the Port Huron Statement with being an inspired document offering a basis for vital political reform. My personal reaction is that it represents a hodgepodge of political confusion and naivete, based largely on the personal drive for power and importance that characterized Hayden and his associates. What they had striven for was a ringing statement of a new freedom, a resurgence of the importance of the individual, and a union of the powerless against the powerful. What they produced was a sophomoric document characterized by superficiality, half-insights, and, as events would later prove, no effective program or tactics at all.

Nevertheless, a group of the committed proceeded to try to translate these ideas into action. In the ensuing three years, they launched several programs that sought to use the skills and ideology of liberal college students to begin to reform or radicalize the system. One of these involved attempts to form an interracial organization of the poor, with the students spending their summers as community organizers trying to bring the message of power and reform to various of the poverty-stricken and underprivileged. This effort failed largely because most of the organizers could find no workable common ground, either psychological, economic, or political, with their chosen clientele. Later attempts to work with established power groups, such as labor unions, foundered for the same reasons, and also because the students were not taken very seriously by the more experienced and pragmatic unionists. At about the same time, the black leadership of the civil rights movement, deciding that white liberal college students had little of a practical nature to offer them, largely excluded white intellectual liberals from their future efforts.

Thus, the movement projected by Hayden and his SDS compatriots failed in its efforts to gain a broad base for social reform. When the student rebellion at the University of California at Berkeley occurred, the leaders began to shift their attention to college campuses, which seemed to promise more fertile ground. SDS gradually became more and more a college-based operation, giving increasingly less attention to the ills of the general society. Slightly later, the Vietnam War became the single preoccupying issue around which SDS rallied, although there were still sporadic attempts to tie that issue together with more general evils in society. Gradually, however, the early focus of the movement on matters of general social reform deteriorated, the SDS was infiltrated by traditional leftists, and its activities became more and more a matter of scattered disruption by college students and hangers-on. Whatever idealism had existed in the original group rapidly disappeared among the exigencies of finding issues by means of which the campuses could be kept astir, and their legacy was left in the keeping of the even more disorganized and nihilistic radicals who are the major focus of this book.

In the hearts of the early radicals still seems to beat the conviction that their revolution without program, substance, or effective tactics will somehow succeed, and that they will someday be hailed as the inspired architects of a new society, which will provide them with the recognition, importance, and influence they yearn for. The fate of the early SDS is hardly encouragement for this delusion. The notion of a uniting of the "underclasses" never materialized. The concept of participatory democracy was foredoomed by the personal disorganization of the few who were attracted to it. The mass radicalization of college students has not occurred. Many students who became radical activists during the 1960s have turned to other tasks— the practical problem of making a living; the escapist path of the dropout, the counterculture, or the drug scene; or even to a more

42

practical participation in the process of changing the system through ordinary political activity. Some few of the more extremely frustrated have become Weathermen (the violent direct-action wing of the SDS), gone underground, taken up terrorism as a political tool, or extended their liaison with Algiers or Hanoi in an active effort to destroy the system, which was not impressed by or responsive to their pathetic demands.

To the extent that the radical activists continue their direct political efforts, they have evolved into a loose confederation that continues to be preoccupied with the recent Vietnam War, damning the free enterprise system in any of its ramifications, assaulting the universities, and finding transient involvement in anything else that promises the possibility of alienating anyone from any aspect of our established life. The radicals are entirely without a program, and are now even lacking in effective tactics; their personal discontent and their inability to deal with problems in a practical way are more and more apparent as the original cause of their supposedly idealistic radicalism. As in the past, they comprise only a tiny minority of their generation, but they persist in a program of mindless destruction of our social institutions. By attacking the colleges and universities, by infiltrating and subverting the high schools and now even the junior highs, by taking opportunistic advantage of the legitimate goals of black people, by attempting to make common cause with every group that has failed the system but wishes to believe that the system has failed it, and by attempting to discredit every locus of reason, honest social progress, and authority, this tiny minority still seeks nothing less than the total destruction of society as we know it.

It is tragic that this handful of committed revolutionaries can succeed, even to a very limited degree, in their goal of disruption and disorder, particularly in our educational institutions. It is even more tragic that in the face of their continuing provocation, some Ameriians have come to believe that their antics and attitudes characterize the majority of young people. Nothing could be further from the truth. Day after day, the overwhelming majority of our young people go quietly about the practical business of building a better society. This vast majority is purposive, dedicated, loyal, rational, and moral. They make little noise, throw no bricks, imprison no deans, assault no

43

teachers, and prompt no sensational headlines. Yet in their numbers, their aspirations, and their energies, they are the heart of our society and its hope for the future.

How, then, could such a tiny minority have gained even limited successes? Part of the answer lies in some very basic conditions of American society, which I deal with at length throughout this book. But a contributor of equal importance is the fact that they have attacked the system at its weakest points, both ideologically and structurally. Their basic tactics have involved appeals to freedom, justice, and individuality, and they have presented themselves as idealistic, reasonable, and committed to good faith and mutual trust. At the same time, they have been prepared to lay aside any such commitments whenever it suits their purposes, and to engage in emotionalism, deceit, repression, threats, and violence as the occasion allows. Their basic points of attack have been the colleges and universities, where the assumption of good faith dealings and mutual trust is very strong, and more recently upon younger and younger children, who possess neither the objectivity, strength, nor wisdom to balance the radicals' appeals to total freedom and instant gratification.

Even though the radicals' tactics are now being applied to broader and broader segments of the society, it is in the colleges and universities that they have found their greatest success. In those institutions, the tactics and successes followed an almost set-piece formula. In the early days of student activism, a series of issues and problems were used as a basis for developing the pattern of rebellion and disruption. Among these were purely local matters, largely pertaining to the students' relationships to the university, and revolving around the question of whether the university had any legitimate right to impose conduct regulations on its students. Many of these were familiar areas of concern, and included such matters as hours, sexual conduct, the regulation and operation of motor vehicles, dealings with landlords and managers in off-campus housing facilities, and so on. In other instances, the issues were more clearly political, concerning questions of free speech, the right to assemble, the right of the university to regulate the use of its facilities, and related matters. Still other issues involved the relationship between the university and the larger society. Should the university cooperate with the Selective Service System; should it have anything to do with companies engaged in war production or involved in countries where flagrant racial discrimination was practiced; should it conduct research for any arm of the defense establishment? Ultimately, the issues broadened to include the basic nature of the governance of the institution, the role the university played in the system generally, and the demand that the universities be politicized and reconstituted as active agents of the revolution.

Whatever the issue, the general tactic remained the same. At first, an effort would be made to gain control of the established forms of student participation in the affairs of the institution. This seldom failed, because typically, no more than 10 or 15 percent of the students actively participated in the processes of student government, and even these were easily influenced by power tactics and propaganda. While most students went about their primary business at the institution, namely, getting the education it provided, the minority generally succeeded in gaining control over the established form of student government. In the few instances where this tactic failed, the responsible students who retained control of their governments were either discredited, condemned as tools of the administration, or subjected to tremendous personal pressure, sometimes including threats, in order to bring them into line. Without any real constituency, and under the constant pressure and ridicule of the radical minority, these groups either buckled and gave in, or gradually withdrew from the scene. Once in control of the student government, either by election, intimidation, or cooptation, the radicals had a quasi-respectable forum from which to circulate their propaganda and a tool for accelerating the rebellion.

A similar tactic was used in the case of the student newspaper. By a process of self-selection of staff members, or by application of pressure, the student newspaper would be captured by the radicals. Once in their hands, the paper became an active vehicle for fomenting rebellion and undermining the strength of any faculty or administrative group that had the temerity to oppose them. Any objections to even the most flagrant distortion, vituperation against persons, deceit, or violence-inducing propaganda was condemned as an affront to the freedom of the press. Many college newspapers became exercises in intellectual and journalistic dishonesty, and were turned to the destruction of the institution that, ironically, provided the reputation and support on which the paper's operation depended. In those few instances where control of the paper was retained by students possessed of a fundamental integrity and devotion to truth, an underground newspaper or political leaflets served the same purposes.

With these tools in hand, the radicals were ready for a confrontation. Typically, they sought some issue that had a broad appeal. If one could not be found, a contrived issue was developed, and attached to some principle that had broad appeal. Thus, whether a faculty member or administrator could be called a liar or worse in public was not regarded as a matter of slander, but as a question of free speech. Whenever possible, even the most unreasonable and irresponsible demands were couched in terms involving appeals to justice, fairness, individual freedom, or one of the items in the Bill of Rights. The pattern detailed in Chapter X was then pursued, with the eventual goal of disrupting the institution, weakening its contribution to the larger society, and reducing it to a political tool to be manipulated by the radicals.

These tactics succeeded because the universities were poorly prepared to deal with even a tiny minority that was willing to abandon good faith, to proceed with mutual trust only so long as it served their purposes, and to violate the fundamental conditions on which the operation of an ordered society of free men was based. When these conditions were added to the facts that few universities were willing to take a stand until it was too late, and that the majority of students did not involve themselves, it becomes clear how a determined minority of only a hundred and fifty or so students could successfully dominate a major institution. It is equally clear why a similar minority is able to terrorize a high school, radicalize a portion of junior high school students, intimidate teachers and principals, and effectively disrupt the process of education at almost any level.

Because their standard tactics and original issues have worn out from overuse, the radicals have gradually shifted the style of their operation. While considerable effort still goes into attempts to radicalize young people in every setting, they have gradually become frustrated at their lack of success and have consequently moved to tactics of desperation. Arson, bombing, threatened kidnappings, assaults, and other flagrant criminal actions have replaced sit-ins, disruptions of institutions, and mass confrontations with the police as the dominant tactics. There are continuing attempts to steer legitimate protests into violent and destructive channels, efforts are made to seize or collaborate with other groups involved in revolutionary activity, and there has gradually appeared a series of paperback and/or underground publications advocating the violent destruction of the system, or its subversion through various countercultural activities. By and large, these activities show the same disorganized, vague, part-time qualities that were apparent in the early statements and actions of the SDS, and the number of radical activists involved remains at less than 1 percent of the total sixteen- to twenty-five-year-old age group.

A major contributor to the radicals' successes, however limited, is the fascination with them in the public communications media. The militant antics of the radicals have almost always been responded to favorably by members of the fourth estate who are intrigued with action and titillated by violence. Because the (most often self-appointed) spokesmen for the radicals are loud, emotionally intense, and expert at the art of the wordy harangue, they intrude themselves emphatically into the senses of the viewer or listener. Their impact on the public consciousness is increased by their personal appearance, and their superficial rhetoric is precisely the kind of copy needed by a newsman who wants a quick story in a few words. It is common practice for the radicals to arrange ahead of time with the news media so that their activities will be prominently covered. It is not unusual for the radical managers of a demonstration or protest to wait a considerable length of time, before engaging in actions supposedly driven by the demands of their outraged consciences, in order to insure that they will gain coverage on the evening television news. As a matter of fact, I have seen demonstrations postponed because the cooperating newsman was not able to be there with his TV camera on the day originally scheduled.

The fascination with the radicals is not confined to a few gullible newsmen. A substantial segment of the liberal intellectual community persists in the belief that the radicals are nothing but idealistic reformers, seeking truth and beauty, and sincerely concerned about the future of our free society. Such implicit support raises radical activity to an undeserved level of

47

dignity, and poses a substantial question about the ability of the gulls to know the difference between sincere efforts to improve a system that has served the nation well, and irrational actions frankly intended to destroy it. Too frequently in the history of revolutions, the failure of liberals to recognize what was going on, and their lending of support to activities designed to promote the eventual overthrow of the system, has provided radical revolutionaries with enough temporary sympathy or support to permit them to suceed in their goals. The final scene in the piece finds the liberals waking up just as the gates of the concentration camp slam behind them, or remaining mercifully asleep so as to be spared hearing the swish of the guillotine as it falls on their sympathetic necks.

In all the activities of the radicals, from the smallest disruptive sit-in to the mass violence of the 1968 Democratic National Convention in Chicago, a consistent pattern of behavior reveals much about their underlying personalities. Most prominent is their absolute conviction that they are right. This characteristic is freely admitted, and is rationalized on grounds of superior insight, conscience, or moral conviction. This in turn gives rise to an unbelievable level of arrogance: they assume that no one can see the truth so clearly as they do, that no one can find insightful answers with equal facility, that no ordinary person can be expected to comprehend the complexities of their ideas and approaches. It is true that many of them are quite bright, and most have a kind of skill in argument and a degree of verbal facility. But they are at the same time exceedingly vague and superficial, given to loose abstractions and sweeping generalizations, unable to deal with complex issues in a rigorous way, and totally lacking the ability to handle practical or operational challenges to their unusual proposals and ideas. As a part of the same general trait, they reveal a deep fascination with their own self-importance, attributing profound meaning to even the most puerile ideas and actions, seeking credit for developments in which they have had no real part, and attributing to themselves the characteristics of profound wisdom, philosophical depth, political skill, and personal cleverness. They have a fantastic belief in their own ingenuity, and it is not unusual for them to believe that some idea or political tactic is their unique invention, when in fact the same notion has been proposed repeatedly

48

throughout history, and is familiar or even trite to a normally intelligent and educated person.

As a part of the same superficial intellectuality, the radicals also show a great fascination with oversimplified, quick, easy solutions to problems. One constantly sees matters of great complexity approached with a simple-minded clarity, and solutions proposed for an immediate problem that fail to take into account more than one or two of the underlying relationships, or to consider the broader implications or the future effects. Once the quick, superficial answer is proposed, the radicals come to see it as God's own truth, and unconditional demands for its immediate adoption are pressed with zeal and intensity. At the same time the radicals seem totally incapable of dealing with any of the tricky problems of implementation, which they avoid at all costs. They see themselves as inspired philosophers and theoreticians, and leave to lesser minds the practical matters of how to get from where we are to where we want to be.

There is also a nearly universal inability to tolerate frustration. They must have their demands met *now*, any questioning of or resistance to their wishes is intolerable, and any blocking of their actions represents not only an insult, but a psychological catastrophe. They are impatient beyond belief, and any caution or delay for reasoned discussion and deliberation is seen as purposely dilatory and representative of lack of sincerity. They are very much creatures of the moment, with little consideration of the future and total disregard for history or past experience. They must have what they want, when they want it, without regard to consequences, implications, or accountability.

The pattern of the radicals' relationships to authority is another most interesting matter. Authority in any form is nearly intolerable to them, and is reacted to with hatred, contempt, or anxiety. The law is something for other, inferior beings, and their hatred of police is nothing short of monumental. They cannot stand to be called to account, they feel justified in whatever they do on the basis of their own conviction, and they regard themselves as the final, omnipotent authority in all questions and actions. In spite of this aversion to authority, there is evidence of a basic authoritarianism within them, which often emerges when one of them obtains a position of real power.

Pervasive in the rhetoric and actions of the radicals is a

constant demand for total freedom. Accepting limits or boundaries of any kind is extremely difficult for them, and one gains the impression that the raising of any barrier to their wishes is seen by them as equivalent to total political repression. They have in some manner become accustomed to having the world bow to their slightest wish, and any suggestion that they must restrain themselves, in the interests of the group or of future consequences, is impossible for them to deal with. At the same time, it is clear that the freedom they demand lacks much sense of concomitant responsibility. Their attitude seems to be that they will do what they want when they want to do it, and that anyone who tries to impose even reasonable limits or demands for accountability is a complete fascist pig.

Finally, there runs through their behavior a strong suggestion of deep anxiety and helplessness as individuals. In spite of their emphasis on freedom, they find functioning as individuals in any area of political confrontation exceedingly difficult. There is little indication of solid belief in their ability or competence to do anything of a practical nature. Group operations, mass demonstrations, the fantasy of involvement in political movements of great collective power, all indicate a deep sense of underlying insecurity. In some ways, their demands and tactics have always borne a mark of personal desperation, rather than secure individual strength.

In composite, these characteristics represent a recurring syndrome, which is hereinafter termed the "radical personality." Even taking into full account the dangers of overgeneralization, this cluster of behavior patterns appears with sufficient frequency to justify its being identified as pervasive among our young political radicals. The typical arrogance, conviction of the validity of their own conclusions, self-importance, lack of frustration tolerance, impatience, fascination with easy solutions, need for immediate relief from tension, difficulty with authority, strident demands for total freedom without responsibility, and evidence of underlying fear and insecurity, are almost universally seen in their individual and collective psychological makeup. In subsequent chapters, we will examine the peculiar social conditions and family relationships in their backgrounds, which help to explain why and how this particular variety and expression of radicalism has developed.

For now, it is enough to ask what the young political

50

radicals propose for America. On the surface, they would have us believe that all that they seek is a better, fairer, more peaceful society, in which individual freedom and worth may be reasserted, materialism submerged to deeper spiritual values, and the profound problems of the nation and the world quickly solved. Worthy goals, these, and ones with which no reasonable person would quarrel. But we need to look beyond these statements into the actions, the means, and the philosophy of the young radicals in making our judgments about their value to the society. Taken collectively, the various radical groups propose no practical means to these goals, offer a philosophy both nihilistic and reactionary in the deepest sense of the words, and engage chronically in actions that belie even the narrowest commitment to the goals they allegedly seek. The intriguing thing about the behavior of the young radicals is that, while they profess to be deeply concerned about the problems of our society and the world, their actions fail to do anything effective in removing the self-evident threats to our civilization. If anything, their actions tend to increase the possibility that the very things they are worried about will come to pass. Many examples of the peculiar self-defeating nature of their behavior can be observed; a few will suffice to illustrate the point. The militant's answer to the threat of nuclear destruction seems to be to promote the development of political systems either of the far left or the far right whose characteristics of rigid totalitarianism or volatile anarchy would place a highly unstable finger upon the nuclear trigger. Their answer to the problems of loss of individuality and bureaucratization is to drop out of the society through drugs, hippie-ism, or sullen alienation. Their answer to the problem of poverty is not to be economically productive in their personal lives. Their answer to the problem of race relations is to foster hatred and a new racism between two groups that desperately need reconciliation and understanding. Their answer to the problem of difficult communication between the generations is to shout polemic diatribes and state non-negotiable demands. Their answer to the problem of managing a complex technology is to press for total individual participation in every decision. Their answer to the problem of meeting massive educational needs is to disrupt the universities and subvert the high schools. And their answer to the problem of maintaining freedom is to tear down a system that has offered greater individual freedom and opportunity than any other devised in the history of mankind. Finally, their answer to a world of problems requiring profound and rational thought, deep personal commitment, unending work and patience, and a total dedication to purposeful programs is to advocate a formless, mindless revolution based on emotion, designed to destroy what exists, and to worry later about what will replace it.

Peculiar? Irrational? Dangerous? Certainly, the actions of the young radicals are all of these. Certainly also, such actions can only be understood in terms of psychological disturbance so intense as to be personally disorganizing and incompatible with logical reasoning. This supposed political movement is barely political at all; it is much more a peculiar expression of deep psychological disturbance, in which uncontrolled emotion interferes effectively with the rational capacity of the victims. As such, it poses a particular and unique threat to the essential basis of our system. When even a tiny minority of persons can find even limited acceptance of actions based on characteristics antithetical to those required for the maintenance of a free and orderly society, we have cause for concern. When deceit comes to replace good faith, when paranoia succeeds mutual trust, when emotion overrides reason, when integrity and honesty are replaced by the notion that the end justifies the means, when immediate relief from tension becomes more important than any consideration of the future, and when freedom with responsibility is translated into insistence upon doing precisely everything one wants without respect to the consequences, we are in serious trouble. Herein, rather than in their programs, their philosophy, or even their tactics of violence, lies the danger of the young radicals to the American system. For in their personal characteristics and in their basic psychology, they are the precise antithesis of the kind of citizen required to carry the heavy responsibilities of a free society.

In my academic and administrative experience at the University of Michigan, and more recently as a practicing psychologist, I have had a close personal association with a large number of radical young people. My exposure to the liberal-intellectual community as a faculty member was intimate—I knew well the personalities and goals of many of the early radicals on the Michigan campus, and at the time sympathized with them. I was one of the early faculty sponsors of a student organization called "Voice," which was a precedessor of the SDS, and was freely accepted as a confidant of such radicals as Tom Hayden. Later, as vice president of the university, I confronted many of them across the battle lines of protest and disruption. Out of these experiences, on which much of this book is based, came a close acquaintance with some of these radicals and a knowledge of their underlying psychology. A considerable understanding of the general pattern of the radical personality may be gained from a brief accounting of some of their more obvious qualities, especially as several of these individuals have since gained prominence as public figures.

TIMOTHY LEARY. Leary first gained broad public attention while he was a psychologist on the faculty at Harvard. There, while conducting research on the effects of various mind-influencing drugs on levels of consciousness, he supposedly administered LSD to several students, with insufficient attention to accepted ethical and scientific standards. His relationship with Harvard, and with the scientific community generally, suffered, and he eventually returned to California to establish a quasi-legitimate center where he continued his "studies." This eventually evolved into a kind of commune, with Leary as the "spiritual leader," and allegedly was little more than a gathering place for persons who were heavily into the LSD scene. Out of it came a more and more bizarre commitment to the "Turn On, Drop Out" philosophy advocated by Leary, paralleled by increasing attention to a vague revolutionary philosophy, in which Leary fancied himself the high priest of a new antiestablishment, antimaterialistic spiritual movement. For a period of time, Leary was popular as a speaker on college campuses, where he would hold forth on his "philosophy" during a kind of mumbo-jumbo seance, advocate the use of LSD, and preach a weird combination of spiritual actualization and revolutionary action. Later, after several drug-related encounters with the law, he escaped from a prison facility in California. He fled to Algeria as a "political refugee," was met there with a less than enthusiastic reception, and at present, after an unwelcomed sojourn in Switzerland, is back in the United States, perhaps to face charges.

When I first knew Leary, in 1953, he had recently finished his Ph.D. at the University of California at Berkeley, and was working as a junior researcher in one of the facilities in the San Francisco area. On the surface, he appeared to be shy and somewhat retiring. He suffered from a hearing handicap, about which he was quite sensitive, and it seemed to contribute to his sense of uneasiness in personal relationships. He was married, but the relationship between him and his wife was obviously full of tension and difficulties, and her subsequent death, allegedly a suicide, contributed further to his tendency to withdraw into himself. Beneath the surface, Leary carried a conviction that he was a genius destined to make a revolutionary contribution to the understanding of human psychology. To some degree, this fantasy was encouraged by some of his colleagues, who reacted with fascination to his troubled eccentricity, or with sympathy for his obvious personal problems. His great wish at this early stage of his career was to gain a position on the psychology faculty at Berkeley, and to assume a leadership position there while developing a reputation for sensationally creative research. Frustrated in that desire, he attempted to pursue a similar path while at Harvard, but found the demands for scientific respectability inconsistent with his driving need for sensationalism. Unable to fulfill his fantasy of fame as a philosopher-king within the confines of the regular academic role, Leary gravitated into more and more bizarre activity, building a sub-culture of his own to support his conviction that he was a genius with superior insight.

Leary represents several of the commonly seen characteristics of the radical personality. He suffered from a basic sense of inadequacy and had great difficulty in dealing with interpersonal relationships. He compensated for these inadequacies by developing an internal conviction that he was a genius with unique insight into the problems of human relationships. Frustrated by the realities of his own limitations and by tragedies in his personal life, he set about constructing an environment where he would be recognized as someone of importance and influence. He came to see himself, in the grandiose and perhaps even delusory manner of many radicals, as above the law, uniquely gifted and insightful, and as the leader of a new and mystical movement, which would destroy the forces that had denied him his proper fame and power. His fascination with revolution can be best understood as a means to elevate his own influence and power, and as an attack upon a society that refused to take his initial strivings seriously. Beyond the unfortunate effects on his own life, the tragedy is that his personal pathology came to be translated into a drug cult that has brought even greater destruction into the lives of a great many young people.

TOM HAYDEN. Hayden has already been mentioned as the author of the Port Huron Statement and as one of the early leaders of the SDS. My acquaintance with him dates from his undergraduate days at the University of Michigan in the late 1950s. His career followed a pattern typical of many of the early radicals. While an undergraduate, he was active in many of the liberal causes of the day, and as an editor of the student newspaper at Michigan, he was chronically involved in efforts to undermine the positions and actions of university authorities. One of his particular targets was the dean of women, toward whom he held a particular antagonism because of her traditional views concerning discipline. He prompted a number of amateurish investigations of this woman, built what he thought was a convincing case, freely impugned her character at private gatherings, and was immensely frustrated when she was not summarily dismissed. Somewhat later, he turned his attention to larger issues, and became active in the civil rights efforts of SNCC. He stayed with SDS for several years during and after his days at Michigan, serving as field secretary, project director, and so on. His work as a community organizer in Newark coincided in time with the Newark riots. Hayden's politics gradually drifted more and more to the left, he became increasingly preoccupied with the Vietnam War as an issue, and his activities took on a flavor of greater willingness to engage in, or provoke, violence. He was one of the organizers of the demonstrations at the Democratic Convention in Chicago in 1968, and he was eventually convicted, as one of the "Chicago Seven," of violating the Civil Rights Act of 1968 in connection with his activities there. (Recently the U.S. Court of Appeals for the Seventh Circuit reversed Hayden's conviction. The three-judge panel also voided those of Rennie Davis, David Dellinger, Abbie Hoffman, and Jerry Rubin.) Since that time, he has maintained a close affiliation with various end-the-war groups, he has kept up an active liaison with the Hanoi government and the Viet Cong, and has steadfastly associated himself with a great number of anti-establishment groups and activities.

Hayden's early characterization of himself was as an intense, altruistic, idealistic reformer. Like Leary, he fancied himself to be unusually bright and insightful, and he was strongly motivated by a wish to be personally important. He was endlessly frustrated by the "apathy" of his contemporaries, and he was always searching for some issue or other that he could use to propel them into outraged action. Underlying his actions were two prominent and obvious motives. He was a dreadfully insecure young man, who saw cause for alarm, apprehension, or dread in any person or situation that threatened his personal security or ideas even in the slightest way. At meetings or discussions, so long as Hayden was in control, or speaking about matters with which he was familiar enough to be persuasive or looked up to, he was quite comfortable. But when challenged, frustrated, or called to account, he would show marked symptoms of fear and insecurity. I saw him many times with tears streaming down his cheeks when things were not going to his liking. His hands trembled, his voice broke, and he would lapse into abject discouragement and despair, or, on occasion, become insistently righteous. In addition, he was always motivated by an intense underlying resentment of authority. When convinced that he was right, nothing else mattered, and he was verbally facile enough to adduce rapid, if often sophomoric and superficial, arguments to support his total conviction that his view was correct. He viewed challenges to this omnipotent belief in the validity of his own position as the mistaken rantings of inferior beings, or as arbitrary impositions of fascist beasts.

Hayden thus epitomizes the personality characteristics so commonly seen among the young radicals. At the base of his personality is deep insecurity, a sense of personal helplessness in the face of frustration, and great resentment of authority. This is covered by a compensatory veneer of self-assurance, a dogmatic belief in the correctness of his own position, a sense of superiority in relationships with ordinary human beings, and a willingness to move through varying stages of protest toward violence when he fails to get his own way. His career offers a dramatic illustration of the process of fear, frustration, and anger through which the radical personality moves in its quest for power, influence, and recognition. At each stage, when the system (the university, the government, the established practices of civilized society) fails to grant recognition and comfort, which the radical seeks, he moves a step further in his attack. In fifteen years, Hayden's personal problems have moved in their expression from a wish to destroy a dean of women, through a wish to radicalize college students, and finally to a wish to destroy an entire system of government—all so that he may finally be accepted as the profound intellect and powerful leader he fancies himself to be.

WILLIAM AYERS. Ayers was one of the "second-generation" radicals whom I encountered frequently while I was vice president at the University of Michigan. Several years younger than Hayden, he nonetheless was strikingly similar in his background and basic personality. Although somewhat less ideological than Hayden, and somewhat less bright, he more than made up for this in possessing a deeper anger and a tendency toward violent confrontation. By the time I knew him, he was already totally committed to the destruction of the system, by whatever means necessary. He saw injustice everywhere and took the slightest challenge to his position as a personal affront. While he could be superficially pleasant, his underlying hostility was never far from the surface. He regarded his parents and most members of their generation as "plastic" hypocrites who cared nothing for principle or the problems of others. He spoke often and freely of his intentions to bring about radical change in the system, although he was lacking in any clear statement of alternatives, means, or implications. He took it as given that anything evil should be eliminated, and that something better would automatically arise as a result. He was typical of the young radicals who flocked to the SDS in the mid-sixties, promoted and participated in campus disruptions, and gradually gravitated into more and more violent and frankly revolutionary activity. While he was still in Ann Arbor, he made sporadic efforts to promote radical activity among public school students, engaged in some quasi-legitimate political activity by seeking to organize a radical party, and participated frequently in antiwar activity. Not finding sufficient success or relief from his frustrations thereby, he eventually became associated with Weatherman, the violent-action arm of the SDS, and allegedly was a participant in several of the more serious confrontations between members of that group and the law enforcement agencies in Chicago and elsewhere. Ayers is presently "underground" with other Weatherman associates, and is on the FBI's Ten Most Wanted list.

DIANA OUGHTON. Like Ayers, Oughton was a student at Michigan during the 1960s. Her radical career roughly paralleled that of Ayers, and she also eventually became associated with Weatherman and its activities. She was identified as one of the persons who died in the New York townhouse explosion, discussed later in this book, which resulted when explosives being manufactured into bombs for terrorist attacks were inadvertently set off, with destructive results to those involved. Out of respect for the dead, and for her family, which has already suffered tragedy beyond belief, I have decided not to comment on her personality or on the forces that shaped it. Shortly following her death, a syndicated series of newspaper articles more than adequately analyzed the evolution of Oughton from a privileged child of the liberal middle class to a violent revolutionary dedicated to the destruction of our system. This series is extremely interesting, and is recommended to the reader of the present book for the added insights a detailed study of an individual case can provide.

ROGER RAPPAPORT. While Rappaport was never himself active in the SDS or other organized campus radical organizations, and while he never personally participated in violence or disruption, he nonetheless represents an important element in the radical activity of the 1960s. Like Tom Hayden, he was an editor of the student newspaper at the University of Michigan, and, again like Hayden, he gave the surface appearance of great idealism and principle. Rappaport's contribution to the radical cause grew out of the fact that he found personal enjoyment and satisfaction in seeing and promoting conflicts that eventually escalated into confrontation. My first exposure to Rappaport came when he was a junior editor on the paper. One of his reporters (who eventually became a flaming radical activist, but at the time had some commitment to objectivity) had done a story on a program being run by the fraternities and sororities on campus, which tended to illustrate their good will and interest in some matter of social reform. When the story appeared, it had quite another flavor to it, and communicated the notion that these groups were self-seeking and cynical in their interest in the program. When I questioned the reporter, he alleged that Rappaport had encouraged or ordered him to change the story, because of Rappaport's wish not to publish anything favorable to the fraternities and sororities. Rappaport, for himself, never denied the allegation, although he had numerous occasions to do so.

Later, still in pursuit of the sensational, Rappaport undertook an investigation of one of the university's regents. This man, who was a highly respected citizen of the state, had devoted a good portion of his adult life to building and serving the university, and had given or pledged several millions of dollars to the institution. Rappaport apparently was convinced that the man had profited from the relationship, and undertook to demonstrate a financial conflict of interest. In the final event, one item of less than five dollars was uncovered about which there was a remaining question of conflict of interest. The individual, rather than suffer further embarrassment, resigned, and Rappaport was gleeful in his reaction, believing that he had served as an instrument of the right and the principled.

At every opportunity, Rappaport's journalistic approach was to heighten conflict, emphasize differences, encourage dispute, and raise doubts about the credibility of university officials. By his handling of the "news," he could keep an issue alive until it flared into confrontation. By his sympathetic response to almost any demand from the radicals, he served, perhaps inadvertently, as an agent of every cause they espoused. By his staging of editorial attacks, and by his timing of these efforts, he was successful in helping to create and maintain an atmosphere of crisis on the campus for a long period of time. The supreme irony of his situation was that he consistently denied that he had any such intentions, and insisted he was not doing anything other than trying to run an honest newspaper within a long-established tradition of a free press on the campus.

Whether Rappaport was simply naive, self-deceptive, or totally lacking in integrity was impossible to tell. Whatever his motive, his method of operation was clear. Whenever he approached an individual on a news or editorial issue, it was obvious that he had a well-established position on the matter. His interviewing style consisted of making assertions about how the person being interviewed saw the issue, and unless these were explicitly contradicted, the response was taken as confirming his own already formulated evaluation. When translated into a news story, the interview became much more an expression of what Rappaport had already established for himself as the truth than what the situation actually was. Compounded over several occasions, and further bolstered by a series of editorials in which his bias was even more flagrant, this tactic was an effective means of supporting the radical position and keeping the campus in turmoil.

I have since lost track of Rappaport's whereabouts or activity, although I understand that he is pursuing a career in journalism. I can only hope that added maturity has come to him, and that he is turning his obvious talents to a more objective pursuit of the truth than was apparent in his formative years. I further hope that his personal fascination with the sensational, his omnipotent belief in his own wisdom, and his budding notion that the end justifies the means have moderated sufficiently to take him out of the company of the radicals with whom he formerly found common cause.

There are numerous other figures in public life, prominent in one or another aspect of the radical movement in America, who reveal a similar or closely related pattern of personality and behavior: zealous conviction of the rectitude of their beliefs, bitter hostility toward our established way of life and toward authority generally, complete impatience with any challenge to their position or to any delay in responding to their demands, heavy emphasis on the importance of their personal freedom, little attention to the existence of any concomitant responsibility, and so forth. Scarcely a day passes when one of this group does not burst into the public eye with another demand, supposedly based on the conviction of his or her conscience, for instant redress of some grievance. To this group, the system is evil, manipulative, exploitative, and insensitive to the needs and concerns of the people. To them, also, there is an easy answer—tear down the system, and hope that something better will emerge, based on the twisted concept of conscience that characterizes many of them. Pretending a concern for humanity, these noisy jackdaws are artists in the marketing of hatred and craftsmen in the destruction of a decent and ordered society. Armed with an astounding lack of understanding of the complexity of our problems and the difficulty of solving them, these purveyors of the easy solution through the destruction of the system rank as the poorest advocates of the people they claim to represent and serve.

Among the more noteworthy examples—and giving due notice to exceptions to the pattern in minor details—are such individuals as Jane Fonda and Jerry Rubin, William Kunstler and the Fathers Berrigan, and Allard Lowenstein and James Groppi. The reader is invited to make his own list, and to examine the behavior and backgrounds of the persons on it in the context of what is said about the radical personality throughout this book. It is an interesting exercise, if somewhat sobering when one considers the prominence granted such persons by the media and the influence their antics have on our youth.

Some beginning insight into the origins and development of the radical personality may be gained from considering briefly a composite description of the several score young radicals with whom I have had contact in my clinical practice. Again, details vary from individual to individual, but there is a strikingly similar general pattern. In their behavior, they exude deep hostility toward authority figures, which in most instances has been generalized to include the system. They are antagonistic toward school, characterize it as "boring" or irrelevant, and are generally defiant toward or contemptuous of their teachers and their parents. They insist on having total personal freedom, and are resentful and hostile toward parental efforts to set limits. They respond in a stereotyped, negative way toward the national government, nonradical public figures, the law, the armed forces, police, religion, limits on sexual behavior or drug use, and requirements that they accept the consequences of their own decisions. They affect a hippie style of dress, claim to reject hypocrisy and materialism, and talk much about love, meaningful relationships, and "getting their heads together." Their political attitudes are extremely superficial, consisting largely of slogans, but pointed generally in the direction of "revolution" and "destroying the system." Their grasp of complex problems is highly superficial, and they are generally persuaded that we are prevented from solving them only by the stupidity or evil of powerful persons in high places. The general pattern of their activity is aimless and purposeless, but usually directed toward some momentary personal indulgence or escape. They have little view of or hope for the future, beyond a continuation of the pattern of freedom without responsibility and indulgence

61

without work or effort, often embodied in a vague yearning for a pastoral existence in some pre-Columbian nirvana. As individuals, they are dismally unhappy, lonely, embittered, and generally purposeless, pursuing a revolution that is only vaguely political, only haphazardly conceived, and hardly understood by them at all. In short, the teen-age radical, much like his earlier and older precursors, is suffering from a pervasive psychological disturbance, which is allowed expression in political and social form by a society whose commitment to political freedoms is so complete that even illness, masquerading as principled objection to our way of life, is permitted to flourish.

The clinical histories of the young radicals whom I see in my practice also contain some surprising uniformities. Almost inevitably, they come from liberal middle-class homes, where permissiveness and self-indulgence have been a way of life. As a child, the budding radical is almost worshipped by his parents, or at least by one of them, and is permitted his own way; if either parent attempts to impose some reasonable limits, he is forced to back off by the other. The child is regarded as superior—either intellectually, physically, or aesthetically. The home is characterized by a heavy emphasis on the accumulation and consumption of material goods. The parents themselves are often highly self-indulgent, many times to the detriment of a continuing and close relationship with the children. The home frequently is marked by political attitudes expressing the typical intellectual views of current social issues. Attitudes toward school and school achievement are "progressive," and the notion is communicated that education can be accomplished better by one or the other parent than by the school. Later, when the child's demands for indulgence, total freedom, and no responsibility become distasteful to the parent, a disciplinary crunch is suddenly applied, with the result that the child becomes totally rebellious and alienated. The most striking single feature of the parents' attitude is a helpless air of inability to do anything effective about the child's unacceptable or self-destructive behavior.

While these are only a part of the total spectrum of causes for the development of the radical personality, they emphasize what I see as the central factors in the parent-child relationship underlying that development. In the remaining chapters of this book, a more detailed consideration of these and other factors will be presented.

62

III
THE GREAT DIVIDE

We have recently been hearing a great deal about something called a "generation gap," a supposed sharp division between the attitudes and values of young people and those of their elders. This notion has been advanced both by serious analysts who seek to explain the communication difficulties that sometimes exist between parents and children or students and teachers, and by others who often try to justify the alienation felt by some youngsters, particularly the young radicals, toward authority, parents, or the Establishment. The idea that our youth are somehow a race apart, or a homogeneous subgroup isolated from the rest of society, has also been fostered by the extremist minority, in the hope of accentuating differences between older and younger Americans for the sake of furthering alienation and broadening the base of rebellion. "Never trust anyone over thirty," a phrase which has become a watchword for the young radicals, in fact illustrates both the deeply defective personal relationships that characterize their own lives, and their effort to involve their entire generation in a paranoid distrust of older persons.

Like all generalizations, the idea that the difficulties faced by our society, and particularly those in relationships between younger and older persons, are due to something called a generation gap, is deceptively easy and simple, and largely incorrect. As I will illustrate in more detail below, parents and their children, for the most part, still share the same basic values and outlook on the important issues facing them and society.

For the most part, too, the relationships between American parents and their children are excellent, and contain strong elements of mutual trust and respect. In the great majority of American families, alienation between the generations is the result of the normal stresses of adolescence, and typically disappears with the passing of that period of the younger person's life. When severe alienation does occur, the generation gap is only one of a large number of causes and often merely reflects the operation of other and more important variables.

It is nevertheless sensible to look more carefully at the implications of this now common term "generation gap," since it is frequently used to explain everything from minor youthful dissatisfactions to major episodes of violence and destruction. Anyone with common sense and the ability to view his own youth in perspective realizes that the idea is not a new one. No one can grow up without at some point experiencing a disagreement with his parents over something he wants to do. Differences in judgment about the young person's maturity and capacity inevitably occur, and just as inevitably lead to normal disputes, with the younger person pressing for more freedom and self-determination, and the older seeking to hold the line until he is satisfied that freedom will be safely and responsibly exercised. In times past, before we found it necessary to coin a scientific term for even the most common occurrences, most young people found it sufficient to mumble about "old-fashioned ideas" or to act disgruntled over "horse and buggy" parental attitudes. Likewise, most parents and teachers contented themselves with quiet murmurings about "those crazy kids" or wondered "what the world was coming to." Almost always, attitudes on both sides softened as time passed, and before one knew it, the former children, who were now parents, were sharing most basic attitudes with their parents, who were now grandparents, and both coined new unscientific phrases to bemoan the immaturity and foolishness of the latest generation of young persons.

Differences in viewpoint between successive generations are virtually certain to occur. The conditions under which persons grow up, the problems they face, the opportunities offered, and even the basic structure of society inevitably change through time. Even in a perfectly static society, fundamental differences between age groups dictate variations in outlook and

64

values. The differences in levels of physical strength and energy, how long one has to live, sexual interest and capacity, general health, and other physiologically based factors determine attitudes and behavior in a variety of spheres. Few women over fifty become mothers, and few girls of twenty-five become grandmothers, and their respective attitudes are accordingly different. A man who makes his living as a longshoreman is certain to put increasing concern into pension plans and job security as he nears sixty, while a man of twenty-five with a young family will typically be more interested in mortgage rates and the quality of public education for his children. Equally important distinctions grow out of experience, increasing historical perspective, changing social roles and responsibilities related to age, and long-term opportunities to view and evaluate the operation of the political and social system. Thus it is unreasonable to expect the interests and goals of university students, whose involvement with their school is quite transient, to coincide with those of the permanent faculty or administration, who typically have a long-term equity in the institution.

There is no reason to expect that members of different generations will ever share precisely the same attitudes and outlook. In fact, it would be disastrous to progress if this were true. Civilization must change, and the impetus for this change has typically come from the infusion of new ideas generated by younger, often unconventional persons. Thus, "conflict between generations" is a natural part of an age-old process and need not be a cause for consternation or for recrimination between the parties. In recent years, however, a new quality seems to have appeared in the relationships between at least some members of the older and the younger generations—a hardening of attitudes verging on bitterness. Today, some radical members of the younger generation seem quite prepared to condemn nearly all older people and some adults seem quite ready to give up entirely on the young. As I have already said, it is natural for young people to feel that their parents' ideas are anachronistic, and equally natural for parents to feel that children are rejecting ideas and ethics that have served the parents perfectly well. On the other hand, it is a most destructive and unnatural thing to have extremists, both young and old, take these natural differences so seriously that they are eager to resort to mass head-busting of younger people, or preventive euthanasia of older ones. This is not to say that the ideas and actions of militants characterize the general attitude of any generation, but it is alarming to see the degree of bitterness sometimes expressed by a few members of each of the two groups.

Some of this extreme vindictiveness, which exists among a small minority of both younger and older persons, can be better understood simply by describing in stereotyped terms the way in which each group characterizes the other. For embittered older persons, the radical young are seen as dirty, disrespectful, arrogant, and disruptive. It is thought that they want to tear down established institutions and ways of life; that they have no appreciation for the efforts of older people to provide a secure and comfortable life; that they put their own immediate satisfaction ahead of consideration for others, stability, and order; and that they are vicious nihilists who really care nothing about the heritage of our civilization. Older people, on the other hand, are seen by alienated radicals as hypocritical, self-seeking, and materialistic; as devoted to shallow, narrow, and deceitful human relationships; as being without social conscience and a concern for the preservation of a decent environment; as militaristic, imperialist, chauvinistic boobs; in short, as being prepared to sacrifice the future for the sake of their own immediate pleasure in the form of bigger cars, more fattening foods, more bestial police, and more rewarding stock dividends. If these be accurate characterizations, they certainly represent a tragic comment on the social character of Americans both young and old. Indeed the fact that one finds a growing number of people on each side willing to characterize the other in this fashion is already a tragic matter.

Let us examine further how such essentially vicious attitudes have come to exist, albeit only among a tiny minority of the younger and older groups. Anthropologists have long recognized that very pronounced and even destructive differences can develop between peoples who grow up in extremely different cultural settings. By now no one is surprised that a native Balinese and a native Jivaro have drastically different outlooks on life. The Balinese are passive, warm, friendly, and affiliative people, or at least were when their culture remained virginal. The Jivaro, on the other hand, were aggressive, militant, notorious as headhunters, and altogether unfriendly toward anyone outside the immediate group. Such differences are directly traceable to the operation of the total environment within which each group exists. Differences in the natural environment, the level of technology, the nature of social organization, and the long-standing mores of the groups all interact in a complex way to produce something like a tribal or national character. While it is beyond the scope and purpose of this book to identify in detail the nature of these determining factors and the complexities of the interaction among them, it is necessary to recognize that such things as a consistent group attitude and a pervasive style of life grow out of a group's total natural socioeconomic-technological environment.

This principle, even though it has been formally recognized and articulated by scientists only for the past four or five decades, has been implicitly accepted by every civilization the world has ever known. Every culture develops implicit and generally accepted ways of dealing with the environment surrounding it, and the operations of the various social institutions interacting with the natural environment are designed to develop individuals who will fit into and carry on the life styles that have proved to be effective for that particular civilization. Thus, the Plains Indians of North America, prior to the coming of the Europeans, based their survival on the protection of territorial hunting areas, and deliberately developed in their children characteristics of aggressiveness, daring, and physical endurance that made them successful hunters and warriors and thus contributed to the welfare and survival of the tribe. In a less hostile environment, such as the lush tropics of the South Pacific, cultures developed in which pacifism, communal cooperation, and individual passivity were valued, and child-rearing practices were designed to support the development of such characteristics. In the modern world there are several examples of nations in which, utilizing a more sophisticated understanding of psychology and anthropology, governmentally controlled programs have been deliberately designed to produce the kind of citizen deemed necessary for the national purpose. Hitler's Germany sought to develop a racist, arrogant, warrior generation of young men in order to provide the human raw material for militaristic conquest and national expansion. The USSR, from Lenin to the present, seeks to secure the perpetuation of the Communist ideology through similar although somewhat more subtle means. Any modern-day totalitarian government worth the name most certainly is engaged in a conscious effort to produce citizens whose attitudes and values will support its ideology. A final example of this method, carried to its logical extreme, is found in the terrifying book *1984* by George Orwell. The incompatibility of these manipulative approaches to the development of human beings with the concept of a free society and a democratically determined political system is obvious, and we must proceed very carefully if we are to avoid the loss of our freedoms through the development of a process of indoctrination that is designed to produce a kind of citizen and a set of social attitudes that fit conveniently some demagogue's notion of the ideal society.

Thus, differences in attitudes, ethics, group characteristics, and general outlook on life are known to grow out of different cultures. The notion of the generation gap can be more readily understood if it is recognized that cultures need not be separated geographically, but only *in time*, to produce significant differences in the views of the persons who grow up within them. To whatever extent the total environment of younger people during their formative years differs from that of their parents and grandparents, there will be significant differences in their values, morals, and general attitude. If a society were completely stable, that is, if there were no changes in technological level, social organization, the nature of the political system, and so on, then there would be little generation gap, since the factors shaping younger people would be essentially identical to those that shaped the attitudes of their ancestors. Since everyone young or old would have the same problems and the same prospects there would be little basis for disagreement, and relationships between young and older people would be quite harmonious. To those of us who are experienced in living through periods of change and find change an exciting experience, things would also be unbelievably dull. Can you imagine what it would be like to live in a society where every day and every week and every year promised nothing but a repetition of yesterday, last week, and last year? Few of us would find that situation very much to our liking, no matter how much stability, order, and comfort it promised.

For thousands of years man existed in most of his cultures in just such a very slowly changing environment. Imagine yourself to be a serf toiling on a piece of land in A.D. 1100. Your father and your grandfather and his father before him had tilled the same land, with the same tools, raising the same crops, and serving the same family of overlords, for generation after generation. Each faced the same fate and future. Agricultural technology remained what it had been since ancient times. Innovation was virtually unknown and boundaries were narrow. The stultification of the human condition was chronic but the generation gap was very small. It is possible, of course, given the great ability of man's brain to view things in relative terms, that such tiny changes as did occur loomed large and threatening in the minds of those who were committed to the established ways. It is equally possible that changes viewed today as revolutionary will appear insignificant to those caught up in the perhaps even more rapid change of one hundred or a thousand years from now. Was landing on the moon a matter of more consequence than the invention of the wheel?

In any case, beginning about three hundred years ago developments occurred which vastly accelerated the rate of change in the nature of our civilization. While the basic causes of these developments are probably forever lost to us, a complex of forces began to operate to produce vast social and technological shifts. As he emerged from the Dark Ages, man began to comprehend and to master the physical world around him. Competition among the national states of Europe led to a golden age of geographic discovery and exploration; the scientific and technological revolution took its start with the discovery or rediscovery of basic laws of physics and mathematics; communication among peoples increased and discoveries made independently began to be shared, at least through Western Europe and later among European colonists in the Americas. The revolution of technical and geographic discovery led to an equally important revolution in social and political affairs. Man was on the move after an interlude of more than a millennium, and his movement eventually developed the proportions of a critical mass, which exploded in the late nineteenth and early twentieth centuries into a transformation of gigantic proportions. Throughout the era of discovery forces were operating to accumulate the effect of change, and the rate at which things were being altered began to rise geometrically. In many ways, however, until the mid-twentieth century these changes had relatively little effect on the nature of mass society and the lives of its individual members. It is true that improvements in technology and means of production gradually made life easier, at least in Western Europe and North America, but most of the rest of the world remained isolated and the changes did not produce very much of a mass effect. In the United States there was a gradual shift from a rural-agricultural to an urban-industrial society, but even this had the quality of an evolutionary process rather than a dramatic revolution in the lives of individuals in the nation.

Around the year 1945, however, factors that had been at work for several decades came together in the United States and Western Europe, and to a degree throughout the world, to produce extremely rapid alterations in the total social, political, and technological environment. For the sake of convenience, and because so many highly dramatic new configurations of forces emerged in that year, 1945 may be viewed as the year in which the present gap between the generations took its start. In that year changes occurred or were predetermined that produced an environment quite different from the ones that had preceded it, and as a result the culture within which children grew up began to bear only little resemblance to the one in which the now older generations had developed. Out of this remarkable and rapid shift in the nature of our society came a culture which, while separated in time by only a few years from its predecessors, was marked by differences at least as significant as the geographic separation between the culture of the French bourgeois and that of the Chinese coolie in 1935.

Scarcely a single aspect of American life has been untouched by the events of 1945. If an intelligent person, fully aware of the circumstances defining our national life, could have been magically isolated from developments beginning, say, in 1939 and then could have been returned by the same magic only ten years later, he would have found himself in a situation so significantly changed that he would have had difficulty in comprehending it. In 1939, which even today is less than one-half a lifetime in the past, American society was still largely characterized by a simple, rural, agriculture-dominated, isolated, provincial atmosphere. There was little general intercourse with other nations or peoples; the county seat was the center of political life; the issues that had meaning to masses of people were the economic depression and the sheer problems of sur-

70

vival. Even in 1940, after World War II had begun, the majority of Americans remained isolationist in their international views. It took a week to cross the country by automobile, three days by train, and only the hardy or the foolhardy would consider making the trip by air, which itself was a two-day proposition. The small-town newspaper was the principal medium of communication, supplemented by the beginnings of a national radio system. Adolf Hitler's voice was a metallic crackle on the shortwave, and the respondent "Sieg Heil" could not be distinguished from the roar of the crowd at a Joe Louis championship fight in Madison Square Garden. Knowledge of the Belgian Congo or Singapore existed only in geography books—mine still showed Czechoslovakia as a part of the Austro-Hungarian empire—and Hiroshima, Salerno, and Phnom Penh did not even exist.

Six years later, all was changed forever. Hiroshima once again did not exist, but it had—for one searing, blinding, atomizing microsecond. But the rest of the world did exist and America was in and of that world, committed in a thousand ways not to return to its pastoral, parochial problems. The world of our children was now the whole world and the whole nation and the whole set of the world's and the nation's problems. And it is these problems with which the younger generation has grown up, and because of the intensity and immediacy of their exposure to the problems, young people attach to them a higher order of importance than they do to the problems of the 1920s, the 1930s, and the early 1940s.

With this background, it is now reasonable to review briefly not only the manifest problems that everyone recognizes as having surrounded the younger generation during its formative years, but also certain less obvious differences in the conditions of our society, which have had at least an equal impact on the developing attitudes of young people. We shall also consider the major events of the earlier period of our nation's history as they affected the attitudes and outlook of the older generations of Americans, reserving for the next few chapters a more detailed discussion of the effects of both sets of conditions upon whatever conflict has developed between older and younger people in America.

The major events and conditions that shaped the outlook of most Americans thirty and over are well recognized by historians and have been discussed at length by some social scientists. Keep in mind that a person who is seventy today was born in 1903, and was sixteen the year after the end of World War I; that a person who is sixty today was born in 1913, and reached the age of sixteen in 1929, at the time of the economic crash; that a person who is fifty today was born in 1923, and became sixteen in 1939, the beginning of World War II; that a person who is forty today was born in 1933, and became sixteen in 1949, one year before the Korean War. Note also that anyone who is under thirty has no first-hand recollection of World War I, the Roaring Twenties, the Great Depression of the thirties, and World War II, and few memories of the important events of the late forties and early fifties, each of which was highly instrumental in shaping the attitudes and outlooks of persons who lived their childhoods and youths in those contexts.

For the sake of brevity, I will not attempt to trace the effects of the events of their early lives, during which time their view of the world was forming, upon each of the ten-year age groups mentioned above. While that would be an interesting exercise, it is one that the reader is invited to undertake for himself, by picking any period in our recent history and then imagining how the exposure of a young person to the events of that period would have shaped his attitudes toward subsequent events. For my purposes here, it is sufficient to highlight some of the crucial conditions and events in the lives of persons now between the ages of thirty-five and sixty, who today represent the dominant generation in our country in terms of economic and political power, social influence, and decision-making responsibility. Of the events of the past fifty or sixty years, two stand out as major influences on this older generation. These are the economic depression of the 1930s and the fighting of World War II. Through its exposure to the depression the older generation became intimately familiar with the meaning of economic insecurity. Many of us can remember not having enough to eat, not being able to find a job, or having our fathers out of work, with all the accompanying material wants. Out of this experience, which weighed on us for more than a decade, came an implicit resolve never again to allow ourselves to experience similar deprivation. Out of this resolve in turn developed a very strong urge toward material security and a commitment not to allow our children to suffer the same unpleasantness. Thus it is not surprising that to the present older generation the sheer fact of "having things" looms as extremely important, and that what some of the younger generation deride as immoral materialism represents to us a highly symbolic desideratum.

America's participation in World War II had at least an equal importance in shaping the attitudes of the older generation. Our whole way of life and the democratic process was threatened with destruction by the totalitarian imperialism of the Axis powers. A total unified national effort was required to prevent a national debacle, which if not avoided might well have resulted in our being enslaved and exploited by the enemy, or at least reduced to a position of national impotence within which we would have been forced to deal with the enemy on the most severe terms. Out of this experience developed a strong sense of national unity, a preoccupation with national strength and defense, and an appreciation of the value of the military-industrial establishment in protecting our established way of life. There also came the knowledge that people could and did survive wars, and that the outcome of wars could lead to an improvement in the national condition and in the level of personal satisfaction.

If the depression and World War II were the paramount problems in the earlier lives of the now older generation, the outcome of these events represented a highly convincing piece of evidence that the nation and its system of government could and would deal successfully with crises, and there thus developed the faith that we possess the means to solve the problems that face us. Having seen the system solve these two major problems, we became convinced that it was good, and that it could deal with such other problems as might arise.

Certain other conditions and forces in American life in the twenties, thirties, and forties also influenced the attitudes of the generation over thirty-five. These are treated in more detail in subsequent chapters, but they are mentioned briefly here to provide context for the intervening discussion of factors shaping the outlook of the generation under thirty. Up until the end of World War II, and to a degree even into the late 1940s and early 1950s, our technology was considerably less sophisticated than it is today. In fact, it is only since the mid-fifties that we may be said truly to have entered the age of technology. The speed and ease of transportation and communication was significantly less than it is today. It was harder to get from place to place, more

73

difficult to be in immediate touch with people who were geographically remote, and the life and activities of the average person were much more limited by geography and local custom and exposure than they are today. There were more isolation and parochialism, but there was also a closer-relatedness among neighbors and nearby communities, plus much more opportunity for the development of loyalty and other affiliative ties than at present. This condition had several other results, including development of a feeling that one belongs to something or belongs in *some place*, and that alone tended to foster a sense of identity and security. Also, under such generally stable conditions, people became familiar enough with the part of society to which they were immediately exposed to develop the feeling of being able to accomplish something, however limited, in that society. Whether one lived in a small town or city ward, one knew where to go or whom to see to get something important done; or, if it could not be done, whose head to hunt to prevent the same kind of failure from occurring next time around. Out of this came a sense of individual importance, control over one's own destiny, and meaningful participation in the system. Contrast this attitude with the helplessness many young people today feel when faced with the need to get something done or trying to develop a sense of individual importance or consequence.

The level of technology thirty or forty years ago also had the effect of keeping the mass of the people remote from the affairs of the world outside their immediate locale. Prior to World War II, there was no really effective intercontinental communication system, and the American public did not immediately become aware of many important things happening in Europe or Asia. There was a much less immediate exposure to events, and the passage of time between their happening and our becoming aware of them reduced the sense of their importance and gave them a less pressing quality. Again, the contrast to the experience of today's youth, who see in living color in the evening whatever happens ten thousand miles away in the afternoon, is startling.

Other circumstances affecting those who grew up in the twenties, thirties, and forties, which probably had less impact than the ones mentioned above but are nevertheless worthy of mention, include the following: First, the health and physical well-being of the average person was nowhere near as secure as

74

it is today; children frequently died of contagious diseases, mortality rates from pneumonia were high among the aged and the disease was a threat even to the healthy; the advent of hot weather each summer brought with it the threat of infantile paralysis (polio); and every childhood scratch or cut carried with it the danger of lockjaw or blood poisoning. Second, the population was small, and except in the most congested areas of the cities, very few people felt crowded for space or air; in fact, the idea that we might some day have too many people simply did not occur to anybody. The task of development and exploitation of our natural resources went forward without much thought that they could ever be misused or exhausted, and only a few dust bowl farmers knew at first hand what harm the misuse of land could bring to those not prudent enough to avoid erosion-producing practices. Finally, firm in the belief that the individual mattered and that he could affect the course of his existence, Americans paid little attention to welfare plans, school lunch programs, or other expressions of group responsibility for the individual.

The contrast between these conditions and those in which the present generation of young Americans have grown up is striking indeed! Throughout their lifetime, they have been surrounded by economic security and a high degree of general affluence. They have been treated with permissiveness and have been, in one sense, sheltered from many of the harsh realities of the world around them. At the same time, they have been subjected to severe stress from a variety of sources: the threat of thermonuclear warfare; the heavy international responsibilities weighing on their country; the strife of the racial revolution; the threat of personal participation in the Vietnam War; the general uneasiness arising from competition between the free world and the Communist world; the demands of the underdeveloped nations; the pressures of overpopulation; the depersonalizing effects of big government, big business, and big unions; the trauma of political assassination; and the now evident threat to our general survival emerging from the abuse of the natural environment. And not only have all of these problems existed throughout their lifetime, but each has been brought home immediately, personally, and relentlessly by the effective operation of a technologically advanced communications system that makes escape or isolation impossible.

At the same time that these problems have generated stress among our young people, another important series of developments has worn away at their and the nation's ability to deal straightforwardly with them. Our population is highly mobile and many of our communities are highly transient. Increasing opportunities for leisure time and recreation have turned us away from family-oriented activity, so that more and more of our personal experience is in one way or another in the public realm. This has removed some of the family and community stability within which young people formerly developed, with the result that there is a growing feeling of lack of roots, loyalties, and relatedness to those with whom one lives. Thus, as I shall show in detail below, our young people are undergoing highly stressful experiences but have not been provided with the cultural or psychological stability to give them a sense of comfort in dealing with these problems.

Finally, our society is plagued by overpopulation, the frustration of rising expectations, increased crime and threats to personal safety, the debilitating effect of drugs, and a myriad of other evidences of social breakdown.

It is not surprising, in view of all this, that we suffer from some kind of gap between the generations. Nor is it surprising that young people clamor for change, while most older people feel content to enjoy the fruits of a system that has already solved most of the problems that vitally concerned them as youths. This is not to say that older people are not interested in the solution of today's problems; they are. But having seen the system solve significant problems in the past, they feel confident that it will also solve the problems of the present. Young people, on the other hand, having had only the experience of living with the problems and not knowing at first hand that the system is capable of solving them, are understandably anxious, impatient, and occasionally dubious.

Even in the face of this anxiety, impatience, and occasional doubt, the overpowering majority of young Americans find a mutually encouraging common ground and purpose with their elders. Alienation and rebellion are the province of a tiny minority and evidence is beginning to appear that even that proportion is dwindling, although the young radicals would have us and their contemporaries believe that their view of things is produced by a special degree of intelligence and insight, and that it is only a matter of time before the majority awakens to the validity of their position and joins them in tumbling down the established order. Later, I shall treat in more detail the factors that give rise to their revolutionary attitudes and to their absolute conviction of self-righteousness. Here we must decide whether the majority of young people are correct in their implicit assumption that all of us, regardless of age, share common goals and purposes, and have a stake in dealing rationally with the problems facing our society. In short, we need to identify the generally shared issues of our time, and to determine whether they represent a valid form of joint interest that can justify us in a total commitment to mutual purpose and effort.

First, as far as the preoccupations of the older generation are concerned, we may ask the following questions: Should all Americans, regardless of age, have a concern about national strength and security, and about the military defense of our nation? The answer to this is obvious, when one considers that the question is really whether or not we have more common interest among ourselves, regardless of age, than we have with other nations, particularly potential enemies. While the world may have made some progress in maturing toward a general altruism, we are very far from the point where all of humanity, or even a substantial segment of it, is bound together in a common quest for love and peace. The harsh realities of international existence include the fact that there are strong impulses to grasp power, secure material goods, protect national interests, and acquire political positions, all of which would assist the "have nots" of the world in securing for themselves the material benefits already available to the "haves." Impulses toward creature comforts, material acquisition, territorial possession and protection, and group security are deeply ingrained in the human character, and we have unfortunately not yet reached such a stage of worldwide comfort and affluence that there is no longer any coveting of our neighbors' goods, wives, or possessions. The argument that by maintaining our national strength we only encourage similar competitiveness among other peoples may be momentarily persuasive to those who would escape from the realities and responsibilities of international life, and it is of course desirable that we do not foster conditions that encourage a military solution to world problems, but it is also realistic to recognize that motives for conquest and subjugation exist around the globe, and that our cherished way of life and our ideals of love and peace would not long survive were we to sacrifice our national defense as a high-priority item. Thus, most reasonable people would agree that we have a highly important common interest in maintaining a sufficient military defense to prevent our exploitation and subjugation by other nations.

Should all Americans, regardless of age, have a concern about economic and material security? This question, the radicals allege, is the one that most sharply divides the generations. It represents in fact at least as firm a common ground for older and younger Americans as does the need for a strong national defense. Economic security may be a meaningless concept so long as one does not have to do without it. But in spite of our present affluence and the lack of experience of many younger people with economic deprivation, we can all recognize that enough to eat, a warm and secure place to sleep, sufficient clothing and furnishings to protect ourselves against the elements, and a modicum of material accessories to make the matter of survival and productivity a bit easier and more comfortable are not automatically provided to us off the nearest banana tree. The road to economic security in our country has been long and toilsome, and our hard-won gains would not be long maintained if any substantial segment of our population decided to return to hunting and gathering as a way of life. The attitude among some young radicals, that care, comfort, and personal and group welfare are somehow automatically provided for, without effort, is a reflection of a frightening lack of contact with reality, and as it is put to the test in various kinds of small-group experimental communal settings, it is having the effect of establishing (in some for the first time) the idea that it is not a totally evil thing to have a warm dwelling, comfortable and utilitarian clothing, and a few of the lower-grade luxuries that were formerly decried as immorally materialistic. Thus, older and younger people again have a group investment in maintaining the stability of an economic system and a productive capacity that even now is only a short step or two beyond providing us with the bare necessities for survival.

Do younger and older Americans share any stake in the maintenance of conditions that insure our general health? Again, it is almost sufficient to state that the great scientific and medical advances of the past three or four decades have not been automatically provided to us and that their benefits have not yet been incorporated into our genes. For this reason, all Americans obviously need to maintain a concern about our basic physical health, and to recognize that it would not require much of a retrogression in the state of our civilization once again to unleash the terrors of poliomyelitis, tuberculosis, plague, tetanus, and other horrors upon us. The alarming recent increase in the occurrence of venereal disease and infectious hepatitis among segments of the younger generation is sufficient evidence for any reasonable person that we had best maintain a general national commitment to the protection of our individual health, and to make us recognize that these problems of yesterday could easily become problems today with only a very little neglect of practices and precautions we have come to take for granted.

What about the concerns of the younger generation? Can the older generation step aside and leave it for our children to find solutions to the problems of world peace, racial reconciliation, and protection of our national environment, as well as the burdens of international responsibility, the maintenance of the power and dignity of the individual in the face of a mass society, the mastery and constructive use of our technology, and the problem of overpopulation? Do we share a mutual concern in these matters, as we do in regard to national and economic security, health, and other areas of concern? No one over forty with a whit of idealism, responsibility, or even self-interest could possibly take the position that our generation does not have a continuing stake in dealing with these issues. From a pragmatic and totally selfish point of view, many of us still have thirty or forty years to live, and it should be apparent that the fruits of these problems, if left unsolved, will be nothing short of a personal as well as a national disaster. We simply cannot turn aside from the continuing responsibility of dealing with things as they are today, and we must not be so satisfied with the successes of the past that we shut our eyes to the needs of the present and the future. There can be no question that the concerns of today's world are the concerns of all of us, and that the responsibility for dealing with these concerns is shared by the entire population.

Fortunately, neither younger nor older persons are tied helplessly to views of the world that developed out of their youthful experiences. While attitudes formed in 1930 and 1940

79

have a continuing effect in determining the older person's outlook, he need not be rigidified and imprisoned by them. A rational man is always capable of modifying his views, and he can respond to new inputs and opportunities. Nor are the attitudes of younger people merely a reflection of how they are experiencing the world today. In spite of the disdain for history prevalent among many young radicals, most members of the younger generation are capable of absorbing and profiting from the experience of the past; even, with effort, of developing a deep empathic understanding of the effects of that past on our present condition. Thus, the ability of older people to benefit from new knowledge, and the ability of younger people to incorporate the knowledge of the past, represents a broad bridge across the generation gap, and should provide a source of deep encouragement to those who sometimes despair of finding common purpose with our children. And both groups have the ability to anticipate future events, to weigh alternatives in the light of their consequences, and to decide things with more than today's comfort in mind.

Finally, do all of America's generations have a common cause in maintaining intact the existing political system? Do we have a basis for joining together to reject the threats and demagoguery of the new radicalism, and in setting the nation once again on a course to unity, strength, and decency? The answer to these questions is conditional, and depends on whether we wish to reestablish the worth, dignity, and competence of the individual to determine his own course and to stand up to the consequences of his own actions, freely taken; whether we believe that reason, logic, and diligent application of one's efforts are preferable to emotion, demagoguery, and instant relief from discomfort as a means to solving problems; whether we are willing to make momentary sacrifices for the sake of a future goal; and whether we are secure in the belief that individual freedom is best achieved in an ordered, organized society. Insofar as I am convinced that virtually all Americans are committed to these propositions, I am confident and hopeful that the gap between the generations will be successfully bridged.

IV
THE RED GLOW
OVER DETROIT

This chapter is the first of several that examine the psychological and social factors underlying the behavior of the young radicals. The frustration, anger, impatience, and arrogance, and the tendency to move to direct action, all of which are typical of their behavior pattern, have already been mentioned and will be dealt with more extensively in later chapters. For now, we focus on another characteristic, which is seldom openly revealed by the young radicals but clearly underlies many of their attitudes and actions. This characteristic is fear.

In the extensive contact I have had with young radicals, both as a university administrator and as a practicing psychologist, it has been clear that virtually all of them suffer from an underlying fear, apprehension, and uncertainty that often verges on panic. Although this fear is typically covered over by bravado and a surface appearance of great confidence, there is no question whatsoever that the psychological makeup of the young radicals contains an unusual amount of insecurity, and a sense of personal helplessness. The characteristic need for group support in even the most bland confrontations, the need to bring oneself to a pitch of anger in order to deal with even the most unthreatening situations, the total lack of ability to examine critically the merits of their arguments and position, except in the shelter of a like-minded group, and the mass reappraisal of their commitment to violence resulting from the New York townhouse explosion and the Kent State killings, all support strongly the notion that fear and panic, rather than courage and

81

personal fortitude, are near the core of their personalities. The apparent super self-confidence and arrogance is a thin compensatory mask for underlying uncertainty and paralyzing self-doubt.

In the last chapter, the stresses and problems of American life in the 1950s and 1960s were identified as among the sources of differences in outlook between the younger and older generations. These same problems may also be viewed as a source of the deep anxiety that runs through the character of the young radicals. The most frequently proposed explanation of the stress under which our society operates is the existence of the hydrogen bomb, and its psychological impact deserves examination.

In 1945, the United States used nuclear energy to obliterate the major part of two Japanese cities. The immediate effect of this action was to bring a quick end to the ravages of World War II, and undoubtedly to save several times as many Japanese and American lives as were lost in the bombing. For Americans who lived through that war, there was scarcely a moment's doubt that it should be ended by whatever means possible, and that President Roosevelt's decision to produce the bomb and President Truman's decision to use it were totally justified. In more recent years, it has been suggested by some critics that to have used the A-bomb was an immoral act for which we should be forever condemned. Such pious preachments, an aggrandized form of second-guessing, are the province and luxury of those fortunate enough not to have faced the agonizing responsibility of making the decision.

Whatever its retrospective fault or justification, the use of the A-bomb at one stroke reshaped the nature of international relations and recast grotesquely the meaning of war. For thousands of years war had remained in its basic concept a mortal contest between two men, each of whom took shelter against the projectiles of the other, and each of whom sought to penetrate the shelter of the other with something sharp or explosive before his enemy could do the same to him. Alterations in technology and tactics only varied the scale of this operation, not its fundamental quality. Had it been no more than a quantitative expansion of explosive force, the nuclear bomb would only have altered again the scale of the basic process, since the bombing of cities and the deliberate destruction or terrorization of noncombatants had long been practiced. But the nuclear bomb introduced a significant new qualitative dimension to the process of war. Not only could combatants be killed, noncombatants terrorized, and cities and the means of production eliminated, but large numbers of people and uninvolved nations would be directly damaged, and many others would probably be slowly destroyed over a period of time by the bomb's ubiquitous half-life poisons. It is one thing to face the destruction of a city, an army, or a nation. In that process there is a victor and a vanquished, and the victor's civilization prevails and the vanquished's subsides. It is quite another thing to conceive of a war in which there is no victor or vanquished, but only a vast glazed cinder with the poisoned bones of mankind parching under an isotope-laden sky.

Certainly the specter of that dismal end to civilization as we know it, and perhaps of mankind in toto, is cause for deep concern. And certainly younger people, who have lived their entire lifetime with no surcease from the specter, must feel a special alarm. But it is one thing to feel an intelligent concern about a possible catastrophe, and another to allow this anxiety to reach a proportion that creates panic, causes emotion to override reason, and leads to general disorganization and irrationality of behavior. My clinical and administrative contacts with radical extremists suggest that underlying concern over the potential threat of destruction in a nuclear war is a factor in producing their deep panic, disorganized thinking, and general irrationality under conditions of even normal stress. In this connection, it is interesting to ask oneself whom he would prefer to have control of the nuclear trigger in a time of national threat—Mario Savio, Mark Rudd, Timothy Leary, Bernadine Dohrn, David Eisenhower, or even Richard Nixon?

From time to time, the general anxiety over nuclear war finds specific focus and expression in an issue facing our nation. Since the late 1940s, events have periodically caused pressure on our national and personal panic buttons. For several years immediately following the end of World War II, the United States maintained its monopoly on nuclear weapons, and our national security was almost absolute. As a result of a massive espionage effort in the United States and Great Britain, however, the Soviet Union by the early fifties developed a significant nuclear capacity, and we were suddenly faced with the fact that a potential enemy could mortally threaten our survival. Events throughout the fifties, such as the Berlin blockades and the crushing of the Hungarians in their effort to secure freedom from Soviet domination, reminded us that we were confronting an enemy who was prepared to use considerable force in dealing with international problems, and the launching of sputnik in 1958 was sufficient evidence that the USSR could deliver its nuclear weapons to our cities if the occasion arose. Thus, throughout the childhood of people now eighteen to twenty-five years of age, there were steady reminders of nuclear menace.

In the fall of 1962, however, the Cuban Missile Crisis brought home to us how shockingly narrow was our margin of safety from a nuclear attack. As events unfolded, the successive reactions of most Americans were disbelief, then shock, then great apprehension. Most of us can remember vividly how friends and neighbors stockpiled dried foods, water, sleeping bags, and other bare necessities. If apprehension accurately describes the reaction of adult Americans during that week, the reactions of children aged eight to fifteen are more aptly characterized as puzzlement, helplessness, and near terror. For many young people in that age range, the Cuban Crisis was a frightening introduction to a reality from which they had been generally protected, in spite of the chronicity of the tension about it, by the comforting indulgence of the easy life in affluent America. The children who were between eight and fifteen during the Crisis of 1962 are the young men and women, aged eighteen to twenty-five, of the present moment, and the traumatizing effect of the fear and helplessness they experienced then contributes to the apprehension they experience in connection with any present-day international tension. Periodically, the anxiety over the bomb surfaces in connection with a specific issue, such as the recent surge of alarm over the deployment of an ABM system.

When World War II ended, the United States was the most powerful nation in the world, and we inherited the role of custodian of Western Civilization, which had resided in Western Europe since the Renaissance, and had been largely held by the British for the last two hundred years. This power and responsibility removed us permanently from the relative comfort and remoteness that had permitted isolationism to flourish even into the early years of World War II. Things that happened in Moscow, Beirut, or Delhi could no longer be thought of as curiosities

84

of remote places; they were immediately relevant to the welfare of Montpelier, Centerville, and Los Angeles. With world power and responsibility inevitably came world awareness and involvement. This awareness and involvement comes home immediately to us, not only through the evening news report on the color TV, but even more personally. For older people, it means heavy taxes for national defense and foreign aid. For younger people, these national responsibilities may mean military service, enforced delay in forwarding plans for marriage or career, personal threat or trauma, and neglect of other priorities. Thus the nation's international responsibilities intrude into the daily lives of us all by calling for certain personal sacrifices and inevitably produce anxiety and discontent among those asked to make such sacrifices. Further, when the style of our national life is such that personal comfort, safety and security, and material indulgence are extremely high-priority considerations, and when the mass of our young people have become accustomed to taking such conditions for granted, it is not difficult to understand that calls for personal sacrifice, even in the long-term national interest, are not going to be very popular.

The key example of how international involvement has brought stress and crisis into our national life is, of course, the Vietnam War. Whatever final judgment history provides concerning the merits of our involvement in Southeast Asia, it is a fact that four separate national administrations, over a period of fifteen years, have judged that America had an important stake in preventing North Vietnam and the Viet Cong from seizing power in the South. It appears that President Nixon's policy, which has removed all of our forces from Vietnam, was made possible only because we judged the South Vietnamese able to protect themselves from a Communist takeover. There is, of course, no assurance that Presidents Eisenhower, Kennedy, Johnson, and Nixon have not successively made a total misjudgment concerning the importance of a non-Communist South Vietnam, but it is strange that first a Republican, then two Democratic, and now another Republican administration would come to the same conclusion about the nation's interest without that policy having some merit.

However, even if the American combat presence in Southeast Asia had been 100 percent justified, and even if our general policy there had been 100 percent correct, the conditions of American life and the interpretation of the policy to the American people foredoomed our actions there. First, whatever national interest or political principle was involved was never adequately explained to the American people. Second, the effort always had the character of something we were doing with our left hand, rather than something to which we were fully and strongly committed. Third, our national leadership never made the war a prominent rallying point for a unified national effort; rather, the sacrifices required fell on a very small segment of the society, primarily college-age youth, and the rest of the nation conducted business as usual. Under these conditions, it is not surprising that many of those on whom the burden fell would become resentful about the bad deal they were getting. Fourth, as the years stretched on, and as the goals of the war were stated in only the most ambiguous terms, it came to seem that there was no conceivable end point and thus no finite goal toward which to strive. This is in striking contrast to World War II, where the enemy was clearly identified, the goal of his unconditional surrender completely unambiguous, and steps toward that goal in the form of territorial recovery specifically stated and understood. Fifth, each succeeding step in the escalation of the war-without-progress remobilized the always present anxiety that we would be led eventually into an all-out nuclear confrontation. Finally, the conditions of our society, under which the generation supposed to fight the war had been raised, were not such as to foster acceptance of the need to make personal sacrifices for any cause, much less a half-hearted national effort in an uncomfortable and inhospitable country twelve thousand miles away from suburbia. While affluence and permissiveness were among the important conditions creating the general reluctance to put aside personal comfort for the sake of the nation, a great many other factors were also at work, as I shall show in detail below.

Other aspects of our international relationships also contribute to the experience of threat and anxiety with which the younger generation has grown up. The end of World War II and the emergence of the United Nations foreboded the breakdown of the colonial system, under which great portions of Africa and Asia had been governed for more than two hundred years. The principle of national self-determination, which had been one of the rallying points of our cause during World War II, was so

86

manifestly incompatible with the colonial system that the emergence of the so-called underdeveloped nations became inevitable. Largely inexperienced in self-government, with masses of their populations undereducated, with technologies and productive capacity grossly insufficient to respond to the aspirations of their people, these new nations have injected a new element of uncertainty and even volatility into world affairs. They are swept by a militant nationalism, are distrustful of the Western nations that were formerly their colonial masters, with which they often associate us, and are more concerned with the practical problems of feeding, clothing, and housing their people than with considerations of individual freedom, USA-style. As poorer peoples they envy us, and their friendship is hard won and harder maintained. Our actions toward them, no matter how purely motivated, are subject to suspicion and criticism as harking back to colonial exploitation. Out of practical considerations of international politics and world power, we jockey with our major competitors, the USSR and China, for favor with these nations, and the uncertain course and outcome of our efforts gives rise to a national uneasiness. Additionally, these efforts reflect another aspect of sacrifice that Americans of all ages are called upon to make, in the form of taxes, voluntary service, foreign aid, and military assistance.

The special aspect of our international relationships with the Soviet Union and China is not limited to the threat of nuclear confrontation. In 1945, Winston Churchill stated clearly a truth that the less sophisticated among us came gradually to recognize: The Soviet Union, far from being any longer an ally, was in fact a competitor if not a downright enemy. The conflicting ideological system of the USSR, coupled with its emergence as a military power on a par with the United States, introduced a source of stress into the world and our national life that we have found most disconcerting. From the harassment of the Berlin Blockade and the threat of the Cuban Crisis, through the crushing of the Hungarian freedom-fighters, the race to explore outer space, the struggle to maintain military parity, and the invasion of Czechoslovakia, to the potential confrontations in the Mediterranean, the Middle East, and the Asian subcontinent, we have been tested and challenged and threatened by the Soviet Union. As Vietnam once did, this situation appears destined to go on forever. The drain upon individual energies and national

87

resources has been immense, and is another contributor to the profound experience of threat and uncertainty that has characterized the lifetime of our young peole.

When the Communist revolution succeeded in China, a highly militant, anti-Western third force emerged on the international scene. The existence of a Red China controlling more than a half-billion people and influencing an equal number poses a significant threat to the dominant position of the United States, a threat that has found only modest expression in Korea and Vietnam. Backed now by a growing nuclear capacity, an impressive if not yet superior technology, and a nearly inexhaustible supply of manpower, the sleeping giant that was China is awakening, and as it stretches, it further adds to the personal and national apprehensions felt by Americans. While we may at last be finding and adopting an international policy that will effectively deal with the problem posed by Red China, the mere existence of this force is a source of continuing threat to our established concept of world order.

Our nation's international problems and responsibilities are not the only source of stress and threat impinging on young people. Domestically as well, a host of problems and events add to our apprehension and adversity. The younger generation's introduction to our domestic political life was at least as traumatic as its introduction to our international problems. Whereas internationally we had the Cuban Missile Crisis, domestically we had the assassination of President Kennedy. To understand the psychological meaning of this event, it is necessary to recall once more that in 1963, when the assassination occurred, today's eighteen to twenty-five generation was from eight to fifteen years old. Take a young man who is now twenty-two as an age-representative case: he would have been twelve in 1963. Twelve is hardly an age of great political awareness or sophistication, but given the effectiveness of our communications technology, he would have been aware of the 1960 election, and would have known something of the Eisenhower years, of the inspiration of the Kennedy rhetoric, and certainly of the Cuban Missile Crisis of only a year before. His life would already have been touched by the stresses of our chronic international problems, but he would otherwise have been comfortable, sheltered, and probably indulged. And he would by all odds have been touched by the charisma of President Kennedy. He would have heard the call to "ask not what your country can do for . . . "; seen the Peace Corps perhaps as an opportunity for his personal contribution to world peace; heard JFK's *"Ich bin ein Berliner"* at the Wall; and been thrilled by the loveliness of Jackie, the charm of Caroline, and the cuteness of John-John. He would, in short, have identified strongly with the articulate, handsome young man who had become our President and our leader.

Kennedy's appeal was broad, but it was especially strong for most of the young. Even his inaugural address, in which he said, "Today the torch has been passed to a new generation . . . ," was a pointed appeal to young people. To them he projected a youthful image and a youthful vision of idealism. His family, whatever their private problems, radiated charm, beauty, grace, and quality—leavened properly by humility and bolstered by the strength that comes of adversity conquered. To the young he was the stuff of which legendary heroes are made—indeed, he was already an established hero—and a legend began to grow up around him. He had strength and physical courage—had he not saved a man in his crew from drowning, dragging him by mainforce away from the wreck, and did he not fancy playing touch football, prevented from indulging this active interest only by the misfortune of an ailing back? He was a brilliant intellectual—did he not read everything (he had mastered speedreading), did he not speak German, and did he not dominate the brilliant minds with whom he surrounded himself? He was a solid family man —did he not have a beautiful and faithful wife, lovely children, equally brilliant brothers and sisters, and did he not love his mother, whose life had been so sorely scarred by tragedy? Was he not, in short, a prince among men who had been elevated by the people to the throne of leadership, and were not Jackie his queen and Carolyn the little princess, and did they not live together in the beautiful castle of Camelot, on the Potomac?

Whatever history says of John Fitzgerald Kennedy, he made and left behind a fantastic impression on most of the youth of America. For the hypothetical twelve-year-old, Kennedy's election, his personality, his approach to problems, and his successes were the continuation of a fantasy of comfort and pleasure and security and indulgence that had been the youngster's lot throughout his life in middle-class America. There was even the promise that the plaguing stresses of his earlier years would be removed, because the threat of nuclear destruction had been faced and turned back during the Missile Crisis of only a few months before, and a brighter, more secure, even more comfortable future seemed promised. And then suddenly, on that dark November morning in 1963, while the sun shone in Dallas, the unbelievable tragedy came. Harsh reality spurted from Oswald's gun, and Camelot came tumbling down, not in noble combat over some great cause, with the hero's struggle, albeit unsuccessful, leaving behind a heritage of valor and a vision of more successful, nobler struggles carried on by an equally heroic successor, but in the cowardly, senseless, and savage action of an obsessed leftist. To the boy of twelve whose hopes of relief from tension had been built around the heroic fantasy of Camelot, this introduction to reality was doubly cruel and base in the extreme. Small wonder that cynicism and despair came to play a part in his later view of the world.

Then in Kennedy's place stood another kind of leader. Lyndon Johnson had a very tough act to follow, and he brought to his task few virtues that had any appeal to romantic and idealistic youth. Big-eared, crass, vain, pragmatic, and politically tough, Johnson too had a vision—of a great society, of liberal progress in the tradition of his idol, Franklin Roosevelt, and of himself as a great man. But he was hardly a romantic figure, hardly an articulate visionary, and hardly an altruist. The characteristics that had made him a successful politician, and which, I believe, in history's view will have him judged a successful President, were anathema to the young people, who needed either the relief of instant solutions or the tranquilization of idealistic rhetoric. No man could have provided the first, and Johnson did not offer the second—partly because he lacked the ability, partly because even in his arrogance he was no demagogue, partly because he knew he was in a tough fight and had always met a fight head on, and partly because he sensed that it was time to bring home the reality of international life to the American people. But in the end, he failed to win the fight and even failed to bring home the responsibility. His plain mien and manner, rather than connoting honesty, came to be evidence of his stupidity. His pride in himself and his nation seemed churlish and anachronistic. His cleverness was translated into accusations of a "credibility gap." And in the end, he fell—brought down by the panic of the radicals, the disdain of the sophisticates, and the failure of many among us to grasp the real significance of the fight he was in. All of these were aided and abetted by the cynicism of academic and journalistic jackals, who, once his star began to fall, saw an opportunity to feast upon his and the nation's misfortunes, and to appear to be humanists in the process.

Thus the Kennedy myth and its destruction, and the years and fall of Lyndon Johnson, added to the tension of our youth. Thus also, through those years, were multiplied the nation's domestic problems, each one of which adds its share to the threat to the younger generation's comfort and security. Chief among these domestic problems is that of relations between black Americans and white Americans. Beginning with President Truman's order to desegregate the armed forces in 1948, we rededicated ourselves to the proposition that all men are created equal, and over the past twenty-five years we have made halting progress in translating that proposition into reality. But progress is slow, and associated with the effort are great conflict, deep tension, and significant personal threat. The threat arises not only from open violence, as has occurred in Detroit and Newark, but also from the latent hostility in many of our schools and neighborhoods. How many black children could walk alone through an all-white neighborhood without feeling afraid—of insults, rejection, or physical assault? How many white children could comfortably walk through an all-black neighborhood without experiencing danger of the same kind? How many completely comfortable and open relationships exist between a white person and a black one—relationships where race is of no consideration whatsoever? The tension of racial relationships and unresolved racial problems is ubiquitous in our society, and it is a part of the everyday experience of a great many young Americans. Whether experienced personally, as a fear of insult or physical abuse, more remotely as a concern that the ghettos will erupt in a frenzy of racial violence spreading into the suburbs, or distantly as an abstract concern about equality and brotherhood, it creates a significant and chronic threat to all of us. For the older person, who has the perspective to see progress being made and the faith to believe in an eventual solution, the tension is considerably more tolerable than to the youth, who experiences it as a more immediate and inescapable frustration.

The pressures of overpopulation represent yet another

91

source of threat. One has only to take a rush-hour drive in any major city, or try to find a place to camp on a summer weekend, or endeavor to find solitude at all to realize that we are crowded and becoming more so. People are everywhere, and competing for mere space to stand or live. Some recent research suggests strongly that animals forced to live in overcrowded conditions become irritable and combative. In 1930, the census revealed slightly more than one hundred million people to be living in the United States. Forty years later, that number had nearly doubled. By the turn of the century, it will have increased by another hundred million. Population pressure is clearly forcing changes in our way of life. Even now, the tradition of the one-family home is slipping from the grasp of the average citizen. Pressure on our food and energy supplies has not yet reached the critical point, but it is within sight. In many nations around the world, population already exceeds the capacity of the productive system to support it, and we seem to be heading for a worldwide Malthusian catastrophe. The margin of protection of personal health and safety narrows with every added birth, and our success in reducing mortality rates and extending the life span adds to the demands for food, space, and sheer oxygen to breathe.

Population pressure acts in more subtle ways to create tension in our children. If one's home base is an eighty-acre farm, one has a comfortable feeling of room to move, area to explore, and fresh air to breathe. If one's home base is a forty-by-eighty-foot lot, he has more a feeling of containment, limits, and pressure, as well as a narrower concept of the world and a lessened understanding of the vital experience of freedom. Crowded neighborhoods, crowded schools, crowded parks, and crowded highways not only frustrate the individual's wish for his fair share of whatever there is, but also, in a more subtle way, reduce the respect and value we place upon ourselves and our fellows. When an area or a nation is sparsely populated, every individual is valued as a contributor to the strength and productivity of the group; in the opposite case, the added individual becomes an encumbrance or nuisance, whose mere presence is a handicap. Thus, as we become more crowded, we not only lose in terms of whether there is enough of everything for all of us, but perhaps more importantly, we lose in terms of maintaining

92

mutual respect and individuality. The individual's lot in a mass society is not a happy one, and today's children are finding it difficult to maintain much sense of value as individuals in the face of mass pressures. In a subsequent chapter, more attention will be given to other factors that have reduced the value of and respect for the individual in our society, but overpopulation is certainly a major factor in the demise of individuality. And overpopulation is a chronic source of stress in the lives of the younger generation.

Before closing this chapter, one other source of alarm about our national condition needs to be mentioned, and that concerns the state of our natural environment. One only need look about him to recognize that we have done, and are doing, some dreadful things to this tiny planet which is our home. Our littered streets, highways, and parks testify to personal slovenliness and disdain for aesthetics. Our slimy rivers and clogged lakes reveal our short-run concern for convenience and our long-run neglect of natural resources. And our polluted air reflects again that we would apparently prefer cheaper artifically air-conditioned cars to somewhat more expensive naturally air-conditioned air. When our children think about their children, they are understandably concerned that they have clean air to breathe, clean water to drink, and some aesthetic surroundings in which to live. Recognizing as we all do the interdependence of life forms, the younger generation is concerned, and properly so, with insuring that the condition of the ecology will allow them and their children to survive, and sees the connection between the "silent spring" and a silent—that is, dead—planet. Thus, another anxiety is added to the existence of American youth, which already is bearing more than its share.

Similar anxieties exist in connection with many other problems. In an era of great personal comfort and high economic security, it is ironic that so many things threaten the safety and stability of our lives. Some of these, to be dealt with more extensively in other parts of this book, deserve passing mention here: Will the poor undertake to seize by force the things the middle class has labored to secure? Will the Red Chinese contrive to inflict more and more Vietnams upon us? Will the great bureaucracies and the mass society ultimately crush the individual to dust? Will the Soviet Union overcome us, economically, militarily, ideologically? Will our unbelievable technology turn us to a newer, higher path, or will it transform us into mindless, meaningless cogs in a great empty utopia? Will we survive and find purpose and flourish? Or will we drop out and die?

Such are the great fears and anxieties besetting the younger generation. I am convinced that much of the disturbed behavior of young people, and much of the irrationality of the radical movement among the minority of them, is directly motivated by such fears, and that this behavior can be better understood and managed if it is recognized that great stress, operating over long periods, makes personal adjustment very difficult. There is ample clinical evidence that most young people today operate under high stress. Once past puberty, the young person seems to become inordinately serious—indeed, almost somber. His intensity about problems, relationships, and ideas belies the traditional image of frivolous youth. Even among the vast majority of adolescents, who are adapting well, there is clear evidence of persistent worries, pressures, and strain. The deep concern about the problems of our time seems to run heavily among our youth, dampening their sense of humor, sometimes souring opportunities for satisfaction, and accelerating the rate of involvement in matters for which their experience has not well prepared them. If the great majority of young people, who are making a normal and successful adjustment to life, are influenced by serious fears, the evidence for the existence of almost intolerable anxiety among the small minority of militant revolutionaries is even greater. Fear and anxiety are of such force in this small group that its members are driven to highly frustrated behavior: to direct, forcible, irrational action, and to activities that do little to remove the real causes of their fears. But anxiety alone is not sufficient to explain the behavior of our young radicals. Their contemporaries face the same threats with steadfastness and confidence in their eventual solution. And men have for ages faced difficult problems that create anxiety by threatening their survival. Sometimes, such anxiety becomes a source of effective or even heroic behavior. The difference is that the young radicals have been ill-prepared to deal with the great stress they face, and thus they cannot bring their energies effectively to bear on solving the problems. In the next two chapters, we probe more deeply into the conditions of their life and upbringing that have made it impossible for the young radicals to deal with today's problems with reason and purposive action.

V

FOLDED, SPINDLED, AND MUTILATED

The American approach to social organization and government has traditionally placed great value on the individual. The Jeffersonian image of democracy, which runs deep in our heritage, assumes that the individual will use his unique talents and intelligence in pursuit of the general good, and that the common sense of individuals, expressed through an electoral base, will assure rational group decisions. We have pursued the Jeffersonian ideal in ourselves and it has been reflected in our methods of attacking social problems. Our history and our folklore are replete with examples of how free men, relying on their own resources and ingenuity, manage to deal with difficult problems, in the process developing a sense of self-respect and pride in accomplishment. The embattled farmers at Concord Bridge, Ben Franklin, Johnny Appleseed, the Wright brothers, Paul Bunyan, the solitary pioneer carving his existence out of the wilderness, Henry Ford, and Charles Lindbergh all exemplify the ability of the determined individual to direct the course of his own life, and to master his times and events rather than be mastered by them. This is a heritage of strength, belief in one's own worth, and a steadfast resolve to do what needs to be done to survive and prosper.

It is not an exaggeration to say that the golden age of American progress was simultaneous with the point of highest expression of American individualism. Some will argue that our greatest progress has come in the past twenty years, with the advent of revolutionary technological advances achieved through group effort in the setting of corporate or governmental organizations of great complexity. This may be true, if one considers progress to be merely a matter of technological advance. But if one includes in his definition of progress the expansion of culture, rising group satisfactions, increasing unity, and growing mutual respect, the point of our zenith must be placed considerably before the advent of the technological revolution. The commitment to excellence of individual craftsmen, the fierce devotion to independence of the American farmer, the solitary dedication of the traditional American scholar, and the enterprise and risk-taking willingness of the independent businessman all illustrate both the personal pride and the communal benefit that emerge when free men meet and overcome the challenges of existence. In these circumstances, the value of the individual is enhanced and the respect for the individual's ability to overcome adversity is compounded. Moreover, the life of the individual has vital meaning not only to himself but also in terms of how his efforts contribute to the common good. When the things the individual does matter vitally to the comfort, safety, or quality of life of his fellows, and when his contribution is in any way unique, then the individual also matters. Questions of purpose and direction find immediate answer in the day-to-day contributions of the individual to the good of other individuals who also matter, and questions of identity and self-doubt are not likely to arise. One's life finds meaning in the personal appreciation of others for one's honesty, energy, and contribution to a better life for all.

Over the past few decades, both the concept of individualism and the individual himself have suffered a bad beating in American society and politics. The individual and his uniqueness have come to be mistrusted as dangerous or evil or both. The popular view regards the individual as greedy, without social conscience or group interest, and as something to be submerged within a leveling conformity. His eccentricities, no longer seen as promising a refreshing or inspiring departure from a dull norm, are interpreted as threatening stability and order. Hewing to the accepted and familiar, rather than daring the risks of unploughed ground, is the virtue that has become paramount in our society. We seem to have lost a place for the man who wants to try things on his own and in his own way. Our programs for the solution of social problems assume that individuals

96

do not and cannot know what is good for them, cannot or will not help themselves, and will not or must not find a solution outside the bureaucratic directives provided by someone who implicitly believes that his way is right for everybody.

As faith in the individual has declined, all of us have lost in self-respect, confidence in one another, pride in what we do and how it contributes to the common good, and ultimately in unity, purpose, and national strength. Finding one's own way through a problem may not guarantee efficiency, may not result in a generally applicable program, and may not even insure that every problem will be fully solved. Yet the effect on the individual in terms of his own satisfaction, his view of himself, and his willingness to try to attack future problems may be more beneficial than a more nearly perfect solution imposed by someone else.

The collectivist philosophy, which is more and more dominating our approach to social problems, is in itself a declaration of no-confidence in the individual. Each time we turn to a larger unit of government or a more complex bureaucracy of any kind to deal with our problems, we are admitting and contributing to an individual inability to affect the course of our own lives. It is an interesting paradox that liberals and radicals, who are quick to condemn the power of government to dominate the lives of individuals, are in the forefront of those who would turn over to such bureaucracies the power to determine what is right, just, and socially desirable in ever-broader sectors of our personal and national lives. All of this is, of course, done with the intent of bringing speedier resolution of major social problems, but in the process, a social malaise involving the total loss of individual determination of events, and even more devastating loss of individual identity and self-respect, is promoted. In short, each time we act as if the individual, acting within the framework of the Jeffersonian ideal, is incapable of dealing with the pressing issues that confront him and his contemporaries, we further detract from a sense of individual strength, worth, and resolve. At this point in our history, we have reached a state of such little faith in the worth and competence of free men that we assume almost automatically that individuals must be forced to act in the common good, and that collectivist solutions, which override the rights of individuals to pursue their own way, are our only recourse. How these attitudes have developed, and how they contribute to the emergence of radicalism among the minority of young people, will occupy us in the remainder of this chapter.

The evolution of our economy from one based on a rural-agricultural system to one based on an urban-industrial system is one of the central reasons for the individual's loss of power and esteem. In preindustrial society, a man's survival and status depended very largely on his individual effort. The harder he worked, the more ingenuity he evidenced, and the greater his willingness to sacrifice immediate personal comfort and indulgence, the more productive he became and the more he was able to win the respect of his neighbors through his contribution to the mutual purpose of the community. Efficiency and progressive techniques resulted in direct, immediate, tangible benefits to himself and his associates. Innovation and experimentation, if they succeeded, brought quick benefits in the recognition and admiration of his colleagues, as well as more reward and security to himself. Similar tactics, if they failed, were his personal responsibility and he paid a direct price for his misjudgment. Consequences followed quickly upon decisions, for good or ill, and were largely confined to the individual who made the decisions. Out of this, a strong sense of being one's own master and of control over one's own fate emerged. A similar set of psychological conditions surrounded the enterprise of the craftsman or the small commercial operator. Evidence of success or failure was immediately forthcoming in the form of community response, which was a reliable basis for deciding whether to pursue the same course or shift to a different one. The skill and energy of the individual directly resulted in his prosperity and yielded the admiration of his associates, and thus it fed directly into a sense of self-respect and achievement.

There is no fundamental reason why the same psychological force s cannot operate within the framework of an industrial society. However, for a variety of reasons, they have not come to do so in ours. Two basic factors have subverted the worth of the individual in our industrial society. The first of these is the demand of the consumer for more and more goods at cheaper and cheaper prices. Out of this demand has grown an overriding commitment to efficiency. The response of industry to consumer pressure for greater productivity at lower cost has led to methods, under conditions of mass production, that treat the individual as a low-priority consideration, and value his personal satisfaction only in terms of whether it further enhances his productivity and efficiency. The simplified operations of a mass production system require that individual members of the production team become highly efficient in an extremely simplified and limited skill. The opportunity of the individual to bring a special skill, talent, or insight to bear on such a highly limited operation is virtually nil, and even such special ability as he might reveal through personal speed or energy is discouraged by his less talented associates. Because the welfare of all is tied into a common purpose—namely, to avoid the exploitation of the group by other sectors of the industrial complex—the premium on and reward for individual accomplishment are reduced.

The second factor reducing the value of the individual in mass production industry is the fact that few people can claim to have an individual effect on the social worth of the product, at least not in any way that is apparent to their associates. True enough, if a production worker fails to perform his job, there is a short-run effect on a few units. But such a worker can readily be replaced without causing much of a stir in the overall productive efficiency and in the reaction of the consumer to the product. Thus, rather than having a sense of personal importance and contribution to the general good, the individual worker is left with a feeling of little consequence and diminished self-respect, at least as far as his work life is concerned. In times of national emergency, it has been possible to create a direct sense of the relevance of the individual's effort to the national good, but the argument becomes tenuous indeed when the worker is asked to abandon his individuality only in the interest of providing a higher standard of living to a mass of consumers who are already living very high on the hog. Small wonder that there is a growing lack of identity and increasing discontent.

Directly related to the process of industrialization was a change in where the majority of Americans lived. While the movement from the farms to the cities had been underway as an evolutionary matter for several decades, there was a brief period in the early 1940s during which population shifts produced a fundamental alteration in the form and style of American society. These shifts, stimulated by the needs of the wartime economy, caused a reorientation of our society from one whose political and social life had been dominated by farms and small towns to one dominated by urban centers and suburbs. This

99

development was of great importance, for it both mirrored and produced significant changes in the nation's outlook, attitudes, and way of life, particularly as they affected the value we placed on the individual.

Prior to World War II, the dominant cultural and political orientation of America sprang from its rural-agricultural past. True, by 1940 the nation was already highly industrialized. At the same time, the majority of people still lived on farms and in small towns, where concepts of Jeffersonian democracy, with their emphasis on the value of the individual, were strongly entrenched. Further, the governmental system favored the dominance of our political and social institutions by rural and small, and nearly everyone knew everyone else. Thus, the functionaries of social institutions were usually known personally, slowly and relatively undisturbed by outside forces. Under such circumstances, the general form of the society and its impact upon individuals was very clear. Relationships between the individual and the institutions of society—government, law, schools, church, etc.—were well understood, closely related to the goals of the community, and personally meaningful to individuals. The effective size of the community was quite small, and nearly everyone knew everyone else. Thus, the functionaries of social institutions were usually known personally, and were quite directly responsive to the attitudes of their constituents. In many ways, the pioneer ethic was little changed. There was much stress on individual freedom and resentment over intrusion from the outside. There was great interdependence among community members, and mutual support developed rapidly within communities in times of crisis.

Geographic and social mobility were limited, and for better or worse, members of the community had a sense of belonging and permanence. Home and family, school and church, politicians and policemen, were largely united as to goals and provided meaningful psychological reference points for individuals. Out of common purpose and fate developed ingroup loyalties not only among individuals but to the social goals and means held in common. Alienation from society was rare, and when it did occur, the alienated person became an outgroup of one treated variously with charity or ostracism. Thus the social system of rural and small-town America, however admirable or despicable its total value system, did insure a meaningful place

100

for its members, a sense of stability, and loyalty to a local system that was rather faithfully reflected in the national system, and avenues of access to the decision-making process as it affected individuals and the community were open to all. Such conditions mark an effective social system, and a society based upon a myriad of similarly functioning local communities offers a firm foundation for the development of individuals characterized by a sense of self-respect, dignity, and importance.

Many of the same conditions existed in pre–World War II cities. Here, the important social reference points might be nationality groups, neighborhood organizations, unions or political groups, or religious congregations and schools. Here, mobility might have been slightly greater and the tie to land or personal property slightly less. But the goals of individuals and their social institutions were largely consistent, and therein individuals found security, self-worth, and identity. One knew personally the cop on the beat, the neighborhood grocer, and the minister, priest, or rabbi. The social unit was the neighborhood, and if there was less economic independence, there was also great loyalty to the neighborhood group and interdependence among its members. And again, as on the farms and in small towns, the functions of the social institutions were well integrated with community and individual goals and aspirations. Even though one might curse city hall or the bosses, one had a sense that he, or his neighborhood, union, or party, knew how to fight them. The Jeffersonian ideal was not as potent a force as outside the cities, but many of its major elements were present and served to provide goals and purposes. With these clearly available, individual identity was firm, even though personal alienation from subsectors of the total society did occur. Certainty and clear reference points for one's life thus existed in cities as well as in the towns and on the farms. The individual took value from his uniqueness and from his ability to influence events that directly affected his life.

The heavy population migrations, which reached their peak during World War II and have continued to the present time, effectively disrupted the stable functioning of the social system based on farms, small towns, and city neighborhoods, and thus have contributed to the decline in the value placed on the individual. The value system of rural and small-town America has lost its prime effect on the outlook of the nation.

101

The stability and psychological reference points of the city neighborhood have also been lost or weakened. The central cores of the cities have come to be populated by black migrants, largely of southern origin, whose lack of adequate education and familiarity with the formerly effective social institutions of the cities create a situation where effective social institutions are absent, where the individual has little access to the decisions affecting his life, and where individual alienation from the larger social system is almost unavoidable. Further, the suburbs into which urban middle-class individuals have escaped, and into which rural working-class whites have moved for job access, are so relatively new as social and political units that they have not yet developed effective social institutions for the expression of individual needs, worth, and identity. Thus the urban revolution has been a major force in establishing conditions in which the individual is less highly valued, social mechanisms to provide him with points of reference and access to the decision-making process are lacking, the Jeffersonian ideal has not yet found effective expression, and the devotion to individuality and personal independence moderated by mutual support in time of crisis has gravely declined. Thus, our traditionally accepted ways of dealing with social problems have been dangerously weakened, at horrible cost to the value we place on the individual.

The cities themselves have undergone significant qualitative change. The upwardly mobile European immigrant groups, which formerly populated large areas of our urban centers and had worked out effective ways for penetrating the mainstream of American life, are gone—absorbed into that mainstream. The southern black migrants and their first- and second-generation descendants, who now populate the central cities, have not yet developed such mechanisms. Already isolated by the burden of racial discrimination, the black slum-dweller bears the added handicaps of a long history of inadequate education, generally unstable family patterns, and lack of job skills. He thus has great difficulty in developing any economic leverage upon the total society, without which his efforts to participate fully in the system are likely to be unsuccessful. He also finds that the social institutions to which he related and through which he could obtain some redress in the South do not exist for him in the slums. Thus the black slum-

102

dweller does not have a basis for direct participation in decisions that have an effect on his life, and, lacking that, he has little on which to base a sense of personal strength or individual value.

Nor has life been the same for middle-class and working-class whites who have remained in the cities. Through their economic power, they do have somewhat greater access to the decision-making machinery. However, the traditional social organizations and mechanisms, through which they formerly solved local problems and participated in the attack on larger ones, are no longer totally intact or effective. They are subject to the manipulations of the giant bureaucracies of government, industry, and unions. Their economic strength is sapped by a growing burden of taxes. Their means of pursuing personal and small-group goals have been submerged within the mass society. All of this has made them more subject to a loss of individual identity, personal freedom, and effective participation in the society. Thus, they do not provide a firm social base on which a national culture and a national action pattern may be built.

The development of the suburbs was a direct and almost inevitable consequence of the migration of an economically underprivileged class into the central cities. This in-migration, because it was not followed by economic assimilation and parity, inevitably led to a decline in the economic position of the cities. With further growth prevented by land saturation and encirclement by other political units, and faced with a declining property value and tax base, the cities became unable to provide a level of public service, public education, and aesthetic and cultural conditions that would have enabled them to remain attractive to the upwardly mobile and increasingly affluent working class and middle class. Under these circumstances, emigration of these groups to the suburbs became almost inevitable.

The suburbs have become the center of concentration of mass economic power. Heavily populated, politically influential, filled with skills, energies, and articulate leadership, the suburbs are rapidly becoming the dominant political force in American life. It would seem natural for the suburbs also to become the locus of development for a new basic culture pattern and a new set of person-to-institution relationships on which the new American society could be developed. But the suburbs are a relatively new phenomenon, and much like the Negro slum areas, they have not yet developed an effective set of cultural

103

patterns, institutional relationships, and action-oriented political structures.

Thus, while the suburbs remain as a potential force for the positive solution of problems in society, their potential is at the moment far from being realized. The same self-indulgent urges that caused the suburbanite to emigrate from the city in the first place, maintain him in a relatively uninvolved position. For their residents, the suburbs remain something of a way station. There is little involvement with matters outside a rather comfortable day-to-day life. The suburbs are almost bereft of a meaningful culture, a vital ethic, or a personally satisfying set of relationships to those social institutions through which individual influence on the larger society becomes possible.

Nor do the conditions of life in the suburbs contribute much to a sense of uniqueness or personal worth. Crowded together on tiny pieces of land, living in houses that communicate a routine sameness, driving interchangeable cars with interchangeable parts to interchangeable jobs, the suburbanite finds little to set him apart as an individual from his equally interchangeable neighbors. Most of his day-to-day problems of survival are taken care of by one or another impersonal bureaucracy, and his sense of vital participation in the affairs of his time is extremely limited. Drive through a typical residential suburb and observe the efforts the inhabitants make to express something of their individuality—a slightly different tree on the extension, a minor deviation in color scheme, a plastic flamingo standing among the petunias—note also that the dominant activity pattern in the suburbs involves getting out—for an evening, a weekend, or a vacation. There is little permanent commitment to home, neighbors, or community, and lacking that commitment, the suburbanite has lost an important base for a sense of individual worth, participation, and unique contribution.

It is noteworthy that the majority of young radicals have come out of the suburbs. In some ways, their behavior may be viewed as an outgrowth of the overcomfort, overindulgence, and underinvolvement of their suburban heritage. With little sense of permanence or individual value, little respect for history, traditions, or heritage, an urging toward immediate, easy solutions to the first really difficult problems they have had to face, the suburb-bred young radical is in many ways only an extreme expression of the peculiar subculture from which he has come. As the suburbs represent a society in search of culture, purpose, and individual means for self-expression, so the young radical is searching for an escape from sameness, impotence, and lack of purpose.

In a simple society, it is quite possible for the vast majority of individuals to retain a high degree of personal independence. Primitive hunting-gathering cultures require little by way of social organization, and interdependence with others is limited to a family or at most a small tribal group. The structure of social institutions under such conditions is similarly simple. The family head or the tribal leader is the government. As the nature of man's activity changes, as cultivation becomes a significant activity, and, gradually, as trading and finally industry grow, members of the society become increasingly interdependent. It is of course possible for an individual in any type of society to retain almost total independence, but usually he pays the price of not sharing all the benefits available to full members of the society.

In terms of the interdependence of its members, American society has become vastly more complex in the last twenty-five years. This change has many facets. Ninety-seven percent of the population does not produce its own food, and is totally dependent in that sense on the other three percent. Only a handful build their own automobiles or homes. The self-educated man is nearly a thing of the past. Even in the area of recreation, which one might think of as a relatively independent kind of action, we are increasingly dependent on persons and facilities provided by the group. And it becomes more and more difficult to imagine only one person, or a small group, or even a simple organization putting a man on the moon, finding a cure for cancer, or rehabilitating a slum.

As our interdependence and the complexity of our problems have increased, we have developed more and more complex arrangements for trying to deal with them. These arrangements have generally taken the form of gigantic bureaucracies, whether in business, government, unions, or educational institutions. The bureaucracies have gradually gathered to themselves vast power, in the form of money, productive capacity, governmental directives and regulations, and negotiating leverage. They represent another expression of the mass society, and

105

even though they have been initiated for the purpose of solving problems, the effect of their operation is very often to take away from the individual any chance of dealing with his problems on his own.

When a decision is made to attempt to deal with problems by collective means, the emergence of a bureaucracy becomes inevitable. The process goes as follows: someone, or a group of people, recognizes a need that is not being met (or not being met quickly enough, or not in a way that suits the ideas of the affected group). Next, an operating group is established and given power in the form of funds, legal authority, or decision-making responsibility, with the goal of solving the problem. Typically, this operating group is not directly affected by the problem, but is involved only to the extent that its job is to deal with it—in the case of governmental bureaucracies, the interest of the operating group is often quite academic and remote from the actual problem as it affects people's lives. At this point, a new set of forces begins to operate, and the bureaucracy begins to take on a life of its own. Its original reason for existence often becomes secondary to the perpetuation of its own existence. The members of the operating team begin to think in terms of personal advantage in the form of building a larger operation, obtaining more power, having more persons responsible to them, and so on, all of which adds to their own importance, and assists them in developing a sense of purpose, identity, and worth. This development is easily rationalized, because the unsolved problem remains; it still represents a pressing social or organizational need, and more of whatever is being attempted is needed. In quite a real sense, if the bureaucracy succeeded in its original intent, it would lose its reason for being. But if it did, the persons involved in its operation would lose, in terms of job, status, and a sense of involvement in something important. Thus, the survival of the bureaucracy and the satisfaction of its members depend fundamentally on *not* solving the problem, but rather on making a sufficient appearance of trying to solve it so that other members of the organization or the society do not eliminate the "problem-solving" operation. The long-term effect of such an operation is to focus greater and greater power in the hands of people who have no real stake in solving problems, and thus to perpetuate an arrangement in which not getting too much done is at a premium.

106

The existence of massive bureaucracies has several other important effects. Such bureaucracies are difficult to penetrate, with the result that an individual who wants to deal with them directly is heavily disadvantaged. They also are remote—usually geographically, and always interpersonally. And they have immense power—to disburse funds, to regulate directly the actions of individuals, to discourage innovation and individual experimentation, and to impose general solutions across vast areas of the society. The bureaucracy also has the effect of placing decision-making power in the hands of technical experts. The justification for this goes as follows: most decisions affecting people's lives in the matter of public policy involve a multitude of variables and infinite detail. Simply on the basis of the time involved, few people are able to accumulate the raw knowledge sufficient to permit them to make intelligent decisions. Sometimes, in a flurry of eagerness to democratize the process, invitations are extended to the nonexpert to sufficiently acquaint himself with the facts that he may become enough of an expert to make some contribution to the decision. This argument is in part reasonable, but it is too often used to keep nosy people out of places where they don't belong, or to cover the tracks of an errant expert whose decisions were based not on reason, fact, and a desire to solve problems, but on arbitrary, capricious, or self-interested attitudes.

The cumulative effect of the existence of massive bureaucracies is disastrous. The bureaucracy becomes immensely powerful. It adds layer upon layer of organizational complexity and resists efforts at penetration, criticism, and change. It has the capacity to control individual lives, and it rationalizes its activities as being in pursuit of the common good. It is remote and most often unresponsive to immediate human needs. It proceeds on the basis of general policies that attempt to treat highly dissimilar situations as essentially identical, and worst of all, it contributes to the lack of respect for the individual by removing both motive and opportunity for him to solve his own problems in a unique and personally satisfying way, and it subtly subverts his freedom in the process. The bureaucratic system has become a stifling, conformity-demanding force in our society, and, as such, it contributes significantly to the growing sense of personal helplessness and powerlessness. The price we are paying for complexity is a growing centralization of authority, and a gravitation of real decision-making power away from the individual.

Since the New Deal period of the 1930s, we have undergone a rapid evolution in the direction of collectivism. Social Security and general social-welfare systems represent an excellent illustrative case. Under the Social Security concept, the central government has assumed the responsibility of providing basic care to elderly, disabled, or retired people. This assumption of responsibility has been accompanied, as it inevitably is, by an assumption of extensive power, in this case in the form of taxation to support the system, regulatory authority over earnings and conditions of living, and so on. The original goal, of course, was admirable—to insure a basic level of support to older people whose life experience had not been fortunate enough to make them financially secure in their later years. But the Social Security system has had an effect on attitudes about the individual's responsibility for himself, and the responsibility of families, neighborhoods, and communities for their associates, which may well override its beneficial effects. Irresponsibility has been encouraged by the subtle promotion of the idea that the program will meet the basic needs of the elderly. Remote, impersonal, collective, bureaucratic responsibility has replaced personal commitment, family and neighborhood loyalty, and self-respect. The sense that whatever happens to the individual is either to the fault or credit of someone else has increasingly taken away from the individual the sense that he can do something about his own condition and his own future. The economic and psychological price we are paying, for providing a couple of hundred dollars per month to allow an older person to live in less than adequate public facilities, is immense.

If the Social Security system is bad, the general social-welfare system is even worse as a factor in detracting from individual pride, self-respect, and contribution to the general good. Here, the pattern is the same—growing centralization, increasing concentrations of power in remote bureaucracies, less and less capacity to respond to individual situations and more and more tendency to treat everyone alike, and skyrocketing costs, which result in truly onerous taxation on the productive sector of society. If it is proper to raise gentle questions about the success of the Social Security system, it is quite appropriate to condemn the general social-welfare system as an abject failure. Its results are clear—it has failed to deal with individuals in terms of their unique needs; it has fostered, rather than reduced, the dependence of hundreds of thousands upon continuing public handouts; it has come to reward inactivity and non-productivity; it has dehumanized its clients by denying their capacity to do anything about their own condition; and it has accomplished all these remarkable ends in the name of the common good. Further, it has become mired in its own muck to the point that it is virtually unreformable, and represents the perfect example of how a centralized, massive, remote, self-perpetuating bureaucracy fails to solve problems, and contributes to individual malaise, loss of self-respect, discouragement of initiative, and the absence of individual responsibility in the process. And the greatest irony is that the currently proposed solutions all involve steps in the direction of even greater assumption of responsibility by larger and larger, and more and more remote, units of government.

We see a similar attitude operating in other crucial problem areas. We are being encouraged to move away from local support of education and to rely more heavily on statewide financing systems as a means of avoiding differences in the quality of educational opportunity in various areas. If this is done, it will further reduce individual interest, local participation in control, and commitment and involvement of communities and other small units of society in the educational affairs of their children. And if the experience with other massive bureaucratic programs of social improvement is any indication, it will also lead, not to an improvement in quality and opportunity, but to a massive, lowest-common-denominator mediocrity. A similar philosophy that someone else knows best is evident in the manner in which governmental units and the courts propose to solve such problems as school desegregation. We are now being told that the general good will be served if all units of massive metropolitan educational systems are formed into one gigantic supersystem, with interchangeable children and interchangeable buildings being bused together for the sake of another bureaucratically defined common good. Before taking this drastic step, we might be wise to inquire whether the good produced is worth the price—loss of personal choice, of neighborhood identity, of local pride and commitment. We might also inquire more deeply into the consistency of our court system, which contends on the one hand that it is expanding the liberties of the individual, while on the other, it chronically upholds the right of the governmental bureaucracy to direct the actions of individuals in areas of very basic personal concern. It is hard to see how the cause of individual freedom is served by programs that tell people where they must send their kindergarten children to school, and how a sense of neighborhood loyalty and small-group self-determination is fostered when the neighborhood school becomes valueless as a local reference point.

The operation of the mass society, and its effects on the worth of the individual, can be seen in many other areas of our national life. A few of these deserve passing mention. The sheer size of the group or organization within which the individual operates has an important effect upon how he feels about himself and the kinds of satisfactions available to him. If one lives in a small community, or attends a small school, or works in a small plant, his individual talents and abilities have a greater chance of being recognized and rewarded. Not only is the intimacy of personal contact greater, but the competition is less fierce, and the number of opportunities for recognition and approval are proportionately greater. In a high school class of fifty, nearly everyone can find a place, or a role, or a relationship, which brings the recognition and appreciation of his colleagues. But in a class of five hundred, the number of such opportunities is hardly greater than in the class of fifty, and the remaining four hundred and fifty are much less likely to find means of satisfying their urge to uniqueness and individual self-expression. A parallel situation exists in communities, clubs, or social organizations of any kind. In addition, when the size of a group becomes so large that broad mutual acquaintance is lost, the individual fails to find the continuing support of enough other individuals to help him to deal with the increased pressure of large-group life. Add to this problem the fact that many of us are geographically transient, uncommitted to community or neighborhood life, and the result is that we lose most of the vital group relationships that could help to sustain us in times of stress. As is shown in the next chapter, certain developing conditions have lessened the relevance of the family as a point of personal reference, self-respect, and individual satisfaction.

With the pressures on us, and the depersonalizing effect of the mass society, has also come a growing tendency toward cynicism about many of our social institutions. We have already seen how the individual finds little sense of participation in the affairs of government which affect his life. We are more and more distrustful of other forms of group life, or, at least, less and less committed to them. Social clubs, neighborhood organizations, churches, schools, and other institutions are much less central in our lives than formerly. The extended family group, as well, involves us less, either because of geographical separation, growing disparity of goals, or preoccupation with our own definition of the good life. As we have come to neglect or view cynically our participation in these social institutions, we have also lost some of the major social props for our own individuality. Casual acquaintances, fleetingly held, do not provide the individual with continuity of self-image and a basis for self-respect, as do intimate relationships, fostered within reliable social institutions, and cherished over a long period of time. It may seem funny to the intellectual cynic that his neighbor's aspiration is to become secretary-treasurer of a lodge or club whose total membership is eighteen, but to the neighbor, such an accomplishment has vital meaning in telling him who he is, in giving him a sense of place and consequence, and in maintaining some opportunity for individual expression.

In this chapter, we have seen how developments in American life over the past several decades have gradually eroded the importance we attach to the individual. Among these factors are the loss of the rural, small-town, and city neighborhood base on which the Jeffersonian ideal of democracy was erected; the industrialization of our economy, and the move toward mass production; the emergence of the mass society, which is an outgrowth of our growing population and of increasing pressures toward conformity and interchangeability among individuals; the historical trend toward collectivism, and the stifling effect of bureaucracies upon the individual's power to determine his own life and to take responsibility for his own actions; the increasing mobility of our population, with a consequent decline in the importance of stable social institutions and reliable reference points for the individual; and the effect of urbanization and the development of the suburbs, which have produced a breakdown in the effectiveness of social and political institutions, and the individual's relationship to them. Out of all these developments, I have attempted to show how individuals have gradually lost in freedom, self-respect, pride, and sense of personal worth. As problems have become complex and as real decision-making power has gravitated away from the individual, a parallel encouragement of irresponsibility and detachment has been seen. The individual has been encouraged to take less and less responsibility for his own actions, and as the real prospect of his doing anything about his condition has been reduced, he has fallen into an attitude of helplessness and powerlessness, which further weakens his resolve and his capacity to attack the problems around him.

In the face of the immense problems faced by this nation, it is absolutely imperative that we develop a means for the individual to reestablish a sense of personal power, confidence, and control over his own destiny. To do otherwise is to foster withdrawal and futility, and ultimately to cause us to lose our will to deal with our problems. Further, it is important to recognize that the sense of helplessness in the face of threat, which is a product of the decline of individualism in our nation, is a salient factor in the personalities of members of the radical minority, and that the combination of threat, helplessness, and lack of conviction in their worth or power as individuals produces much of the frustration and irrational behavior in which they engage. In the next chapter, we shall look at conditions in American life that more specifically are determining factors in the development of radicalism among our youth.

VI
GETTING READY FOR
THE BIG GAME

There are tough times ahead. The problems and dangers that face America and her people today will be with us for a long time, and some of them may get worse before they get better. It does not take a prophet to foresee that such problems as war and peace, pollution, and race relationships are not going to be solved quickly or easily. Thus, we and our children can look forward to a long period of tension and trying challenges. Preparation for an adult life filled with stress and unsolved problems is a difficult task, and the basic question facing us in our dealings with our children is whether we are doing an adequate job of providing that preparation. The characteristics the young generation will need to deal with these problems are obvious. They include the ability to maintain courage in the face of danger, patience in the face of trying provocation, reason in the face of emotional strain, and steadfast resolve in the face of frustration and disappointment. These attributes do not develop automatically, and they are especially difficult to foster when an individual must face problems that pose threats to his security or even survival, and thus tend to create a pervasive fear. As the experience of danger, provocation, and emotional strain continues through time, the individual inevitably becomes frustrated, and when fear and frustration are combined with a sense of personal helplessness, he may easily become erratic, desperate, and irrational, just as we see happening in the behavior of the young radicals.

Psychologists have long recognized the conditions required

to produce people capable of dealing with great stress over extended periods—that is, people who are basically stable and secure; who can tolerate frustration without blowing up or giving up; who are capable of reasoned discussion and action; and who can mobilize and apply their personal energies over long periods of time. To develop these qualities, one must be exposed during his formative years to conditions that require him to accept responsibility, to experience some frustration, to view objectively and realistically the conditions around him, and to develop an internal discipline that will maintain him when the going is rough. Yet over the past two decades, conditions of life in American society, and particularly in many liberal middle-class families, have not favored the development of these qualities. In the place of discipline, we have had permissiveness. Instead of helping children to grow in their ability to handle frustration, we have had unbelievable indulgence. Instead of encouraging objectivity and reason, we have contributed to irrational emotionalism. And instead of helping children to mobilize and apply energy over long periods, we have expected less and less effort and have led them to believe that wishing will make it so. This being the situation, we may reasonably question whether we have been giving our children fair preparation for dealing with the world. From the extreme form of this failure results the characteristic impatience, irrationality, arrogance, and irresponsibility of the young radical.

Attitudes toward child-rearing in the liberal middle class, over the past two decades, have been such that the child is not required to tolerate much frustration. Blessed by economic affluence and determined that their children should share fully in the bounty, many middle-class families have come to be highly indulgent of their own and their childrens' material wants and psychological demands. Because of this, the child learns a seriously defective lesson about the world. If throughout his life everything he wants materializes, everything he wishes for comes true, and every action he intends is allowed to occur, he develops a very strong expectation that this will always be the case. Thus, when he later, as a young adult, faces a real-world problem that he cannot solve and no one can solve for him, he becomes immensely frustrated and lacks the necessary tolerance to work patiently and rationally on it. When the problem is a threat to his survival and his helplessness to do anything about it becomes apparent to him, he panics to the point of losing control of his emotions and lashes out irrationally at the superficial source of his frustration. In the case of the radical minority with which we are concerned in this book, he attacks the university, his parents, the older generation, or the system—depending on whom he momentarily holds responsible for his frustration.

Being able to delay the gratification of one's impulses— that is, to tolerate frustration—is one of the hallmarks of the civilized person. This is not to say that one should never be allowed the satisfaction of letting go of his inner controls and indulging his wishes, but that considerations of time and place, the rights and feelings of others, and the ultimate consequences of immediate gratification, to society as well as to the self, must be considered. The margin of civilized behavior, which sets us as human beings apart from other organisms and from the jungle, is narrow—it depends on our ability to reason, anticipate consequences, and base our actions on broad considerations of the general good rather than on the impulse of the moment. When we develop a group of young people whose fear, frustration, and impatience are so intense that immediate emotional release and personal gratification dominate their behavior, we have narrowed that margin dangerously.

These attitudes concerning the importance of reason, anticipation, and considerations of the general good as marks of civilized, sensible behavior have found clear expression in our traditional way of life and in our social and economic system. Coursing through the American heritage was a great emphasis on delay in the enjoyment of life's pleasures. The promised beefsteak was guaranteed to taste better if one had to wait awhile to have it. By harboring resources, by accumulating a reserve for a secure future, and by delaying personal gratification, one's ultimate enjoyment was enhanced, and strength was added to the community and the nation. Indeed, our economic system is based on the assumption that we will accumulate unused reserves of money, energy, and human resources, and that these reserves can be committed to the future, and can thereby contribute to the anticipation of even better conditions. These delays in personal gratification for the sake of a better future find expression in very commonplace events—getting an education rather than immediately going to work at a less remunerative job; waiting to be married until one is economically established; not buying a house until one can have the kind that satisfies his aspirations; making do with the old car, the old clothing, or the less flashy appliance for the sake of immediate security and, in the long run, greater personal and group benefit.

I have already referred to the effects of the economic depression on the attitudes of older Americans. Out of that experience came a preoccupation with making sure that one did not have to put off the enjoyment of the "better things in life." While that attitude has many ramifications in how American society operates, most important in the present discussion is the extreme to which the liberal middle class has gone in its obsession with material possessions and with the satisfaction of personal urges for comfort and pleasure. Indeed, it would appear that the long-standing commitment to self-denial in the interest of a better future has passed from the lives of many members of the middle class, who are now engaged in a flurry, if not an orgy, of self-indulgence. Things of all descriptions are easily obtained, and conspicuously consumed. These things are bright, shiny, fascinating, amusing, and seem to fill more of a symbolic than a literal need. In some strange way, a great sector of the middle class seems to have replaced genuine self-respect and a sense of personal worth with the stainless steel and plastii gimcracks of the consumer society, and their watchword would appear to be, "If I want it, I will have it, whether I need it or not." Newer, shinier, more powerful automobiles; bigger, deeper, warmer swimming pools; more spacious, more luxurious homes; longer, more expensive, more impressive vacations; and a myriad of other self-indulging extravagances have come to preoccupy the middle class. This pace-setting group in our society seems to have committed itself to a philosophy of immediate reward, of escapism, and of material excess, and its members are quite successfully communicating these attitudes to their children.

Meanwhile, the drive for economic security is expressed in other ways as well. We strive for guaranteed annual incomes, for iron-clad pension plans, for vested retirement programs, and generally for more reward for less work. The easy life, the comfortable life, the self-indulgent life has become the mark of success, through which one is supposed to regain respect and a sense of individual worth, which have been lost, at least in part, in the very process of coming to value guaranteed annual

116

security above all. Moreover, middle-class parents seem to have assumed that the same values and urges characterize their children. The result has been that most children from such homes have been unbelievably overindulged. From early in their lives, they are showered with tangible expressions of their parents' concern that they should not suffer material deprivation. They are encouraged to ask for more and more, so that the parents may gratify their own needs by providing a constant stream of things to show how much they care for and how deeply devoted they are to their children. From new tricycles and the latest plastic gimmick advertised on TV, through the ten-speed bicycle and the electric guitar with quadruple multi-phase-high-gain-cosmic-decible-ultra-phonic speakers, to the motorized cycle, the personalized snowmobile, and the engraved sports car, only the age and the level of extravagance changes—the basic pattern remains the same. And while no child starts out his life expecting such a level of material grandeur, it does not take him long to understand the messages being sent by his parents—namely, that he may have what he wants when he wants it, and he doesn't have to worry about the installment payments. This level of material provision to the child soon comes to define his expectations, and if the same or a higher level of indulgence is not forthcoming, he begins to feel deprived.

The emphasis placed on material objects in the parent-child relationship often leads to a situation in which the child learns how to manipulate the parents in order to gain still further indulgence. As the pattern develops, the child, like the parents, begins to place an unusual importance on obtaining *things*, which have become the stock-in-trade of the relationship. Very often, the child is rewarded for good behavior by being given an extra thing. While one may ask what is extra when virtually everything is provided unconditionally, the child comes to expect that his good behavior will yield even more bounty. If, when the child's behavior is less than good, the regular indulgences are not withheld or removed, this reward system becomes a one-way street, and the child soon learns that he can bargain or extort from the parents even greater indulgence as the price for being good. This one-way street serves as a model for the later radical tactic of the "non-negotiable demand."

If providing the soft and comfortable life for our children were limited to the realm of material indulgences, perhaps the

117

result would be less harmful. Unfortunately, many liberal middle-class parents extend this attitude to nearly every aspect of their child's experience. Throughout his young life, everything that can possibly be done for him is done by his parents. In addition to *things*, they provide services, accommodations, and convenience. Examples of this amazing child-centeredness are easily found, but it is sufficient here to recognize that the experience of deprivation, frustration, or even inconvenience is rare in the lives of many middle-class children. Worse yet, these indulgences are provided with little or no expectation that the child has to do anything to obtain them. The idea that the good things of life have to be earned, that material comfort and security are not automatic, is all too frequently absent in the dealings of the liberal parent with his child. As a result, the child easily develops the expectation that his needs will be met, his demands will be indulged, and his tensions and frustrations removed by the benign intervention of the all-giving and comforting parent.

So long as it is within the power of the parents to control events that affect the child, the appearance of reasonable success in child-rearing is maintained. But when the child encounters frustrations that cannot be relieved through the benevolent service or purchasing power of his parents, the situation is quite different. At that point, a basic sense of powerlessness to deal with things on his own overcomes the child, and he is then subjected to almost intolerable tension and frustration. His reaction is one of rage, disillusionment, panic, and insult at the idea that anyone or any condition or any force can have the effrontery to deny him the easy solution and the relief from tension he has come to expect. In the process of being indulged and protected, he has retained a magical notion of his own power and omnipotence, for he has been able to change the world to his liking merely by wishing it, or by calling on persons who temporarily appear even more powerful and magical, his parents. Out of this experience has come a magnified sense of his own importance, and a truly arrogant belief that the world is his to manipulate, dominate, or consume at his own whim. Thus the overindulgent parent is teaching his child a fatally false lesson about the real world. When the child is never frustrated, he never develops any tolerance for future frustration. When every material want and service is automatically provided for, without commensurate effort or responsibility on the part of the child, he comes to take economic security for granted and sees it as a consideration of no value or concern to him. When the child is made to feel that his wishes are more important than his parents', or other considerations of reality, he develops an overweening, conceited belief in his own superiority, and when faced with problems he cannot solve, he is unable to muster the necessary patience or sense of personal responsibility for actions to deal effectively with real-world tensions. The family and social histories of young radicals, in contrast with those of their normal contemporaries, are replete with examples of this pattern. To the extent that a simple phrase can be used to sum up this aspect of the radical's personality, the term "spoiled rotten" would seem to apply.

Thus we can see how overindulgence leads to personality characteristics that are not helpful to the young person who has to face a lifetime of difficult problems. Such steady providing of immediate satisfaction of the child's wants leads him to expect equally quick relief from later tensions, and an inability to tolerate frustration develops. Extreme child-centeredness produces in the child an unrealistic view of his own importance, which later gives rise to a phony self-confidence characterized by arrogance and self-centeredness. Chronically allowing the child to have his way leads to increased demands and tantrum-like emotionalism. Failing to expect that the child will earn what is provided causes him to take economic security for granted and, later on, to come to regard work and those who engage in it as foolish or despicable. And out of the total syndrome of relationships surrounding the indulging parent and the indulged child there often emerges, in the end, a profound lack of respect for parents, which has important implications for the child's later relationships to authority and to frustrating forces in his environment. This latter attitude grows out of the fact that, even while he is encouraged to believe that he is powerful and omnipotent, he basically recognizes his own helplessness, so that when he is able to dominate his parents, they come to seem weak, easily manipulated, and unworthy of respect.

For many years, psychologists and educators have been advocating a doctrine of permissiveness in dealing with children. Basically, this idea involves avoiding such strict or repressive handling of the child's curiosity and impulses toward self-expression that he becomes frightened, restricted in his ability to enjoy normal pleasures, and overly inhibited. It also involves a parallel setting of reasonable limits, the fair but firm enforcement of these limits, and the application of sanctions with a view to developing internal controls and discipline. Unfortunately, the second aspect of this process has been overlooked, or neglected, with the result that permissiveness has come to mean allowing the child to do what he wants, when he wants it, without limitation, sanction, or parental control. In theory, permissive child-rearing is supposed to produce a stable, well-rounded person, who is capable of expressing his creative urges, enjoying the satisfaction of his impulses, and controlling himself rationally when the situation or the larger social interest requires. As it has come to be practiced, both in the home and more generally in the society, it is tending to produce children who demand absolute freedom as a right, to whom any limitation is intolerable, and to whom any discipline is the mark of total authoritarian repression.

Examples of how the doctrine of permissiveness is applied in many liberal middle-class homes and in society at large shed some light on the development of another aspect of the radical character—in this case, a lack of internal discipline and great difficulty in dealing with authority. In the permissive home, the child is allowed from a very early age to make a whole series of decisions about what is good for him. If he wishes not to eat something, he is allowed to refuse it. If he wants not to eat at a set time, he is permitted to gratify his need for food before or after the family takes its meal. If he desires an added hour of television, or of play before bedtime, he is permitted that. If he decides to stay at a friend's home after school, or finds school work or being in school difficult, accommodations are made so that he will not become frustrated. Later in life, if he wants to stay out late, or to be with persons about whom his parents have questions, or to begin to smoke or drink or use drugs, or to experiment with sex before he is emotionally prepared, he is permitted to do so. The goal of the parents in such cases is apparently to avoid confrontations that might be upsetting to them and damaging to the child's sense of self-determination. The effect is quite different—a child is produced who has no sense of limits, discipline, or secure boundaries. Each time the parent or some other responsible figure backs away from dealing with unwise, immature, or dangerous behavior, the child is made to believe that he is justified in expecting to do what he wants when he wants to do it. And out of this in turn develops the totally unreal belief that he is his own master, responsible only to himself and accountable to no one.

Closely related to such attitudes of permissiveness is a growing loss of discipline throughout society. Expectations for the control of children's behavior in school, for accepting the consequences of one's own failures, and for limiting what one does because of a larger concern for the group interest seem rapidly to be going down the drain. Failure to meet reasonable standards of performance in response to the expectations of parents and teachers is chronically excused. In this regard, we have come to the point where refusal to perform is equated with inability to perform, and a child who does not do his work is regarded as psychologically or socially ill. A more parsimonious explanation in many cases is that the child has never been expected to perform, has never been differentially rewarded when he has, and never been subjected to any real-world consequences when he has not. Certainly, as a practicing child psychologist, I am not advocating a return to the era of punishment and humiliation of the child whose major problems prevent him from doing what is expected. At the same time, I believe that children are not likely to respond with maximum effort if there are no consequences for their not doing so. And I believe that the sense of responsibility and accountability, which is a vital aspect of the civilized character, will not emerge automatically from a totally benign and permissive child-rearing environment.

Permissiveness is also apparent in our attitudes toward other forms of unacceptable behavior. In our schools and courts, the failure to observe even the most rudimentary respect for authority is chronically excused. Defiance of teachers has evolved from general talking back, through flagrant verbal abuse and obscene name-calling, to the point where physical assault is commonplace. Violations of taste, common decency, and standards of personal conduct are justified in the name of free speech or free expression. Insult or injury is visited on authority, public figures, and persons in the street with complete impunity. Crime is rampant and criminals receive more solicitous consideration than their victims. And as consequences fail to result from the commission of irresponsible or unacceptable actions, those who engage in such actions are further reinforced

121

in their belief that they can do anything they want. Consider that the short-run consequences of irresponsibility are practically nil: one can steal what he will not earn for himself; one can live without working; one can have sex without love, personal commitment, or future responsibility; one can be endlessly supported by his parents without care for the future; one can enjoy the fruits of freedom without accepting responsibility; one can slander, or insult, or damage others without fear of retribution; and one can demand, maneuver, or manipulate his way through a large portion of his life without facing many consequences. Such are the results of our permissiveness, and they are evidence of a serious breakdown in our social and personal discipline and purpose, for they forebode the general decadence of society and the breakdown of civilization.

Thus, a child raised under conditions of extreme permissiveness develops another characteristic fundamental to the radical personality. He believes that he may do anything he wants when he wants to do it, and that he must account to no one for his actions. His freedom is the sole consideration, irrespective of the effects on others or even on himself in the future. He is a creature of impulse and immediate gratification—not only must he have what he wants, but because of the previously discussed inability to tolerate frustrations, he must have it *now*. Consequences mean nothing, because there have been no consequences, and responsibility has not developed, because his irresponsibility has been excused throughout his life. He cannot tolerate limits, even in pursuit of the general good. And authority of any kind is rejected, because authority implies limits, controls, and consequences, which he cannot abide. He has grown up in a self-determined fools' paradise, and he lacks the internal discipline to deal effectively with the inescapable constraints of the real world. Instead, he cries out for even greater freedom, less responsibility and accountability, and becomes still more demanding of having things his own way. When faced with a final, immovable obstacle, he becomes successively angry, violent, irrational, and vindictive, or falls into a helpless state of despair and depression and gradually withdraws and drops out.

Closely related to the generally overpermissive attitudes in relationships between liberal parents and their children is an overprotective concern that nothing frustrating or limiting be imposed on the children by outside forces. Through this pattern the parent is not merely a direct agent of overindulgence and permissiveness, but an active ally of the child in trying to shape the world to suit his immediate demands. From an early time, the parent seeks to shield the child from unpleasantness, danger, and demands for performance expressed by others. If, for example, a neighbor or a teacher attempts to set limits on the child, the parent's reaction is often that he has no right to do so, since the child is supreme and can do no wrong. To the neighbor or teacher, the child's behavior is excused or rationalized. If the child later comes into dispute with other agents of society or authority, the parents' reaction may be a similarly overprotective taking of the child's part, and resistance to a reasonable effort to correct the child's behavior. Further, as the child is encouraged to feel little personal responsibility for the things that do not go well in his life, he develops the conviction that forces outside himself produce his distress, and the stage is thus set for indicting the university, the Establishment, or the system. In another vein, overprotectiveness reveals itself in not allowing the child to become aware of other unpleasant events inevitably associated with living, such as illness, injury, death, interpersonal strife, and violence. In this way, the child's view of the world, during his early life, is made unrealistically bland and benign. As a consequence, he is further poorly fitted to cope with the world's unpleasant realities. Overprotection also damages him by contributing to his notion that he is of overriding importance, that his view of the world, however distorted, is correct, and that he will be endlessly sheltered from frustration. Further, when neither the parents nor other agents of society are permitted to make the child face the consequences of his actions, he has no basis for the development of a sense of personal responsibility. Finally, when he is allowed no contact with the small dangers incumbent upon his status as a child, he fails to develop effective courage in standing up to dangers on his own, and as a result future stresses and threats will loom all the more catastrophic.

The argument has been made by parents that the three-pronged program of overindulgence, permissiveness, and overprotection described above has accomplished three vitally important things for the child. The first of these alleged benefits is a basic sense of personal security, the second a full realization of the child's creative potential, and the third a firm and satisfying relationship for both the parent and the child. This argument deserves a response, since it is frequently used as a justification of parental inaction and irresponsibility, especially on the rationalizing grounds that such child-rearing practices are a means for developing sensitive, humane, creative human beings.

On the matter of personal security, it would seem to be true that meeting all the child's needs and offering him a benign, protected environment create a period of considerable comfort and sense of well-being. Closer examination, however, suggests that whatever security is developed in this way is superficial and transient. A kind of security is probably present in a fool's paradise, but when that paradise is lost, as it inevitably will be when the child encounters the stresses of the real world, it takes more than the continuing intervention of indulgent parents to set things right and maintain a feeling of safety. Basic and reliable security must ultimately be a condition of the inner strength of the person himself, and this inner strength must develop at least in part from the experience of mastering age-appropriate challenges as they occur. In addition, the parent who chronically reveals insufficient strength to confront and deal with the inappropriate or irrational demands of his child provides a very shaky model for the child to identify with, and this underlying parental uncertainty is communicated to the child, adding to his basic sense of unreliability about what the world is. At its root, personal security arises from the experience of the world as a predictable, manageable, and reliable place, and from experiencing oneself as an individual who can cope with whatever comes along, not as a fragile, hapless, endangered rabbit. When personal security truly exists, even the problems of today seem capable of solution—when it does not, any challenge is a catastrophe.

As to the effect of these child-rearing methods on the full realization of the child's creative potential, the superficial evidence would suggest that such parents are accomplishing their goal. Certainly a child whose thinking and actions have never been limited by reality is going to bring a lot of new and unusual views to bear on a problem. Certainly also, a child who is rigidly confined by doctrinaire thinking, authoritarian repression of every idea or impulse, and absolutist demands that he conform in every respect, is not likely to be innovative or creative. But we must be sure what we mean by

124

creativity—many conditions of the human mind can produce in-novative, unusual thoughts, among them schizophrenia, LSD psychosis, drunkenness, and senility. True creativity goes beyond the mere production of the novel or bizarre, and requires the evaluation and criticism of what is produced, its logical pursuit and examination, and a rational process leading from the idea to its implementation or execution. Thus, merely to allow a child to grow up thinking his own thoughts and engaging in idiosyncratic flights of fancy, never evaluating them in the context of their relationship to reality and remaining forever at the level of the abstract and the personally symbolic, is not creativity, it is madness. To the extent that we fail to couple idea production with discipline, rigorous evaluation, judgment, and criticism, we are fostering a process that may be momentarily self-rewarding, but ultimately is of little personal use or social relevance. And when we encourage the child to construct a world that fails to take reality into account, as we do when he is left totally undisciplined, to that extent we are committing on him and society a crime of serious proportions. In this connection, I often recall the assertion of one of my radical friends that he had examined all the issues in the world very carefully, and had come to the conclusion that he did not accept anything as valid. As a consequence, he felt, everything would have to be torn down and new ideas and methods developed for every aspect of human existence. After ascertaining that he meant this statement quite literally, I asked him how he felt about the law of gravity. He took refuge in the handy argument that it was irrelevant to the large issues he had in mind, and the conversation soon ended. But while the law of gravity is so ubiquitous in its operation that its reality comes home even to the most undisciplined, many other limits, which are almost equally evident in the real world, have no real impact on them. As a result, the so-called creativity of radical thought turns out to be so highly superficial, fantastically abstract, and lacking in rigor or appreciation of implications that it is truly unbelievable.

What of the argument that this child-rearing style leads to a firm, satisfying relationship between parent and child? In practice the effects are quite different. Parents who can be manipulated turn out to be perceived as weak and unreliable by their children. Parents who provide endless overindulgence end up being condemned for substituting material things for love and interpersonal commitment. Parents who endlessly protect the child are eventually castigated for not allowing enough freedom. And parents who allow their children to do whatever they please are eventually resented when it is no longer possible for them to insure perfect freedom, comfort, indulgence, and relief from tension. Are these the bases on which a firm, satisfying relationship is developed? Are these the foundations of love and commitment and mutual respect? Hardly. And parents who so deceive themselves earn, in the end, the same fate as all who in any way frustrate the omnipotent, self-important fantasies—namely, the arrogant, antagonistic, alienated reaction that characterizes the total world view of the emotionally disturbed young radical. A successful, mutually satisfying relationship between parent and child is built of other stuff—love, concern, interest, and gratification, assuredly, but also strength in the parents, to set and enforce limits, to handle confrontations, and to face the unpleasant realities of life with the child as he is exposed to them. Parents must insure consequences to the child when his actions warrant correction; they must support social agents such as teachers who express reasonable expectations for performance; and in their own lives they must maintain a basic integrity, which is not always easy in a tense and affluent society. From the parents' continuing example, the child builds his own image of himself and the world. Out of truly effective child-rearing will develop mutual respect, constant love, and personal characteristics that fit the child to manage his own life in a mature, responsible way, and give him the confidence to attack the problems of his time with reason, patience, and fortitude. Out of overindulgence, permissiveness, and overprotection come frustrated, irrational, ineffective catastrophe-seekers.

A final word about certain variations in liberal middle-class child-rearing practices that occasionally make a major contribution to the development of the radical personality. Some parents are so caught up in their own self-indulgence that they unconsciously regard their children as a nuisance who deprive them of the opportunity to do their own thing. If this occurs, subtle rejection and denigration of the child are added to his other problems, and he will build up resentment and hostility toward the parents. Since, in his overindulged state, he can find nothing tangible to be angry about, the reservoir of anger finds expression in hostility toward parent surrogates such as teachers.

Sometimes, the father is so preoccupied with his work and the mother with her career or social activity that they are not in sufficient contact with the child to offer him limits, satisfaction, or adequate parental models, in which case other neurotic complications are added to the syndrome. In other cases, the parents may be extremely permissive and indulgent in the area of personal freedom, yet come through as harsh and demanding in others, such as school work. I discuss the effect of this pattern on the child's life and his attitudes toward school in a later chapter. Finally, there are many instances of indulgence and permissiveness alternating with anger and heavy discipline; in such cases the parents early become the focus for the child's anger, and a more typical pattern of rebelliousness and alienation occurs. Obviously, detailed examination of these variations would lead to an extensive treatise on child psychology, but that must wait for another volume.

In this chapter, I have tried to show how certain current conditions in American society and child-rearing styles contribute to the development of the personal traits that characterize the young radicals. The affluent society encourages material indulgence of children, which leads to an inability to tolerate frustration and a consequent impatience. It also encourages a wish for immediate gratification of impulses, and an emphasis on the *now* aspect of life, with consequent lack of interest in the future and disdain or disrespect for historical events. Out of indulgence and permissiveness come a failure to accept responsibility; a replacement of accountability with excuses, hatred of limits and authority, and an inability to treat problems with rigor and systematic effort. The total pattern, carried to extremes, leads to the development of the by now well-recognized personal characteristics of the young American radical: arrogance, insistence on quick solutions, position-paper answers to issues of great complexity, the blaming of forces outside himself for his distress, and deep emotionalism, anger, and frustration underlain by a sense of personal helplessness and fear. Fortunately, we have so far managed to create only a tiny minority with these characteristics, and as a result, we can still hope that the stable majority will deflect us from the road to chaos.

VII
WHO'S STEALING MY OXYGEN?

The basic personality traits of the young radicals, which were identified and traced to their origins in the preceding chapters, give rise to certain secondary behavior patterns. These secondary patterns, which must be discussed for a full understanding of the styles, reactions, and attitudes of the radical minority, are treated in the next few chapters.

The radical's underlying personality syndrome, already described at length, gives rise to a series of characteristic actions and attitudes in relation to certain national events and prominent public figures, and even to some of his own colleagues. Keeping in mind several obvious psychological facts will make it easy to understand this: First, a person who suffers from a basic and pervasive sense of insecurity, inability to tolerate frustration, and a false sense of self-confidence will chronically engage in a search for strength and reassurance, the removal of the source of the frustration, and a sense of personal importance. Second, in the course of this search, he will often engage in actions that do not have anything to do with solving the basic problem, and thus have a prima facie appearance of irrationality—for example, trying to borrow strength from an inspiring or forceful leader, making himself part of a group that has power, withdrawing, striking out violently at what he perceives as the source of danger or frustration, taking so-called symbolic or principled actions, building himself up into a figure of great influence or importance, trying to appear unique in some bizarre way, and so on. Third, the basic problem of insecurity is not resolved by actions directed toward the world around him. Even if the present frustrations, and the present perceived sources of insecurity, were removed, others would appear. Even if the insecure person gained the power he seeks, or could withdraw from the stressful external situation, or could strike down the supposed oppressor, the basic problems of uncertainty, anxiety, lack of confidence, and experience of impending catastrophe would remain. This is so because the essential problem is *internal,* and can only be finally dealt with through a change in the person's attitude about himself. When he is truly strong, secure, and confident within himself, the external problems are remarkably less catastrophic and therefore can be viewed more objectively and attacked more rationally. This is not to say that a momentary sense of relief from tension and a transient satisfaction does not come to the insecure person if one of the sources of tension and frustration is removed, or that a momentary sense of power and self-confidence does not accrue to the radical when he destroys a hated figure, or that the sense of helplessness is not temporarily alleviated by participation in a mass demonstration, a rock throwing, or a "day of rage." However, the plaguing self-doubt, panic, and sense of powerlessness will return shortly, for psychological security is a matter of internal strength and is not significantly connected to external conditions.

One of the clearest examples of how the basic personality of the radicals reveals itself in the area of social concerns is seen in their fascination with proposing or trying to find the simple, easy answer to a problem of great complexity. Surely, their reasoning seems to go, persons as talented and insightful as we are can find a quicker way through the difficulty we are in than those tedious complications constantly being raised by the Establishment. Surely, there is an easier way—one involving a flash of insight that will immediately be accepted by everybody, and will put everything aright. If the possession of the H-bomb by the United States is the source of a portion of the threat to mankind, the United States should immediately dump all of its H-bombs into the ocean, and thus remove the danger. What could be simpler? What could be more principled? Why doesn't the President, if he has any respect for the survival of mankind, do the quick and obvious thing? If people in the ghetto have inadequate and insufficient housing, why not build them more and better housing? Isn't it a simple question of doing what's right? If students don't want to live in the dormitory, let them move out—why should anyone be required to live anywhere he doesn't want to? If the draft law allows certain categories of men to be deferred on the basis of their occupation or marital status or something else, it should be changed—let's change it, since it's not democratic. And so on, ad nauseam. Simple answers? Yes. Simpleminded? Yes again. The radicals generally fail to realize that the simple answers they propose have already been thought of, and were discarded long ago, because on examination they turn out not to be so simple. In their execution, or their implications, these supposedly simple answers reach into very deep water, affecting directly and indirectly the lives of thousands or millions of other people beside those they are designed to help. The cost, or damage, or other consequences of these and/or other quick solutions, arrived at in theory in the middle of the night and translated into a sophomore-rhetoric position paper, are either not considered at all, or are negated as irrelevant in the enthusiasm of the moment.

Why then, in view of the patent foolishness apparent even to the most unsophisticated, does the simple solution have such an appeal to the radical personality? First, because it seems to promise immediate solution and thus relief from frustration. It is totally consistent with the "now" orientation of the radicals, and the lessons of the past or the dangers to the future be damned. Just as his parents provided him with quick relief from the frustrations of the past, without effort or consideration of consequences on his part, so the position-paper solution to complex problems provides him with promise of similar easy relief now. It solves his impatience, requires little toil or rigor, promises instant action, and suggests the return of the momentary nirvana he experienced when he was told—"It's simple; daddy will just go out and get you another bicycle so you won't feel bad." Second, the instant solution appeals to the radical's sense of omnipotence and grandiosity. It usually is cosmic in its sweep—promising to revolutionize an area of social concern—and self-appointedly brilliant in its conception. It momentarily inflates his self-importance—what a rush of satisfaction comes when

130

he is met by an admiring friend saying, "Hey, Eric—I hear you solved the poverty problem last night!" Heady stuff for someone plagued by personal doubt. Third, the position-paper solution presents an opportunity to shriek at those who in their stupidity fail to accept its profound merit or to implement it. It thus can become a vehicle for attacking one or another member of the Establishment as dilatory, inhumane, reactionary, or inane, perhaps even producing a confrontation in which the advocate of the simple solution can obtain further satisfaction of his infantile need for power and recognition.

The phenomenon of the simple solution would not seem to contain a very profound danger to our established way of life, since the test of reality is always available. However, such an approach does contain important consequences which should concern us. For one thing, when the sense of alarm about an issue reaches a high level among the general population, the appeal of the instant solution broadens, and otherwise responsible leaders may pick it up and seriously advocate it, possibly in good faith, possibly in ignorance, and possibly in pursuit of personal or political ends. If the public at large are not careful, they may be swept along, or their majority voice may be outshouted by the alarmist minority, and if the "simple" solution is adopted, as occasionally happens, we may be a long time picking up the pieces. For another, the simple answer may find so much appeal among a minority of like-put-together characters that they will rally in force behind it, and pressure a frightened or overly conciliatory official into adopting it for the sake of quieting the radicals. If this happens, it encourages the radicals to approach the next problem with the same superficiality and the same tactics. Finally, the process is dangerous because it is essentially irrational and anti-intellectual, and whether it succeeds or not, it sets an unfortunate pattern for those even more immature, unsophisticated, undereducated persons to follow in trying to deal with problems.

Closely related to the phenomenon of the simple solution is another, the rise of the irresponsible critic. Americans have always been fascinated by cleverness—the crisp epithet, the well-turned metaphor, the pungent comment. When a society is faced with very serious problems, as ours is, it takes no great talent or imagination to find fault with things; thus, fault-

131

finding is a widespread, probably not basically unhealthy, activity these days. If fault-finding can be combined with cleverness it is doubly appealing. Thus, in the face of our problems and the lack of easy solutions to them, the clever fault-finder can have a field day. Never mind that the problems are difficult. Never mind that millions of people are busting their arteries trying to solve them. Never mind even that substantial progress is being made. Keep your eye on the failings, the weaknesses, the mistakes, or the lack of perfect good will. Make sure you are clever, articulate, and can go to the weakness of a solution or a national figure, and you have the basic qualities required in the critic. And, oh yes, make sure too that you do not get in a position where you have to do anything about the problems yourself—be careful to stay out of the kitchen because it's too hot, do not assume responsibility, ask the questions rather than answer them—you are now ready for the cherished and enviable position of irresponsible critic. The typical habitat of the irresponsible critic is the syndicated newspaper column or the national television news commentary. This is not to say that all newspaper columnists and all TV news commentators are irresponsible—but, clever, articulate, reasonably sophisticated persons all, they sometimes are irresponsible. And they have immense power, influence, and appeal, so the onus of responsible action weighs heavily on them. Fortunately, most take this responsibility seriously most of the time. But should they not, either deliberately or inadvertently, the effect is unfortunate. By an endless picking at what is wrong, irresponsible critics contribute materially to greater alarm, subvert the efforts of those who have the responsibility for solving problems, add to an already intolerable sense of frustration among the young radicals, and do nothing to contribute to the solutions, unless we accept the flimsy rationalization that they are merely trying to alert the public to what needs to be done. Egad! As if the public doesn't already know what needs to be done! The problem is how to do it.

In any case, the irresponsible critic is frequently found among the ranks of the young radicals, and is highly cherished by them. Why? Because the role is perfectly consistent with some of the radical's important personality traits. Finding the holes in what someone else proposes or is doing elevates his sense of self-importance, for if he can see what's wrong with what they propose, he concludes that he is brighter than they are. Being clever or cute in his criticism earns him added self-importance points, and adds to his status among his associates. Seeing the defects in the actions of a person with real power gives him an increased sense of power. Always implied in his criticism is the notion that he, the critic, has a better plan, and that only a lack of power or opportunity keeps him from solving the problem. This activity also helps him to blame others for the distress, and to express aggression in a socially acceptable way toward figures of power and authority in society. Thus, certain psychological needs important to the young radical are met directly by his role as irresponsible critic, or indirectly by his admiration for and identification with irresponsible critics who are more generally in the public eye. When dissatisfaction and negativism become a way of life, those who articulate these attitudes become heroes.

One of the most worrisome things about the young radicals is their desperation about their lack of power. The gaining of power is a transcendent issue among them. Parenthetically, it is interesting to note that their fear of power is also very great, with the result that entrusting power even to their own leaders is very rare. The "power to the people" rallying cry has in practice been translated into "Power to me," and with that guiding credo, it seems unlikely that a very firm or lasting power base, on which a strong leader might build a program of revolution, is likely to emerge among them. Nevertheless, certain other aspects of their character, operating in concert with their concern about power, may be cause for alarm. Their sense of personal helplessness, their failure to establish a permanent sense of themselves as individuals, their need for immediate solutions and instant gratification, their tendency to blame others for their difficulties, their avoidance of personal responsibility and accountability, and their overriding wish for a sense of security all contribute to the potential danger. Under conditions of stress in our national life, and in view of these personality traits, it is not unlikely that the radicals might find a great attraction in a political demagogue.

What would such a leader have to be? Certainly young, since no one over thirty can be trusted. Certainly articulate, critical, and hostile, to offer an object that can be identified with their own needs. Certainly he would have to possess personal strength and courage, so they could gain through identification the elements lacking in their own character. Beyond that, he would have to draw power to him, but make the appearance of sharing it in a participatory democracy with them, and he would have to promise many and produce one or two immediate, easy solutions. And they might well be had in such circumstances, or at least be had for a long enough period for the demagogue not to need them anymore. It is interesting to consider what kind of person could pull it off. Chairman Mao, perhaps? Too old, too fat, and a bit inscrutable. Che Guevara? Too dead, but otherwise a possibility. One of their own number? Not likely, because their own weaknesses would be too apparent in him. Adolf Hitler, if he were alive, young, and vigorous, and not an anti-Semite? Probably. Whoever the leader might be, the substance of his program would not be terribly important, as long as it were liberally sprinkled with references to peace, freedom, and power to the people.

Fortunately, we are well protected from this eventuality by the great majority of our young people, who are sufficiently stable, secure, and rational not to need psychological refuge in the shelter of a demagogue's arms. How long we shall have this protection depends on how long we allow our national life and personal practice to go on spawning characteristics that today fortunately exist only in a minority.

A mild form of such demagoguery can be seen in our public life today. In addition to the abundance of irresponsible critics, an occasional political figure seeks to advance his own career by appealing to the insecurities of the young radicals. While few serious candidates on the national scene base their entire approach on an appeal to our fears, or limit their campaigns to the one or two issues that morbidly fascinate the radicals and their extreme-liberal bedfellows, it is obvious that the temptation is there. With the Vietnam War behind us, no one-issue candidate has the chance of a wax ball on a hot stove. However, a good many serious candidates succumb to the temptation of opportunism sufficiently to discuss one or more issues in isolation—as though unemployment has nothing to do with the SST, or as though busing for desegregation is independent of issues of urban blight, drug abuse, and individual freedom. We shall, of course, always have political opportunists, and the ability of Americans, young and old alike, to see and understand the complex relationships among issues is our best insurance against their success.

Another striking example of how the basic personality traits of the radical are expressed is found in their fascination with mass demonstrations, and with participating in them. The mass demonstration, or, in another vernacular, the mob, has long been recognized as serving a most important set of psychological functions for its members. Membership in a group of any kind provides important gratifications, but these are gained from the usual social group only after some period of participation. Being in a mass demonstration, however, is particularly consistent with some of the underlying needs of the radical personality. This pattern may be analyzed conveniently by considering it from two separate points of view: first, the relationship of the group to outside forces; and second, the relationship of the individual member and the group.

The psychological functions of the mass group for the member, as it deals with outside forces, revolve largely around questions of how authority is comfortably dealt with. Of first-order significance is the fact that the group offers a relatively safe method of confronting or defying authority. In light of the extreme difficulty the radical has in dealing with authority and limits generally, this is exceedingly important. In thus confronting authority, the group allows its members to gain a feeling of bearding the lion in his den—that is, of dealing directly and forcefully with the object of fear and frustration. The mass of the group thereby symbolizes to the members the relative weakness of the power figure as contrasted to the strength of the group. Demands can be expressed in categorical, non-negotiable terms, and immediate accession to them insisted on. The voice of the individual is multiplied by many decibels when the mass shouts, and it is not terribly important whether the mass shouts exactly what the individual would say. The important thing is power—not persuasion or reason.

It is of course true that not every mass demonstration is loud, irrational, and confrontational in the violent sense implied above. Peaceful, orderly demonstrations play a useful function in our society—they are an extension of our basic right to petition for redress of grievances and to speak freely, and as such should be cherished and protected. Such demonstrations, however, have less appeal for the radical minority. They are typically organized and controlled by more stable and mature individuals than the young radicals, and they do not provide the same attraction or gratification to the radicals as do the noisy confrontations.

The psychological implications of the relationship between the individual and the group in a mass demonstration are somewhat more extensive and varied. First, and at the simplest level, participation in the group's action offers a chance for the discharge of energy, and any action has a tendency to discharge tension arising from frustration. Next, the mass demonstration offers the individual an opportunity for an immediate sense of value—his importance to the group is simply in being there, in order to swell its numbers. In this way, the group is like a kind of fraternity with no membership requirements or limits, and the individual gains a quick sense of acceptance and approval. The mass is nondiscriminatory about the kinds of behavior to which it responds favorably; thus the individual can obtain roaring accolades for even the most trite, inane, or irrelevant utterances, so long as they are vaguely pertinent to the emotional state or manifest purpose of the group. In this way, those with questions about their self-importance obtain meaningful, satisfying rewards in the group's reactions to them. Only a person who brings himself into direct conflict with the mass is rejected or criticized by it.

Most important, however, is the fact that the group provides cover, protection, and power. Imagine that you are in the center of a group of only a hundred people, but that they are pressed close around you. Their power seems immense, especially if there is any movement, or if you are too short to see over heads to the periphery. You are enfolded and surrounded by what might be a hundred-thousand. The sense of protection and insulation from danger is intense. You are lost among them. They are moving to remove your frustration. They are vital and alive and strong. This experience and its emotional correlates diminish your fear, remove your sense of powerlessness. There is strength and unity and apparent purpose. In addition, you are submerged as an individual and you do not have to worry about personal responsibility or accountability, because when the group dissolves, the authorities have no one to bring to account, particularly if you have stayed close to the center, concealing your identity. Finally, you are deluded into believing that the group will accomplish what you cannot, namely having things go the way you want them to. In short, the mass demonstration offers an almost perfect psychological vehicle for relieving your tensions, defying authority, providing a sense of purpose and group acceptance, and removing your impotence—all within the protective covering of no responsibility or accountability.

Of related but much less important significance is the common observation that the radical is grossly uncomfortable in one-to-one confrontations. When I was vice-president for student affairs at the University of Michigan, I had a great number of opportunities to deal with the same radicals both in one-to-one and group situations. In the one-to-one, even around the most controversial or emotion-provoking issues, those who in the mass setting had been most bold in their attacks on individuals and institutions, and seemed the most arrogant, confident, and powerful, were transparently unsure, uneasy, and frightened. One who had threatened your destruction during the noon-hour rally, might tremble in his hands during a quiet conversation with you on a bench beside the rallying place an hour-and-a-half later. In clinical settings, where genuine protection, comfort, and security is offered, similar individuals very frequently break down into fits of crying, despair, and overpowering anxiety. This dreadful apprehension connected with having to face issues and persons also gives rise to the frequently observed phenomenon of having a different spokesman for each confrontation, refusing to meet without the presence of an advocate, or otherwise finding means to protect themselves from being alone in dealing with figures of even the slightest power or authority.

The sense of need for an advocate expresses itself in other aspects of American life. The poor seek advocates in dealing with the legal system or the welfare administrators. Children need advocates in order to get a fair break at the hands of teachers or principals. The unemployed require advocates to enable them to approach employers. And the consumer needs Ralph Nader to protect him from the exploitation of a whole chain of selfish operators, from manufac-

137

turer to delivery man. In every case, the pattern is the same; that is, a weak person, or an inadequate person, or a person who feels helpless, is assumed not to be able to deal with someone who is supposedly more powerful, and requires a friendly third party from whom he can borrow strength, intelligence, or power. The idea of getting help where one can, when one needs help, is certainly admirable. At the same time, the rise of the Ralph Naders in our society raises some interesting questions and is based on some equally interesting assumptions. The assumptions are that everyone who thinks he needs help actually does; that there are no informal or personal arrangements he can make to provide himself with the help; that exploitation of the less advantaged by the more advantaged is so rampant as to require a whole new system of dealing with it; and that the advocate is an altruistic benefactor of society who has no personal axe to grind and no exploitative instincts of his own. Some of these assumptions may be valid in some or even many cases; that all are, even in a very few cases, is most unlikely.

The questions raised by the advocate system are even more serious than the assumptions on which its existence is based. These are: Does the advocate system really result in better conditions for the child, or the poor, or the consumer? Do we really get better, safer, more reasonably priced cars as a result of Nader's activities, or do we get added unnecessary expense, with little practical difference resulting? To use a hypothetical example, suppose it cost 10 percent more per car to insure that a certain part of its mechanical system would not break down. Suppose further that the chances of a breakdown prior to the change were one in a hundred, and that once in each hundred times the breakdown occurred, there was a traffic fatality. Finally, suppose that 500,000 such cars were produced a year, at a consumer cost of three thousand dollars, or thirty-three hundred dollars after the improvement. Some quick arithmetic tells us we would save fifty lives per year, at a cost of one hundred and fifty million dollars to the consumer, or three million dollars per life. The figures are hypothetical, but the idea is not. We should know what both sides of the bargain are before we run pell-mell to correct a defect that may not be that important to very many people. The emotional argument is easily made that fifty lives are

138

worth one hundred and fifty million dollars, but I believe the public's decision would be otherwise. And if the defects we are out to remedy are widespread, or fall into different priority areas—that is, if the choice is to remedy the defect at the price of adding to the unemployment rate, or failing to build a new school, Ralph Nader might be surprised at how the public would decide. In any event, the advocate's stress on a single priority deserves to be balanced by a rational decision among all of them.

The second question is immediately apparent: Irrespective of what it may do for the person whose advocacy is taken up, is society as a whole better off than it would have been, all things considered? The final question relates to the issue of the individual and his view of himself. As I have already illustrated, a great many forces and conditions in our society take away from the individual's sense of self-worth, power, and competence. In the end, does the advocate system result in a strengthening of the individual, so that he gains in a sense of ability to cope with things on his own, of pride in his accomplishments, and of security in the knowledge that he can affect the course of events around him? Or does it further weaken his resolve and contribute to his feeling of being a helpless victim of the mass society by cultivating abject dependence on another bureaucracy? Is the advocate really an objective, altruistic partner who temporarily lends his strength, insight, and intelligence to the growth and independence of the individual, or is he engaged in the development of yet another focus of collectivist power with himself sitting at the top and exploiting the individual in another, more subtle way. It is too early to decide what the final effect of the advocate's role will be on these basic issues in our society, but these questions should warn us to be vigilant. It is not too early to see that the advocate concept serves quite well the psychological needs of the radical personality. For as the radical sees it, the advocate system baits the powerful, gives an ally, offers symbolic protection from fear, and offers quick answers to tough problems.

On the practical matter of dealing with the exploitative aspects of bureaucracies, the individual can do some obvious things. He can educate himself to know when his interest rates are too high, or the per unit cost of a product unfair. He can prepare himself for a better chance to compete in the job market. He can resist the inflationary spiral by not buying every knickknack that strikes his fancy. And he can make rational judgments and discriminations among products, social alternatives, and personal priorities. If he knows, or believes, or even suspects that a product is no good or dangerous, he can and should make a personal, individualistic, nonadvocated choice not to buy it, or should paint it lemon yellow if he has found it inadequate. If he is short-weighted by his butcher, he can stop buying from him and can tell others what happened. If his neighborhood is littered, or his park too crowded, or the exhaust fumes from his car too toxic, he can take some small, personal steps to remedy these conditions. The individual's real power lies in his freedom to decide, in his ability to postpone certain immediate gratifications for the sake of a future good, and in his assertion of his own judgment. When we once again begin to act as individuals who are not helpless, we will reexperience the deep satisfaction of our power as free men.

The Vietnam War and the reactions of the young radicals to it exemplify par excellence how public events and psychological difficulties combine to produce actions that influence the direction of our society. That conflict and the demands it made on us represented an immense threat to individuals who had been prepared by social conditions and childhood experiences to feel frightened, frustrated, and powerless. The involvement of the United States in Southeast Asia may or may not have been a catastrophic error—history will have to make that judgment. The actual impact on the lives of our citizens, including the young, was substantial but far from generally catastrophic. Yet the psychological reactions and effects were catastrophic, and we need to examine why. First, to the young man who has been bred to indulgence, the inconvenience and discomfort of service in the armed forces represent a condition of almost intolerable deprivation. Second, if in addition he lacks confidence and basic personal strength, the thought of risking his life or safety, however low the probability of harm, represents an overpowering danger. Third, if he has been encouraged to believe in his own omnipotence, he finds it intolerable to be placed in a position where another person is going to make decisions about what he does. And fourth, if he has been taught to despise authority, he is immensely frustrated in a situation where he can be ordered around. The Vietnam War, or for that matter any limited war in which we might have engaged during the same period, produced conditions that were totally disorganizing to the radical personality. It represented discomfort, a threat to safety, a puncturing of the omnipotent fantasies of youngsters who had come to believe in their own superiority, and the operation of impersonal authority in controlling personal destiny. Further, it demanded the assumption of responsibility, a temporary sacrifice of personal freedom, effort, and sacrifice of personal convenience and indulgence. It deeply frightened those who were already insecure, it introduced frustrations into the lives of some who simply could not tolerate frustration, it removed the aura of protection from those who had been overprotected, and it demanded compliance from those to whom the permissive society had promised freedom without limits.

The reaction of the radical personality was quite predictable. Alarm and apprehension grew into panic. Demands for relief from pressure swelled to a crescendo. Anger at the frustrating force, in this case the national government, grew into rage and violence. The cry was for immediate relief, for a return to the conditions of comfort, indulgence, and unaccountability their life experience had taught them to expect. And these cries and demands raised so much general panic and sympathy, by threatening disaster or disruption, that the national course was changed, perhaps with unfortunate consequences over the long run.

None of this is to suggest there are not serious questions about the wisdom of our policies in Southeast Asia. These issues were never faced squarely, and a rational judgment was never made by the American people concerning alternatives and consequences. The real tragedy is not that we have departed from Vietnam, but rather that the events and circumstances that led us to withdraw were largely the product of irrational demands for relief from tension (made by a minority who were so personally threatened by catastrophe that rage replaced reason) and were conditioned on emotionalism instead of considered judgment. The radicals and the nation thus were reinforced in the view that if you shout loudly enough, threaten vociferously enough, and demand impatiently enough, you can eventually get your way without consideration of future consequences.

Certain other recent events illustrate how emotionalism, and a devotion to short-run solutions as a means of quelling noisy demands, operates in present-day America. In our justified concern about saving the natural environment, there is an unfortunate tendency to jump to quick conclusions and take actions based on the emotional wave of the moment. In these events, one repeatedly sees the operation of various facets of the radical personality—position-paper approaches, demands for instant relief from frustration, a tendency to react to the slightest danger as a catastrophic threat to survival, a propensity to hold outside forces to blame for one's distress. Certainly we had best be concerned about the pollution of our air and water, the destruction of other species of life, and the growing appearance of our life space as a grand refuse dump. Certainly we must take deliberate steps to deal with the situation and certainly there is no place for delay. But neither is there a place for impulsive, unconsidered actions whose ultimate effects may be of greater harm than the course we are now upon. Because we have a problem with air pollution, must we become so paranoid as to believe that our neighbor is breathing too much? Because Lake Erie is a sludge basin, must we immediately tear down our industrial plants? Before we decide to ban DDT, we might ask whether we want the flies back in our soup or the malaria. Before we remove the phosphates from our cleaning agents, we might ask how many infants will be scarred, blinded, or poisoned by the caustic substances which are the present alternative. Before we dump all of our chemical fertilizers, we might wonder whether an organically based agricultural system will meet our basic survival needs for food. And before we scrap the SST, we might ask whether the competitive position of our nation will be aided, and whether other nations will show an equal interest in reducing thermal pollution in the atmosphere. I do not pretend to know the answers to these questions. I do know that they are exceedingly complex, that a decision about small matters most often has very broad implications that encompass seemingly unrelated matters, and that instant relief from tension is the luxury of the overindulged fool or the madman.

The reaction of the young radicals to public figures is deserving of brief consideration as we conclude this chapter. The characteristics previously discussed play a significant role in determining these reactions, and further illuminate the nature of their basic psychology. Quite predictably, the radical minority adore public figures who defy authority, promote irresponsibility, challenge the Establishment, offer instant solutions, despise history and neglect consequences, and promise freedom and indulgence. They also respond favorably to those who flatter their sense of omnipotence, promise to gain power for them, and operate on the basis of emotion rather than reason. For a minority of the minority, whoever offers relief from tension through escape of one kind or another will be popular. By the same token, they will not be pleased with anyone in authority who seeks to impose limits on them, who indicates that problems may be complex, who requires accountability, who fails to make things easy, who tries to balance social good against individual license, who demands explanation instead of excuses, and who suggests that they are anything but altruistic, idealistic, sincere, principled, and honorable. Thus they idolize William Kunstler because he is a symbol of defiance of established procedures. They admire the Chicago Seven because they were able to express obscene defiance to the courts. They respect Chairman Mao because his little red book is a bible of simple solutions cast in philosophical context. They flirt with Timothy Leary and metaphysical contemplation because these represent a way to drop out and escape from tension. They identify with Bernadette Devlin because she is noisy, defiant, and makes the appearance of carrying the "people's" cause. They were attracted to Eugene McCarthy because he was vague enough to sound promising, flattering enough to build their arrogance, idealistic enough to remind them of JFK, and harmless enough not to make them insecure about giving him power.

On the other hand, the radicals find ample targets for their hatred, frustration, and fear. They could not stomach Lyndon Johnson because he tried to face them with responsibility. They abhor Richard Nixon because he offers no quick solutions. They hate the armed services because they represent limits and discipline. They despise Middle America because it is patiently and effectively going about the business

143

of solving problems, and because it does not get very excited about their personal causes and political views. They are revolted by Spiro Agnew because he is not intimidated by them and is tough enough to take them on directly. They feared J. Edgar Hoover because he represented the ultimate force producing accountability in a lawful, civilized society. And, for obvious reasons, they will not like this book.

VIII

"IF OUR CAUSE, IT IS JUST . . ."

Running through the rhetoric of the radical movement are frequent references to conscience and principle as a basis for actions taken by members of radical groups. The principles articulated are always impressive—morality, justice, freedom, individual liberty, and so on. In observing their actions and attending to the dogma surrounding them, one gets the superficial impression that the radicals are guided by the highest of ethical considerations, and thus may develop a natural sympathy for their position and justify even highly destructive or irrational actions on the grounds of principle. Very frequently, if one listens to the rhetoric and ignores the actions, it is easy to believe that the radicals are only trying to improve conditions through a reasonable expression of their rights as human beings, and that anyone who opposes or disagrees with them is an inhuman, stupid, oppressive, fascist brute. At least so they would have us believe. In this chapter, we examine the origins of this tactic, considering its relationship to some of the basic personality traits of the radicals, and looking beneath the window-dressing of principle, which covers a base of the same violence, destructiveness, and inhumanity they so loudly decry in others.

The history of mankind is occasionally brightened by the emergence of someone whose devotion to principle, altruism, and courage enables him to be of great influence on the course of human events. When such a person is guided by conscience rather than selfish or partisan causes, he is truly admirable and sets an example which uplifts the spirit of us all. And when his convictions lead him to martyrdom, he may eventually be regarded as a saint or a prophet. Obvious examples come to mind. Abraham Lincoln is revered as a martyred humanitarian, whose principles led him through immense crisis and tragedy to stand by his belief in the equality of all men. Gandhi, more recently, was so devoted to freedom for his people that he sacrificed personal comfort and indulgence throughout his entire lifetime. Men of peace and love, integrity and honor, in manifestly living by their principles, have influenced the course of events far out of proportion to their numbers.

Americans have always responded enthusiastically to those who have the courage of their convictions. Plain talk, direct confrontation of issues, simple honesty in the face of adversity are qualities that earn our admiration, particularly if the one who takes things on in this way is willing to pay the price of personal popularity and tangible reward. A phrase like "I'd rather be right than President" can only enter the colloquy of a people who fundamentally place principle above personal gain. Will Rogers's pithy humor had such an appeal. Harry Truman's attitude of doing what he believed right, and to hell with the consequences, is another example from recent history. Thus, when an individual comes to us with an appeal based on unselfish principle, we are inclined to listen, and to believe that his actions spring from his conscience. The unbelievably good fortune of the American people in selecting for the Presidency only a few really incapable or dishonorable men is a tribute to the validity of trusting persons whose appeal generally has been to principle, and to our perceptiveness in sorting out the genuine article from the false. Growing up in America, one cannot escape learning well this lesson about the American people, and one knows from the outset that his conscience had better be an important part of his image if he is to persuade many of his compatriots.

In the late fifties and early sixties, as the attitudes of many of the present-day radicals were being formed, and as those who were already committed to radicalism were groping for a legitimate and popular philosophical base, many men passed across the public stage who dramatized the effectiveness of appeals to conscience as a means of gaining popular support. These men projected to their respective publics images of idealism, devotion to principle, and absence of self-interest. Dwight Eisenhower translated the overwhelming patriotic support that had come from his "Crusade in Europe" into a parallel popularity and general public respect in two presidential crusades. Even though Eisenhower was probably as cannily political as the next man, he always managed to stand above the baser scuffles of political campaigning, and twice successfully outconscienced Adlai Stevenson, himself no mean purveyor of the image of humility, sincerity, and conscience.

John F. Kennedy likewise constructed a public image of great popular appeal, with heavy emphasis on the dimension of heroic altruism. As we have seen earlier, Kennedy had a great attraction for most of America's young. They regarded his life as an inspiration to duty, principle, and self-sacrifice. It was easy to forget, under the spell of his persuasive rhetoric, that he was the product of immense wealth, that he was cleverly political, and that he had an abundance of ambition for personal power. The tragic circumstances of his death, and the fact that he fell at the peak of his promise, before the image was much blemished in the arena of political struggle, added to the imposing aura of principle and altruism. Thus, while neither he nor Eisenhower was held in any personal favor by the radicals, the success of each man's appeal to conscience and principle was not lost on the early radical tacticians.

More importantly, both the early radicals and those who have appeared more recently have taken several pages from the book of the civil rights activists. Martin Luther King, at least as well as Eisenhower and Kennedy, developed an image of being a man of conscience and burning moral conviction. He was a man of intense passion and persuasiveness. He summoned his followers to duty in what they deemed a sacred mission—peaceful but insistent, spiritual but relentless. He sought to touch the devotion to principle in which virtually every American believes. Out of this carefully projected personality came the successful tactics of the civil rights movement—massive demonstrations and resistance, gradual

147

erosion of opposition, and using and testing the legal system to its limit. And, above all, the appeal to conscience and morality.

Against this backdrop, some of the early members of the radical movement, who had been close enough to the civil rights movement to observe its tactics at firsthand, began to develop tactics and rhetoric in imitation of Dr. King's style. What had to be done, they felt, was to build a parallel movement, based on a similar appeal to conscience and principle, which would bring freedom to all, provide relief from oppression, and return power to the people, who, they felt, were to be led by them. A set of plausible ideals, if one ignores the obvious personal interest in power. The difficulty was that, apart from black people, who had some legitimate gripes about their circumstances, the radicals found themselves unable to uncover a constituency. The great majority of Americans was not oppressed, had all the personal freedom it wanted, did not feel exploited, and was not particularly troubled by any considerations of where the power lay. Thus generally contented, these Americans were apathetic to the radicals. Ambitious, energetic, and productive by most standards, they were materialistic honkies to the left. And so, secure in their unique insight that there were great wrongs to be righted, and pervasive injustices to be undone, the disciples of the new radicalism went searching for an ideology and a constituency. Early—that is, in the first part of the sixties—they sought their constituency among black Americans. But they were soon amazed to discover that most black people only sought a fair share of the economic action, and had more practical problems than the radicals were prepared to deal with. Also, the finer ideological points of participatory democracy, communal experience, self-realization through the politicizing of the elementary school, and the like, with which the radicals were preoccupied in their intellectual wallowing, were of no interest to black people. Besides that, a passel of black youth, born in the central cities and physically rough, were prepared for a kind of direct action for which the middle-class white philosophical radical did not have, and has never developed, any stomach.

So, greener pastures were sought, and found. The riots on the Berkeley campus of the University of California turned attention to college campuses generally, and raised questions in everyone's mind as to what dire malaise must exist in our society to cause such a horrendous occurrence. The malaise, of course, was the set of conditions already described in detail: a series of national problems causing stress, the loss of individuality, and our children's poor preparation for dealing resolutely with what they had to face as they grew up. But to the new radicals, these circumstances were evidence of a totally sick and immoral society, dominated by an exploitative establishment, failing to respond to demands for instant relief, and deserving to be totally destroyed, so that a new, moral, loving, peaceful, utopian Phoenix could magically emerge from the ashes. Interestingly, a positive alternative never has been developed or stated by the radicals, in either ideological or practical terms. Beyond some very loose and categorical equating of the system with evil, immorality, exploitation, and oppression, and of themselves with right, justice, freedom, and other enticing lollipop concepts, the radicals have never offered a very clear notion of what they seek, how they would have us get there even if we agreed with them, or what the pitfalls or consequences would be along the way. This is partly because they are extremely hard put to find a practical alternative, but also because the particular mentality of discontent, sweeping generalities, abstract remoteness from reality, and basic sense of personal impotence does not co-exist with sufficient intellectual discipline or rigor to devise a systematic ideological statement, much less a translation of that statement into a practical program.

It is also interesting that the radical left has never developed more than a tiny minority of support. As was shown in Chapter II, the active participants in campus demonstrations have seldom included more than a few percent. Of course, as we shall consider later, 1 percent of thirty thousand is three hundred, and three hundred people clamoring to confront the kind, genteel, compromise-inclined president of a university represents to him quite a handful. This minuscule minority, which has managed to disrupt some of our colleges and more recently secondary schools, has not found in radicalism an inspiring new concept, a viable political alternative, or a principled foundation for the solution of our admitted problems. Rather, they have used radicalism as a

149

convenient vehicle for the expression of personal frustrations, rage against authority, an omnipotent conviction that they are right and the world is wrong, and an overpowering demand for freedom and power without responsibility. The radical's lack of contact with reality is truly amazing—it is as if he has managed to construct a new world in his own head—a world where he is free to do anything he wants, where his ideas have total validity, where he is convinced beyond doubt that he is right, and is only somewhat puzzled that the rest of the world does not accept his version. Yet because of his conviction that he must be right, that he and his tiny band of fellows possess a unique avenue to truth by revelation, he feels completely justified in advocating the destruction of society, and frequently in translating that advocacy into zealous, direct action. Further, all this is bolstered and rationalized by statements that he is acting entirely on the basis of conscience and principle.

When this insistence on his own view of the world is combined with an inability to tolerate frustration and a consequent hatred of authority and limits, the radical becomes capable of moving from one level of force to another in asserting his will against objects that pose a threat or barrier to him. His experience with his parents sets the pattern. He habitually found it possible to move them around to his view of things—at first, perhaps, by being cute or clever; next by manipulating or by passive resistance to their wishes; and later by threatening or violent outbursts. In any case, he was typically successful in creating conditions in which his view of how things should be prevailed. Later, in another setting, if the milder of his tactics for getting his demands met fail to work—if, for example, he becomes frustrated because he cannot persuade a member of the Establishment to accede to his demands and agree that he is right, he is quite capable of moving his tactics up the scale of outrage to increasing levels of violence. He will also feel quite justified in doing so. After all, has he not been right all along, and is not the authority stupid for not realizing it? In the end, the radical will justify whatever he has to do to prove himself right, and he will see his violence toward the authority or his institution as totally deserved. So long as this pattern of behavior is confined to popsicles and tricycles and its expression limited to the family situation where it

150

developed, the situation is no worse than unfortunate. But when it is translated into a non-negotiable demand on a university, or moves up the line to be expressed in the bombing of the nation's Capitol because no one had the sense or backbone to arrest it at an earlier level, it becomes a threat to our personal safety, if not to stability and order. And when parents, university administrators, or other apologists defend such temper tantrums as a matter of principle, right, or free speech, it is both tragic and nauseating.

This pattern can be observed on almost any college campus where the radicals find an issue. At the first level, after the demand has been put on the record in the campus or underground newspaper, the effort to persuade is carried on in the soft tones of political negotiation. If the demand should be granted, another appears overnight, and the process begins anew. It matters not what the demand is, or whether it is rational, or what its granting implies for the rest of the institution or the people therein. It is only clear that somebody wants it, usually very badly, and will be deeply frustrated and distressed until he gets it. During the early negotiations, the demand is usually linked with some "umbrella issue," in the fashion described in Chapter II. The next round then starts, and pamphleteering and speech-making begins. In this part of the process there is an effort to suggest that dire things will happen unless the demand is granted. If it is not, the process moves to the stage of quiet mass demonstrations, or peaceful protest. If yet another failure to accede occurs, the protest gets a bit noisier and some violence occurs. Finally, the violence gets serious; police are called, rocks are thrown, arrests are made, and the demand changes to something relating to freedom to assemble, police brutality, or the like. Later, or in concert with the final-demonstration stage of the process, there may be bombings or arson. This almost totally predictable escalation is a striking parallel to the process that occurs when the radical, as a little boy, makes up his mind that it is time for the next indulgence. First, there is an indication that he wants something. He may even ask politely. The parents tell him no, but because he is supposed to be given reasons for everything, there is a quiet discussion between the parties, with the child trying to argue the parents out of their denial. He then goes off and musters other arguments, returns with them, and begins to show a bit of displeasure by pouting or bringing tears to his eyes. Next, he will actively sulk, become passive-aggressive, refuse to cooperate, resist doing what the parents ask him, and generally make himself an obvious nuisance, while communicating threats of real trouble along the lines of, "If you don't get it for me, I'm going to sit here all day, not eat, and make things unpleasant for everybody." When this fails, his anger bursts out into the open, and the direct violence of the tantrum appears. He throws things, tears up the house, destroys property, and rages irrationally at the parents. Finally, still not indulged, he will pursue further acts of violence as vengeance against the parents for their unfair treatment of him. This pattern is widespread, the parallel to the later behavior of the radicals amazing, and it is reinforced each time the actions of the child or young person are rewarded by giving in to his unreasonable wishes.

A corollary aspect of the process just described is seen in the individual's attitudes following the completion of the cycle. Of course, if at some point in the process the demands are met by the capitulation of the authority, there is extreme rejoicing for a short time. The conditions necessary for the maintenance of the child's feeling of omnipotence again exist and his autistic view of reality continues—in short, it has been proven that he was right, and his sense of power and security is restored. The really amazing thing, however, is that his conviction of being right is so strong that he feels totally justified in everything he has done. The property he has destroyed, the persons he has harmed, the institution he has disrupted, are of absolutely no meaning or consequence to him. Out of this grows the expectation that he will not be held responsible for what he has done; that there will be no unpleasantness, discomfort, or punishment directed toward him. So intense is his preoccupation with his own needs that any suggestion that he has to take responsibility for what he has done is met with outrage and incredulity. Again, forces outside him are blamed—they provoked his actions. Again, because he is right, the end he seeks justifies whatever means he chooses. Following on this process and growing out of these attitudes comes the demand for no recriminations and the cry for amnesty. Any suggestion of punishment is so unbelievable as to represent total injustice. From the radical's point of view, things have been set completely right—he has his way, his demands have been met, and what more is there to it? His amazing ego-centeredness is thus illustrated again in his belief that when *he* feels good, when *he* is not frustrated, then everything and everybody should be satisfied as well. The idea that others have rights or equities is simply not a part of his experience, and as a result, he lacks totally in empathic or altruistic urges.

The self-justifying character of the radicals' view of the world is expressed in other obvious ways. Since he is unable to accept any responsibility for his own actions, the radical finds it necessary to arrange situations so that other persons or forces are to blame for any violence which occurs. At one level, this expresses itself in baiting, teasing, or insulting others in the hope that they will become irritated and respond impulsively or unreasonably. If this occurs, and the radical maintains his cool during the process, he can come out of it looking reasonable and conciliatory, and the other person can be painted as arbitrary, oppressive, or unfair. In the running accounts of events that frequently appear in radical pamphlets or underground publications, and in regular student newspapers, much is made of occasions when an official shows anger or retaliates in any way to even the most bitter personal attacks and obscene insults. At another level, provocation of the most extreme kind is heaped on the authorities. College officials are physically attacked, police officers are assaulted with rocks, bottles, clubs, or worse, and any forceful response is castigated as oppressive, inhumane, and brutal. The clearest example of this tactic is seen in the events at the Democratic National Convention in Chicago in 1968. For hours, the police were taunted, pelted, and insulted without offering any response. Threats to their personal safety were plentiful. Men were kicked in the groin, had excrement flung at them, and were generally subjected to conditions beyond human tolerance. When finally they did respond with force, the radicals' cry of police brutality was heard throughout the land, and with some considerable help from the news media, an effort was made to portray the demonstrators as innocent, principled, and peace-loving. It is a most unhappy situation when law enforcement officers overreact or use force without necessity or provocation. But should we really expect absolute self-

153

discipline and self-control from one group in our society, when we permit another group to behave in a totally undisciplined and irresponsible way? Such provocative behavior should remain the province of infants and madmen, and not be aggrandized as the principled expression of the right of free citizens to seek redress of their grievances.

The target of the radicals' animosity shifted in rapid evolutionary steps during the early and mid-sixties. At first, their personal frustration was directed mainly toward the universities. In those early confrontations, a typical pattern was apparent. First a minor official would be accused of arbitrary or unreasonable action. From there, the point of dispute would move to a higher level, perhaps to an assistant dean. Next the dean, then a vice president, and shortly thereafter the president, in a constant search for someone further up the line who might have the power or the willingness to remove the frustration and rejustify the radicals' belief in their own omnipotence. Once that exercise became tedious, and the radicals found that confronting the university did not make them feel better, they moved outside to an attack on society itself. Again, they pursued their wish for indulgence up the line, through the levels of political organization, eventually to the President of the United States. During Johnson's tenure, he was confronted—*he* must relieve them; *he* must restore the idyllic condition of perfect comfort, complete freedom, and absolute domination of the world to them. Then finally, to the attack on the system itself. It was immoral, oppressive, evil. It must be destroyed. It must be pushed out of the way to make room for some unstated alternative, which would magically rise from the chaos and bring peace, beauty, and total satisfaction to their lives.

In this evolution, which obviously did not proceed uniformly throughout the country, one sees in operation the same basic traits that I have already discussed at length. The system has become the target because attacking it offers the perfect opportunity to express all the needs of the radical personality. It is the biggest possible game, so it satisfies the need for grandiosity. It is rather vague, so it can symbolically be seen everywhere, and psychologically meaningful attacks upon it can be devised to suit every pathology. It represents hated authority. It is largely without expression in persons, except

154

that it is embodied in the President. And it is seen by the radicals as the ultimate source of frustration, because it is the biggest and most powerful thing around. When one exhausts all the other possibilities for feeling frustrated, the system remains as a natural and easy explanation. When one has dominated his parents, denigrated his teachers, brutalized the law, humiliated the university, and terrorized society, the only thing left to overcome on the road to total omnipotence is the system. And when parents and teachers and courts and universities have stepped aside from their responsibilities to arrest the radical's mad demand to have his own way, the system appears to him as the only remaining constraint. Thus the system bears the brunt of their anger, and in its own way, with the cooperation of indulgent and opportunistic public officials, it also begins to provide indulgences. Not because this is wise or rationally justified, but because it is momentarily easier or more popular or less productive of confrontation. And if the system gives way, with a consequent loss of general freedom and stability, the radical personality will remain, equally frustrated, equally demanding, and equally threatening destruction. Unfortunately for him and the rest of us, the next system may not find it so necessary to provide indulgence and comfort. For the radical, the fundamental problems of weakness and fear and frustration will remain, because these conditions ultimately have their source not in the world around him, but in the intricacies of his own personality.

Once the radical has come to believe that the system is the ultimate source of his frustrations, he quickly concludes that any kind of attack on it is justified. His great anger is then expressed in acts of violence against society itself. If, as his conception of things leads him to believe, the symbols and manifest expressions of the system are everywhere, then it can be attacked anywhere. And if he also suffers strongly from fear of authority and a sense of powerlessness, as he does, then his attacks will take the form of furtive assaults, hit and run attacks, bombs in public places, arson, extortion, and eventually the terrorizing of completely helpless individuals. The tactics of the radicals have already moved through most of these stages, and it seems only a matter of time until the remaining methods are tried. When we come to the point of open threats to shut down the operations of government or surreptitious plots to kidnap public officials, we are not far from the terrorization of private individuals. When the end is seen as so vital as to justify and excuse any means whatsoever, it is not only the system that is under attack, but the personal rights and safety of us all.

What happens when limits finally are set, and the radical is forced to face his lack of omnipotence and of ability to dominate the world around him? What happens when playing at revolution ceases to be a game, and real danger is posed to his personal comfort and safety? An event in the not too distant past sheds some light on these questions. A group of young radicals had set up a small plant for manufacturing explosive devices in a townhouse apartment in New York City. In some unknown way, probably while one of the devices was being assembled, an explosion occurred and two of those present were killed. One or more others fled the premises. A few months later, an article written by Bernadine Dohrn, a well-known radical who had been a close associate of the departed, appeared in various campus newspapers and underground publications. Part of the article related that Miss Dohrn had been profoundly upset by this event and had spent several months thinking about the consequences of her earlier fascination with violence. But the amazing thing was that the experience had brought her philosophically to a different position; namely, that perhaps she had been wrong all along, not about the need for destroying the system, but about the methods through which that goal should be achieved. Now, she felt, it was wiser to try to go to the people and build a broader base for the revolution. Persuasion rather than force was now to be the way. Hardly the expression of a constant, principled revolutionary, and hardly consistent with the teachings of Chairman Mao or the exhortations of Che. It was as if Che had seen the light the first time he was shot at, and decided to write another position-paper treatise on the abstract value of revolution. Or as if the IRA had seized an Ulster police station and left pamphlets behind to convince the Protestants of the error of their ways. This was the act of a frightened little girl. Faced with harsh reality for the first time in her life, she realized that revolution was a very inhumane game, that there was sufficient force in the world to deny her some indulgence and not be guilty in the process,

156

and decided that personal comfort and safety had more to offer her than did bombing the Establishment out of existence.

Another example of the radicals' general reaction to the determined use of force by the authorities is seen in the tragedy of the Kent State killings. Kent State is a large institution located somewhat southeast of Cleveland, Ohio. It had suffered from all of the growing pains associated with the development of a regional college into a major state university. Yet it was generally well administered and well respected. For a time prior to the tragedy, there had been a series of protests centering around the ROTC program, and other Vietnam-related issues. The typical pattern of escalation occurred, and finally one of the campus buildings was burned. Violence developed, and the Ohio National Guard was finally called in to restore the peace of the campus. The members of the National Guard, mostly young men with little military training, were contemporaries of the students. They were subjected to fantastic abuse and provocation. They were insulted, stoned, spat upon, called obscene names. Finally, reacting to this provocation, their discipline apparently broke and a volley of shots was fired in the direction of a group of students who, depending on what you believe, were preparing to rush the guardsmen, or were peacefully demonstrating. Four students were killed, and the tragedy was played out to its predictable conclusion. This horror might have been avoided—by better discipline among the troops, by applying lesser force earlier, by removing conditions in society that encourage radicals to believe they can get away with anything under the guise of conscience. But it was not avoided, and second-guessing does no good. The result, however, was extremely interesting. Again, the radicals underwent an agonizing reappraisal of their position and their tactics. The violence they had sought, been fascinated with, and provoked suddenly seemed not to be such a good idea. Once again, there was a withdrawal from confrontation into contemplation, and once again there was the conclusion that the revolution should be effected by other means. Was this the altruistic expression of a concern for the lives of others? Was this the rational political tactic of a group that had a principled commitment to humanity? Such concern for lives and humanity had seldom been expressed in the

157

abuse of college administrators—there had been no such concern for the feelings of the law enforcement officers assaulted and insulted. Or was it the recognition finally that demands by the radicals to have their own way would ultimately be resisted, and that temper tantrums would eventually bring unpleasant consequences, even to the omnipotent self-styled revolutionary? If it were the latter, and I am convinced that it was, how tragic that some of the basic lessons about the real world had not been taught the radicals earlier, with less tragic results, and with less force than finally was applied at Kent State. Perhaps the quiet on the campuses since the events at Kent State indicates that reason has finally begun to penetrate the radicals' veneer of self-importance. Or perhaps it is only a lull while they gather more energy and renew the unreasoning belief in their own infallibility; if so, the tragedy of Kent State will be repeated and multiplied.

We have already seen how the emphasis on conscience by a few men influenced the civil rights movement, and how that in turn affected the tactics of the radical left. Because of the long-standing American respect for conscience-based convictions, the radicals realized that using conscience as a justification was an excellent political tactic. To be told by one's conscience that one is right is a powerful support for any belief, no matter how that belief has actually been arrived at. When one's basic relationship to the world requires that he be totally right, and that anyone who opposes him be totally wrong, a conviction of conscience becomes central not only to his tactics, but to his entire style of dealing with events around him. The conviction that one is right can, as we have seen repeatedly, arise from a great many sources other than a mature conscience; for example, from poorly recognized and not at all understood operations of one's unconscious, or from the omnipotent belief in one's own infallibility, which grows out of chronic indulgence and permissiveness. And in many other instances, which have come to my personal attention as a clinician and an administrator, the supposed conscience-based convictions of a good many radicals arise from just such nonaltruistic sources. None of this, of course, deters the radicals from calling on conscience as a justification.

158

None of it prevents the charitable observer from accepting conscience as an excuse for some of the radicals' more destructive or outlandish claims or actions.

The above discussion is not intended to impugn the motives, sincerity, maturity, or conscience of anyone who raises ethical objections to oppression, deplores the taking of life, sees philosophical conflicts in certain of our international policies, or has a moral concern about the underprivileged. Rather, it is intended to state most forcefully that if some completely unethical, selfish, fundamentally immoral person wants to offer an excuse for an action he cannot otherwise justify, the notion of conscience represents a perfect haven for him. And it is also to suggest that we should be more discriminatory in judging who is truly acting out of conscience, and who is expressing his personal selfishness, cowardice, or immorality under its guise.

The emphasis on conscience, as expressed and practiced by the radicals, holds a fascination or usefulness for certain other groups that otherwise find little in common with them. If the radical "conscience" leads to actions that disrupt or partially undermine the system by creating chaos, groups that gain advantage by having us weakened as a nation find common tactical cause with the radicals, and frequently lend quiet support to such actions. Even fundamentally loyal groups may offer some support. For example, though pacifists and clergymen are often offended by the inflammatory rhetoric and actions of the radical minority, they may yet identify with expressions of "conscience" by the radicals concerning personal participation in the Vietnam War. Similarly, if the pollution problem concerns all of us, then radical attacks on the industrial system, based on "conscience" by the radicals, are often applauded. In this way, the notion of conscience offers a handy umbrella under which a large group, with basically little common interest, can be drawn and motivated to action. As a result, a fairly large number of people are from time to time drawn into activity opposed to the national interest and even to their own long-run good, because they are not sufficiently discriminatory about either the relationships among issues or the question of the mature versus the convenient conscience.

Closely related to the notion of conscience is another of

the concepts advocated by the radical left. This is the idea that a person is responsible only to himself. This is one more convenient rationalization for the person who is almost insanely convinced that he is right, and is again used to justify the most antisocial actions. It feeds nicely into the notion that society is evil, and in its more extreme forms, puts the freedom of the individual completely above the considerations of society. It is the ultimate extension of the concept of freedom without responsibility, and when it is bolstered by the vague conviction that the society under attack is evil, it puts each individual in the position of being a law unto himself. Thus, lawbreaking for whatever reason is justified as an attack on the evils of the system, and many acts of no political significance whatsoever are excused or rationalized as being in the interest of destroying the oppressive system. The middle-class radical finds some common ground therein with other lawbreaking segments of the community, including psychopaths and habitual criminals. In the same way, the cause of anyone who comes into conflict with society is taken on by the radicals: prison riots are applauded as blows against oppression, racial disturbances are encouraged, the terrorism of the Irish Republican Army is admired, and there is an ambiguous identification with the so-called people's revolutions in various parts of the world. In short, any action that represents defiance of authority, an attack on the established social system, the expression of an individual urge, or a manifestation of personal license is encouraging to and applauded by the radical personality.

The radicals' reaction to police and other law enforcement officers is another expression of their conviction that they are above the law. Rather than seeing police officers as a shield against harm, as most people do, the radicals view them as a barrier to the gaining of personal ends. Already prone to be frustrated in any dealings with authority, they interpret the mere presence of police as intruding on their infantile search for immediate gratification. Thus the police come to be hated. Because the police also represent force and are in a social role which generally causes them to make categorical judgments and no nonsense about it, and because the imminence of police action against them means that their repertoire of manipulative techniques has run out of gas and

160

that they may soon be faced with a *real* confrontation, the radicals also experience a dreadful fear of the police. Add to that the fact that their supreme arrogance tells them that they are vastly superior to an ordinary man like a police officer, and the characterization of the police as "pigs" or in other terms of contempt and denigration becomes quite understandable.

The fascination of the radicals with supposedly "symbolic" acts of defiance shows itself frequently. Pouring blood over draft records, staging "guerilla theatre productions," linking arms together around an ABM site, and similar acts are matters of great emotional satisfaction to the radical personality. They represent an ideal vehicle for the expression of certain of his basic urges. They present the appearance of being conscience-based, they allow for the discharge of aggression, they attract attention, they evidence the cleverness of the perpetrator, and they can be undertaken with very little risk. Taking sanctuary in churches, identifying with political martyrs, fantasizing that their defiance will set an example for others to follow and that their symbolic efforts at persuasion will finally convert the complacent masses, the radicals in fact end up appearing both ineffectual and naive. Still, the tactical and psychological "fit" between these tactics and their autistic view of the world is so perfect that such events continue to occur in spite of their now obvious triteness and ineffectiveness. And since occasionally, as with the Berrigans and Ellsberg, such symbolic actions gain publicity and/or sympathy, the tendency to persist in them is periodically reinforced.

Some social and political concepts introduced and practiced in recent years have encouraged the belief of the radicals that they are above the law. Certain civil rights activities, although undertaken with a more laudable purpose in mind, contain vaguely similar notions. Martin Luther King knew that he was a symbol, and even though he was obviously prepared to go to jail for his convictions, his symbolic arrest and symbolic punishment were well understood by everyone. Believing in their own sanctity equally with Dr. King, the radicals come to expect that the consequences of their lawbreaking will be equally symbolic. It is too bad that they do not recognize the difference between their own self-seeking and King's approach. It is also too bad that the concept that it is permissible to break the law, if one does so because his conscience

161

tells him the law is unjust, has come to be generally accepted. When the legal system extends its permissiveness to the point where major crimes of a totally nonsymbolic nature are treated the same as a set-piece testing of a questionable law, the message to young radicals becomes vague, and encourages their fantasy that they are a law unto themselves.

Another event contributing to the idea that the individual is above the law—that is, has no responsibility to his society other than what his "conscience" dictates—grew out of the Nuremberg trials. A fundamental principle of the prosecution of the Nazi war criminals was the notion that individuals were personally accountable for acts they committed under the aegis of the national state to which they owed their allegiance. While this was basically a contrived position, it was invented as a basis for insuring that persons who had participated in the mass crimes of the Nazi regime could be "legally" punished. This concept, that the individual owes a higher responsibility to his conscience, or to the world at large, than to the society in which he lives, was then and remains today a revolutionary notion. It has never been adequately clarified, either philosophically, psychologically, or pragmatically. On the one hand, it expresses mankind's highest religious and ethical aspirations. In a society where most people share a similar strength of conscience and sense of human duty, it could probably be implemented. On the other hand, in a society characterized by unreasoning demands for personal indulgence and omnipotent control over the events of the world, it may become a flagrant invitation to anarchy. Again and again at Nuremberg, the defense, "I did it because I was ordered to," was rendered ineffective by the rebuttal, "But you must have known that you had a higher responsibility." Defendants at Nuremberg were hanged or sent to prison because they had responded to the demand of their national society rather than to their consciences.

The issue of where one's responsibility finally lies is essentially philosophical, and some demanding definitions and assumptions must be made before consideration of the basic question can begin. What does one mean by conscience? If it means what Roman Catholicism means when it refers to a "mature conscience" based on the full operation of reason and logic, that is one thing. If, however, the term "conscience" is

162

applied to every momentary and personal whim, to unconscious and therefore imperfectly understood motives, or to self-seeking called by a pleasant name, that is quite another. It would take the combined wisdom of Aquinas, Freud, and Plato to begin to answer these questions, which go basically to the question of man's fundamental goodness or evilness. Since a philosophical discussion at such depth is beyond the scope of this book, we must continue in a more pragmatic vein. It is important to recognize that Nuremberg-like principles are being utilized as a basis for justifying actions claimed to be responsive to individual conscience rather than national or social responsibility. Whatever the degree of mature conscience of those who stake these claims, the argument, when presented in superficial radical slogans, may have a persuasive effect on altruists, humanists, pacifists, and other men of good will. Such an appeal is important in the young radicals' effort to recruit a power base among their contemporaries, and across the society as a whole. And before anyone, no matter what the degree of his good will, gets taken in by the claims of those seeking self-indulgence under the umbrella of conscience, he should look carefully at the fundamental character of whoever is making the claim.

The existence of mature conscience among the young radicals may be assessed to a degree by examining their devotion to certain general principles associated with conscience and conviction. First, do they show a basic devotion to the truth? The answer is clearly that they do, as long as the truth serves their ends. If the truth stands in their way, it is dismissed as irrelevant and distorted. Second, is there a constant devotion to principle among them? Yes, if one limits the principles to the issues of self-indulgence, the seeking of power, and the destruction of the existing society. Beyond that, principles become rather slippery concepts, to be used when advantageous, and discarded when inconvenient. Third, is there a fundamental devotion to humanity and decency among them? Yes, if insults and abuse of other human beings are a criterion, if exploiting weak or naive persons is humane, and if reducing the beauty of human relationships to the gutter vernacular is decency. Finally, are there altruism, and courage, and resolve among them? Compare their lives and actions with the dignity and decency of men like Lincoln and

Gandhi, and compare the willingness of such men to take a principled stand and to accept the consequences with the radicals' tactics of throwing rocks from the rear of a crowd, committing arson in the depth of night, setting off bombs in public school wastebaskets and safety deposit boxes. Now, decide for yourself whether you are willing to accept the radicals' claim of conscience as a justification for their actions.

It is far past the time that we should have stopped accepting destructive nonsense, masked by supposedly high ideals, as something permissible in a civilized society. It is time each one of us began to draw a fair but firm line between reasonable opportunity for personal gratification and license that brings crime to the status of a dignified pursuit. Until we do, insanity will continue to flourish, and our society, which only a decade ago was on the threshold of a golden age, will decay into anarchy.

IX

THE ABC'S OF ALIENATION

The American system of public education has long represented one of the cornerstones of our way of life. Conceived in the Jeffersonian principle that the educated and rational person makes a responsible citizen, our public school system has served us quite well. Its goal has been to offer to every child as much education as he can take advantage of, both to increase his chances of success in a competitive society, and to insure his intelligent participation in the political processes of a democracy. As a people, we have thought education so important that we do not merely offer it, we require it. Going to school is one of the few things Americans are actually forced to do. Every state constitution mandates the establishment and maintenance of a system of compulsory public education, and every state and community contributes heavily in tax support to a system designed to offer educational opportunity to all. As the need has grown for longer and more valid educational programs, to prepare students for dealing with the increasing complexities of life in a technological society, so have our support for education and our educational offerings. Two generations ago, the average person was reasonably assured of an elementary school education. A generation ago, the high school graduate represented the norm. Now, more than half of the general population is receiving education at the college level. In the same evolution, most communities have moved from having only a grade school to the addition of high schools, and now the majority count at least junior or community colleges among their facilities.

Our investment in public education has paid off handsomely, and should make us all proud. We are the best-educated people in the history of civilization. We have accomplished wonders of technology, invention, and productivity in the short span of two hundred years. We have achieved an unbelievable standard of living without domination by our government or the loss of individual freedom. The nation's educational system has played a central part in these accomplishments, by turning out masses of people with the capacity to think, judge, reason, come to logical conclusions, and act generally on behalf of the common good. Given the results we have achieved and the vital role education has played in producing these results, Jefferson's faith in the rationality and judgment of the educated citizen clearly seems to have been justified. Out of our educational experience, we have not only developed the technical competence to advance our civilization, we have also learned the value of responsible participation in a free society.

Some recent developments seem to raise a serious possibility that we may not be commensurately successful in the future. Since World War II, the public schools have faced a series of difficulties, many of which are hardly of their own making. Most prominent among these factors is the exceedingly rapid increase in the population. The "baby boom" of the mid- and late forties struck the schools as an avalanche during the early fifties. Demands for more and more buildings, teachers, and programs ran ahead of the educational system's ability to provide these in an orderly fashion. Inflation, increasing salary demands, and a proliferation of activities only marginally related to the schools' function ate away at public ability to provide support, and more recently has resulted in a decline in public willingness. Within a short time, the population bulge reached the secondary schools and colleges, and this, added to the growing expectation that everyone could and should go on to college, added to demands for staff and facilities. Because of these and other developments to be discussed below, the public educational system came under severe pressure.

In addition to the external forces beleaguering the

166

schools, a series of developing conditions within the educational system added to their problems. Some of these conditions were direct reflections of changes in society; others were the results of decisions and attitudes fostered by influential educators. Taken together, these developments have brought the school system to a point where it is significantly less capable of serving its fundamental purpose, and in some instances have contributed materially to the personality characteristics and attitudes identified in the previous chapters as the emotional basis for radicalism. In this chapter, we consider both the causes and the effects of these developments as they reflect and influence our society.

The pressures of the mass society fall heavily on the schools. Due to the sheer number of children, and their concentration in urban and suburban centers, schools have become mass herding places. Elementary schools housing several hundred children are common, and facilities for more than a thousand are not unknown. This has resulted in a depersonalizing loss of individuality, much as has occurred in the larger society. For the child who begins his school experience already insecure, this condition represents an added threat. The limits, comfort, and security of a small community are lost to him in the mass elementary school. In this way, his first contact with a social institution supposed to develop his individual potential is influenced by the same mass, bureaucratic outlook he later encounters in the world outside. It takes an extremely secure six-year-old not to feel somewhat lost as he tries to make his lonely way down a corridor full of pushing and probably equally frustrated older children. Additionally, the mass educational system tends to impose a requirement of efficiency, which expresses itself in many subtle ways. The kids become interchangeable units, shifted about like identical blocks in order to balance class size. The pressure for efficiency on the teacher may cause her to take a production-line approach to her efforts with the children. The parents, with their pressures for special attention to their own child's needs, come to represent a nuisance, either to be dealt with bureaucratically or to be placated at PTA meetings. In any event, mass education tends to cause the personal equation to take a back seat to the requirement that not too much uniqueness can be managed.

167

Mass needs have been met with mass solutions in other deleterious ways. During the fifties, the teacher shortage was so great that almost any warm body was encouraged to become a teacher. While formal training requirements continued to exist on paper, the selection and education of the public school teacher became a pretty haphazard business. Economic motivation, as it rose in the society generally, also rose among teachers. Resulting from this combination of circumstances is the undeniable fact that many people entered the profession who had no business being there, and the combination of tenure arrangements, under-supply, and union protection kept them there. Morale fell, the devotion to professionalism was gradually eroded, and we ended up with a lot of inadequate and disgruntled teachers grudgingly going about their jobs. Even for the devoted, competent professional, conditions have become such that continuing satisfaction is hard to come by. The attitudes of the teachers are inevitably communicated to the children; thus, subtle messages about society's faults began to be transmitted. Already embedded in a system placing the responsibility for education in the hands of government, and finding no help in solving the problems of mass education in the preachments and gimmicks of the education schools, which were supposed to train and assist them, the teachers took the position that more money, or newer buildings, or something else that could be provided by the bureaucracy would at least relieve them, if not make for a better education for the children. Greater and greater reliance gradually came to be placed on larger and larger units of government; the individual teacher lost in influence, satisfaction, and responsibility; and the pattern of blaming someone outside oneself crept into the day-to-day exposure of the children in the classroom. Thus, the overindulged, permissively oriented, overprotected budding radicals found in these attitudes confirmation of what they were already prone to believe.

Meanwhile, back at the suburban ranch, liberal middle-class parents were busy doing their own materialistic thing. The demands and opportunities of the affluent society kept them extremely busy. So busy, in fact, that they began to move away from some of their traditional, formerly private, responsibilities for their children. Partly because parents wanted it,

168

so they could get away with giving less time to their children, and partly because the schools sought it, because they believed they could do it better, many responsibilities for the general welfare of the child began to be assumed by the educational system. Parents who were, or felt, inadequate, too busy, or handicapped in providing for the child's personal welfare, as opposed to his educational needs, found a ready partnership with educational and social architects who believed that a public bureaucracy could do it better. Responsibility for the child's health, some of his feeding, any defect or difficulty of his person or behavior, was gradually turned over to the school, which evolved into a combination child-care center, physical rehabilitation facility, sex education corral, disciplinary barracks, mental health clinic, home for the handicapped, detention center, and recreation facility. Parents, educators, psychologists, sociologists, and others all thought this a wonderful idea. The result, however, was more bureaucracy, reduced individual responsibility, and a loss of contact with forces shaping the child's view of himself and his concept of his parents' relationship to him. Along with the effect already produced by the institution of babysitting, which enabled parents to gain relief from the intolerable strain of being with their children, and the increasing practice of committing the child to nursery schools as soon as he was out of diapers, a good bit of the social and psychological glue that once held the family together was thus beginning to break loose. Not only were the results unfortunate in terms of the relationship between parent and child, they were disastrous for the schools. Money that was desperately needed for basic educational programs was diverted elsewhere, and school administrators, even at the building level, found themselves engaged in such "relevant" activity as counting milk money.

The schools were in no position to deal with the problems they already had, much less any additional ones. Concurrently, however, another condition began to creep into the schools: the doctrine of permissiveness, which had been preached at parents and teachers by psychologists and university educational theoreticians. For reasons I have already discussed, permissiveness seems to have become the hallmark of the secure, affluent suburbs. Now it began to be widely translated into educational practice, or at least part of it did: the

169

part that said that children grew and prospered, and gained security and creativity, from experiencing their environment freely. The part that said children ought to be exposed to firm limits and predictable consequences when their behavior did not come up to standard was not adopted.

As a matter of fact, the educational system, whether under the impact of the permissive society or for reasons related to its own circumstances, has moved to a position where standards of performance in any area of the child's behavior are a very low-priority consideration. The concept that a child benefits from being held to standards of excellence has been lost in a flurry of excuse-making and rationalization. Teachers who attempt to maintain standards often get little support from their colleagues, their administrations, or the community. Permissiveness offers a special advantage to the teacher who does not or cannot do his job, since if it is the child's option to perform or not to perform, the teacher cannot be held responsible for his failure. "He wasn't motivated," or "That poor child has so many serious problems," or "The social worker [or nurse, or helping teacher, or psychologist, or speech therapist, or reading specialist] just tried and tried, and she simply couldn't get through to him," or "I don't know what's going to happen to that child when he gets to high school, he just hasn't learned any discipline." I know what is going to happen to that child when he gets to high school—he's going to be somebody else's problem, and if he should make it to college, he's likely to become a problem to the whole society.

We should look at some of the manifestations and consequences of the doctrine of permissiveness as practiced in the public schools. One of its corollary doctrines is that no one should be judged or evaluated. This is based on the perfectly humane concept that if a child is subjected to nothing but criticism and negative evaluation, he will soon become discouraged, quit trying, and develop a lack of self-respect in the bargain. Certain educators have correctly cautioned us about not overemphasizing grades at the expense of self-respect. There is an obvious danger in making the grade the be-all and end-all of the educational experience; children become motivated only to work for grades and are satisfied with themselves so long as they get good grades, whether they learn anything or not. Properly, schools have tried to deemphasize the grade as an end in itself. But from an emphasis on grades as an exclusive mark of success or failure, to the concept that evaluation and expectations of quality performance are incompatible with good education, is a long jump. And the idea that being expected to live up to certain standards is a blow to the individual's self-respect, freedom, or creativity is totally ridiculous. When we further and further lower the standard of performance expected of the individual, we teach him that anything he does is enough, and thereby we subtly devalue the effort of the child who is attempting to perform at the level of his capacity. We also, with equal subtlety, degrade the child to whom we are supposedly being kind by assuming that he is a psychological cripple or by giving him the false notion that what he does really doesn't really matter to anyone. When the school communicates this attitude to the potential radical, raised by overindulgent, overaggrandizing parents, it further feeds his developing sense of omnipotence, of being a law unto himself, and of having no personal responsibility to society.

Whether the notion of not evaluating people has its roots in the educational system or not, it is certainly prominently present there. It has gradually spread from a de-emphasis on grades to a de-emphasis on demands of any kind. People who are prepared to make excuses for children who refuse to tolerate evaluation of their academic work are equally prepared to excuse their lack of respect for teachers, their truancy, their assaults on classmates, or their lack of personal hygiene. Whatever the child does is explained in terms of "problems" and the source of the problems is seen as being somewhere other than the child. Perhaps the initial source of his problems is indeed outside himself, but the chronic practice of communicating to the child that, because someone else has made things difficult for him, he has no responsibility for trying to correct them, is fallacious in the extreme. Further, the idea that the first-grader who defies the authority of the teacher, or the high school sophomore who is determined to sneak cigarettes into the school washroom, needs to be "healed" rather than called to account, violates every accepted psychological as well as social principle.

To be fair, it is necessary to recognize that the schools

are to some degree a reflection of the society they serve. In this respect we may note that the tendency to reject the notion that anyone's performance should be evaluated, and that consequences should follow from the evaluation, is widespread throughout the society. More pay for less work, more comfort as a guaranteed right, more security without effort, are the watchwords of the time. A great many people in our society are caught up in this pattern. It is not restricted to pupils or teachers or members of labor unions. Throughout the system, we find examples of the pursuit of the easy way, the admiration of the man who is clever enough to just get by, and a willingness to be slipshod. Perhaps it is asking too much that the public school system and its personnel resist this trend, becoming unpopular in the process, or is it? Do not educators, who are supposed to carry the collective wisdom of our history with them, and who are supposed to be preparing the children for a useful life in a civilized society, have a special responsibility? Granted that without the willingness of parents and the community to cooperate, the job would be difficult. But granting also that educators continue to occupy a special place of influence in society, is it expecting too much that they provide some of the leadership to return to a devotion to quality?

Regardless of where the causes lie, and regardless of who should take the responsibility for beginning to correct the situation, it is a fact that we are becoming a society committed to mediocrity. And it is also a fact that the people of certain other powerful nations, who have maintained their discipline and are ready and willing to make the effort necessary to produce a quality civilization, are waiting eagerly to take over world leadership. While we fritter away our energies and our substance in a revel of self-indulgence, they are responsibly building and growing and strengthening themselves. While we are using up the savings of our heritage, they are building theirs. We had best repair our ways, soon, or prepare for a sad national fall.

The tendency to seek the easy way and to reward mediocrity has other ramifications in our educational system. We seem to believe that there is an easy way to become an educated person, and we transmit this idea to our children. The materials and methods of education, in order to be palatable to the children, have to be packaged and tinseled and

172

merchandised like a shiny new car. Many adults implicitly assume the same attitude, and are not attracted to the excitement of intellectual exploration unless the book is presented in three-dimensional stereophonic living color. From our TV, newspapers, and magazines, we get a once-over-lightly on the issues and the facts, and it seems to satisfy us. "Headline intelligence" is about all many people feel they have time for, and the deeper penetration of matters is left to the irresponsible critic. This attitude of superficiality is picked up by the children, and they come to believe that if they know a few general concepts and the latest cool slogans, they have a sufficient basis for making profound decisions. This attitude is also evident in the way many issues are approached within the educational system. Facts are increasingly less important; the general concept matters. We subtly encourage the child to dabble with everything under the sun, but think it enough if he can mouth a few key words and phrases.

This easy way to education reflects our general commitment to self-indulgence. If you know enough to get by in a cocktail-hour conversation, why make the effort necessary to understand anything in detail? Why worry about intellectual discipline when all the really tough problems are going to be solved by someone else, or by a computer? We can turn all our problems over to the technical experts or the bureaucrats and go on having fun, trusting that they will solve them, or at least will not bother us about them. In these attitudes, one observes the interplay between the loss of a sense of personal responsibility, the decline in the power of the individual, and the burgeoning influence of the bureaucracies.

There was a time when the public educational system contributed materially to the belief of the individual that he could have self-respect, and that what he was learning contributed to his competence to deal with his own problems. It is much less so now. With the decreasing emphasis on quality performance, and the growing devotion to teaching general principles rather than concrete facts and practical skills, the child emerges from the public educational system with a superficial view of practically everything, and not much competence in anything. He may be fitted for the role of clever critic, because he has been trained in the art of asking the impressive question. But he has not been provided with much to make him feel he has an effective knowledge of anything. And why not? Because mastering practical facts requires intellectual discipline, and as we have lost discipline in the schools and throughout society, we are also losing the discipline of our minds. It takes more than cleverness and verbal facility to get deeply enough into a complex question to have much confidence that you can solve it; it takes rigor and penetrating effort. And rigor and penetrating effort are not automatically acquired through the superficial study of general concepts. They are acquired through the mastery of a great number of facts, which is not a particularly romantic exercise, since it takes time and diligent application. And the investment of time and diligent application seems less and less to be emphasized in the public educational system. Small wonder that children emerge from their school experience feeling vague, uneasy, and helpless about coping with the problems of the world. With little experience in bringing their own competence to bear in the solution of the problems they face as youngsters, they lack a basis for expecting that they can handle the tougher, more complex problems of their adult lives. In this way, the loss of discipline and rigor in our public educational system contributes to the general sense of impotence experienced by the individual in our society, and thus plays its part in furthering the sense of insecurity plaguing so many of our young people. If the child never experiences the sense of mastery that comes with developing competence in the simple tasks of childhood, and if no consequences flow at that time from his failure to acquire such mastery, how will he ever believe later on that he can master more adult challenges? On the other hand, if he is set a few tough, uninspiing tasks during his school experience and masters them, he builds confidence through dealing effectively with small problems, and this confidence will sustain him through later, more difficult challenges.

Loss of discipline and the pressures toward further and further relaxation of standards have by now spread throughout the entire educational system. Vocal militants at all levels demand that things be made still easier and that the same total indulgence of demands be provided in school as exists at home. The attitude that no one should be required to accept anyone else's judgment about what is good for him is ex-

174

pressed in many forms. At the elementary school level, the concept of the "open classroom" is pushed, not so much by the children themselves as by educators. The basic idea of the open classroom is not in itself destructive. In theory, it means that a wide variety of different materials, techniques, and kinds of knowledge are provided, and that the student is encouraged to learn from what is made available. The conditions and method of presentation are supposed to be attractive enough to entice the student into active exploration and participation. In practice, the open classroom too often becomes a place where children are allowed to wander around aimlessly, dabbling with the few things that attract them, and otherwise not being required to meet any expectations. If he does not happen to be intrigued by one of the basic tool-skill subjects, in the way the materials present it to him, he is free to ignore it, in the faith that sooner or later he will see the relevance of it to his life, or will encounter it in some other "free" setting, in a form that will make it palatable and intriguing to him. For children who bring internal discipline and mature curiosity to the process, the open classroom can be an exciting opportunity. For most, however, it turns out to be a vague, unstructured, self-indulging reinforcement of the attitude that they may do whatever they want without regard to the meeting of standards. For the inspired, committed teacher, the open classroom can be challenging and satisfying, and can open up opportunities to deal with a wide range of subject-matter areas in an exciting way. For the teacher who wants to avoid responsibility and effort, however, it provides an easy excuse for not doing anything. In the context of the societywide tendency toward permissiveness and short-run satisfaction, the broad application of the open classroom notion is yet another evidence to the child that his personal indulgence is more important than considerations of individual competence, quality performance, and long-run consequences.

Similar developments and pressures are apparent at the secondary school level, with similar consequences. High schools are now being encouraged to operate "open campuses," which means that students are free to leave school during periods when they do not have classes. The supervised study hall is disappearing, under criticism as representing a

175

situation of forced study, which is equated with repression. Attendance policies are being liberalized so that truancy has no consequences. Some schools have gone so far as to put into practice a policy that no student need attend a class that he doesn't want to attend. A scattering of "free school" alternatives to the regular academic program of the high schools are beginning to appear. In the free school, students are allowed to attend when they like, study what they like, and do virtually whatever they like on the theory that their lack of motivation for performance in the traditional setting has resulted from a reaction to its repressive character. The theory is that their innate love of learning, once freed from the unreasonable demands and psychological pressures the traditional school places on them, will produce an intense application of energies to things they are interested in, and they will at last achieve the depth of penetration and competence that has been missing all along. For some few already well-disciplined students, the free school, like the open classroom, offers some exciting possibilities. But such students already find excitement and interest in the traditional setting, since their motivation is such that they will learn in any setting. The student who is attracted to the free school is the one who lacks the discipline to penetrate deeply, who has come to expect that no demands will be placed upon him, and who is seeking further to assert his right to total freedom. As a result, many of the free school operations turn out to be a further opportunity to do little or nothing, and a further exercise in superficiality, under the pretext of "having a set of deep and satisfying intellectual and interpersonal experiences."

Many parallel developments are seen in colleges and universities, for in these institutions the radicals, through threats and endless pressure, have had a more prominent effect, and, for reasons discussed in the next chapter, are more likely to be favorably received. The pell-mell movement toward permissiveness and the abandonment of standards in the colleges is most apparent in the constant attack on required course work. Because of this, the expectation that the liberal arts degree implies a breadth of intellectual exposure is being eroded, and learning through life experience is emphasized, on the theory that wandering around a city or a public school will provide the depth of competence required to become an urban expert or a teacher. Some professors are gradually relaxing demands for performance in their classes, allowing students to pursue their undisciplined way through an "experience." The attack against being judged or evaluated is gradually succeeding, and grading systems are being replaced with a "pass-fail" system under which a student who makes the effort to learn more or go deeply into a subject is not differentiated from the one who does barely enough to get by. All in all, developments in the undergraduate colleges, particularly in the liberal arts, faithfully reflect society's permissive trends, with the result that the failures of the public educational system are being compounded, rather than corrected.

Running through the educational system is another evidence of the influence of radical ideology. The traditional educational system is characterized by the radicals as repressive, dehumanizing, and irrelevant. The schools are held to be a reflection of an evil, oppressive system and the student an unfortunate victim of a conspiratorial effort to rob him of his personal freedom and force him into a conformist niche. As a result, if the revolution is to succeed and total freedom be made available to all, students must rise up and cast off the chains of requirements, standards, and responsibility imposed by the larger society. At the primary and secondary school levels, these ideas are translated into tactics of defiance, deliberate insult and challenge to teachers, demonstration and disruption, and attacks on standards and requirements. At the college and university level, the demand is for the politicization of the institutions; that is, changing them from their traditional role—preparing students for entry into the job market by providing competence in subject-matter areas—into institutions whose goal is political indoctrination, developing dissatisfaction with the existing social system, and preparing generally for the revolution. This "reconstitution" of the universities has actually made some progress, and it is not unusual to find credit courses in the tactics and methods of revolution and subversion. It is possible to learn, under the guise of becoming an educated person, how to make a fire bomb, how to lead a paramilitary operation, and how to disrupt the operations of an institution. Much more common, however, are courses emphasizing the evils of the society, which offer a totally uncritical view of alternative systems of government and generally advocate or excuse violence as a means of bringing about social or political change. And all this proceeds under the respectable mantle of academic freedom!

One hears a lot these days about the irrelevance of much of what students are expected to learn in the traditional educational system. "Relevance" has come to be a catchword of the radicals. It is supposed to mean that the things a student learns should have a bearing on the problems he will have to deal with later in life. Thus, what is relevant is what *he* considers important. For the radical, considering the nature of his personality, it is completely predictable that anything that requires disciplined effort or demands personal application over a period of time will be irrelevant. Thus, foreign languages, which require effort in their mastery, are likely to be irrelevant. History, especially if it emphasizes fact rather than general concepts, is irrelevant. Mathematics, the sciences, engineering, and other subjects requiring intellectual discipline and rigor, are irrelevant. The social sciences are likely to be relevant so long as they are presented in general terms. And learning through life experience is extremely relevant, because it only requires that the person be there, not that he make an active effort. Thus, the sweeping concept, the superficial generalization, and the frothy innovation hold great appeal, and are applauded for their relevance, while the demanding problem, rigorous penetration, and the facing of complexity in detail are condemned for their lack of relevance.

What is really relevant education in today's society? I submit that it is giving students the practical skills that will enable them to deal with the day-to-day problems of their lives. It is important, of course, that people be able to identify social ills, and to think beyond the mundane level of managing their grocery budget. But it is absolutely vital that they have a sense that they can master practical problems, for this alone will give them the confidence necessary to be effective participants in the solution of the larger problems. Thus, it is relevant to the ghetto child that he be able to read, and that he know enough mathematics to manage the everyday economics of his personal life. It is relevant to the middle-class housewife to be able to figure interest rates and read her bank statement. It is relevant to the average citizen to know how to analyze with some rigor the statistics of risk and gain when it comes to making national decisions concerning priorities. And it is relevant to all of us to develop enough intellectual discipline and rigor so that we are not taken in by fallacious argument and attractive propaganda, and to give us a sense of being able to bring our individual strength and effort to bear effectively in the solution of real-world problems. If the radicals truly want to do something about our problems, their best bet is to develop more than dilettantish acquaintance with issues, to gain familiarity with practical methods of attacking difficult issues, and not to delude themselves and annoy others with an endless and pointless exercise in frustration. And our educators might well turn their attention to better methods for developing such competence, rather than continuing to swim in the stream of the "easy way."

If the educational system has some weaknesses that reflect conditions in the larger society disadvantageous to most children, it is an absolutely disastrous environment to the child whose home experience has made him prone to develop the traits of the radical personality. Such a child finds a continuation of the pattern of overindulgence and permissiveness. The child who has learned at home that he may expect to have things his own way, to avoid frustration, and to believe that he is right and the world is wrong, obtains little contradiction of these delusions in the permissive school. When his faulty view of the world is not challenged by his teachers, his sense of omnipotence is encouraged. When his performance is not subjected to evaluation, the feeling that he is above the law is supported. When his superficial cleverness is applauded, he has no incentive to look more rigorously at the issues. And when his lack of discipline is tolerated or excused, his disregard for authority and disrespect for other human beings multiplies. In short, the conditions that exist in his relationships with his parents, which have led him to the feeling of arrogant self-importance, also come to exist around him in school, with the result that little corrective experience occurs. He feels justified in attempting to dominate the people around him, demands more and more freedom with less and less taking of responsibility, becomes increasingly at home with superficial competence, seeks the easy way to becoming an educated person, resists efforts at limiting him, and generally tries to impose the tyranny of his wishes upon the persons with whom he deals. In this way, the radical personality and the permissive environment lend symbiotic support to one another, and the result is a widening spiral of decadence throughout the school system and in society as a whole. The failure of the parents to demand accountability produces children who refuse to be accountable. These children in turn demand changes in society to reduce the possibility that they will be called to account, which in its turn weakens the ability of society and of parents ultimately to set limits, and so on, in a cyclic fashion. In the same way, lacking any sense of competence as a result of their parents' indulgence, they refuse to believe it necessary to demonstrate any, and they resist educational methods that would require them to develop it. They then demand changes that further limit the possibility of their ever gaining the tools that provide a sense of competence, and the cycle is repeated with ever widening repercussions on the educational system and the society. Thus, overindulgence produces demands for more indulgence, permissiveness leads to greater permissiveness, and weakness and insecurity produce behavior that ultimately enhances these characteristics.

In certain cases, variations in the parent-child relationship foster the development of the radical personality, particularly as related to emerging attitudes toward the educational process and intellectual achievement. There is often a great emphasis on explaining at length to the child why even very limited demands are made of him. The parents' goal is supposedly to insure that the child will not be frustrated by the imposition of unreasonable and arbitrary requirements. Sometimes, this is carried to the extent that the parent seems almost apologetic about expecting the child to comply. "I'm sorry, dear but because [of some reason], I have to request that you not play with matches in the closet." Explanations of this kind, and the length to which they are often carried, have several results. First, they encourage the child to ask "why," which in itself is not a bad thing. However, if the child has difficulty in dealing with frustration, as a result of the general pattern of permissiveness and overindulgence surrounding him, the asking of why is not a means of adding to his reasonable understanding, but rather a way of resisting the parents' demands, and turning the situation around to force the parents to justify their requests. Second, such explanations encourage dispute and argumentation, rather than produce the desired action in the child. Third, they again communicate the idea that the child is the equal or superior of the parent, by bringing the parent to the point of having to justify even the most simple request. Fourth, if the child is recalcitrant enough to pursue the asking of why to its ultimate limit, he may find that the parent will himself feel that there is no adequate reason and will back off from the request. Fifth, the parents' willingness to explain their demands establishes the expectation in the child that everyone else will be obliged to do the same, so that he becomes contentious with teachers and others with whom he later comes in contact. Finally, and of greatest ultimate importance, is the fact that the child may eventually coerce the parents into levels of explanation that are really beyond his ability to comprehend, so that he ends up not only dissatisfied, but confused. Consider the simple question, "Mommy, why do I have to go to school?" The ultimate reasons why children have to go to school are very complicated, although they finally come down to the fact that it helps to keep the civilization together. Can a child understand that, even if you take him step by step through all the interconnected logical reasons? And what if he doesn't want to go to school to begin with, because he has come to expect that any effort or inconvenience is undesirable? Do the explanations serve any useful purpose other than to make the parent feel that he's doing the psychologically correct thing? In my opinion, parents have a right occasionally to be arbitrary, to decide what's good for kids because they have more experience and better judgment, and to expect that children will do certain things because, and only because, parents tell them to. There is no real security for the child in being helped to believe that his parents are weak, hapless, stupid, or apologetic about what they expect the children to do. Nor does such a procedure give the child much basis for respecting the authority of other persons or institutions in the future. It makes no sense always to expect instant, blind obedience to every arbitrary demand, and never to explain at the level of the child's ability to comprehend. But neither does it make any sense never to expect compliance without a lengthy, defensive explanation.

Another individual variation involves a heavy emphasis on academic achievement and an overaggrandizement of the child who shows intellectual talent or verbal facility. The preceding discussion demonstrated how verbal argumentation becomes an important aspect of the child's effort to dominate and manipulate his parents, and later, the world. If he is also bright, his parents shower him with appreciation for evidencing such brightness through being cute, clever, or manipulative. If they put concurrent heavy pressure on him to bring home evidence of his academic prowess, two things happen: first, he applies his argumentative questions to the school situation, where he may be able to impress or intimidate his teachers; and second, his antagonism and frustration over having demands placed upon him get focused upon the area where these demands arise, namely, in the educational enterprise. Thus, to the extent that he is bright enough to succeed by some standard in the public schools, and to go on to college, a reservoir of resentment over academic expectations is built up, which is often later discharged at the institution that has become a symbol of the one area where permissiveness was not complete. In the next chapter, we shall explore this and other attitudes of the young radical as they are directed at our colleges and universities.

X
WHY THE UNIVERSITIES?

From Berkeley to Columbia to Kent State, universities have been the major focus of the attack by the young radicals on the American system. To the extent that there has been a conspiratorial or even a collaborative effort to disrupt society, the universities have been a vital target. For reasons that will be made apparent below, their reconstitution, destruction, or general disruption would represent a major victory for the nihilism that commands the minds of many young radicals. Even though the effort to attack our established way of life is now directed at broader targets—the public schools, the churches, the corporations, the military services, and even the family—the universities still serve as the major staging and recruiting area for the revolution-minded minority. And it is in the universities that this minority has been most successful. Why have the universities been such an important center for radical activities? The answer is complex, and must include a consideration of the traditions and internal values of the universities, and of the relationship between the institutions and the larger society, as well as of the personality traits of the radicals themselves.

In its traditional, or idealized form, the university is a remarkable and wonderful place. It is designed to give full opportunity for the free flow of the creative powers of the intellect. It is populated by serious scholars, who, driven by the force of their unyielding curiosity, extend our grasp of the universe in an unending search for truth. A very strong

183

ethical sense prevails, the responsibility of the scholar to abide by a set of rules is strongly emphasized, mutual respect abounds, and the entire system operates on a foundation of good faith and trust. The members of the university community understand the rules and abide by them. There is a well-established procedure for inducting and indoctrinating newcomers, so that those who do not show evidence of sufficient commitment to the truth, or who are lacking in the necessary integrity, intellectual rigor, tolerance, or motivation, are ruled out of full membership. The student is in the position of an apprentice who must demonstrate a similar set of characteristics, and he is given personal attention sufficient to permit him to identify with those responsible for the perpetuation of the system, the professors. All members of the university community recognize and accept the fact that the institution offers a special kind of freedom, provided for by the larger society in the faith that social and spiritual good will emerge, and that this special freedom carries with it special responsibilities. Eccentricity is cherished, because it may give rise to a great new insight. Individualism is at a premium, for who is to say that one man's ideas are not as valuable as another's? The whole process is designed to proceed in isolation from the larger society, and from political and pragmatic considerations, because the search for truth must not be impeded by pressures for consensus or conformity. The members of this community, secure in their insulation from the society around them and experienced in the manners and practices of their particular subsociety, pursue the truth with high ideals, tolerance, and a deep commitment to peace and reason. Dishonesty, expediency, self-seeking, anger, and other kinds of unsettling emotionalism have no place in the ideal university, and it came to be assumed that such attitudes or behavior would not appear in members of the university community. All in all, the university as thus conceived represented an ideal place for intelligent, devoted, sincere men to pursue the truth, to transmit this truth as best they could comprehend it, and to do so in the protective and secure quiet of the sheltering ivy-covered walls.

In this setting, and in the generally accepted understanding that all members of the community, including the students, possessed sufficient integrity and devotion to pursue the truth in the fashion described, discipline and rules were largely left to the conscience of the individual. True, there were provisions for sanctions against persons who flagrantly violated university ethics, by cheating, plagiarizing, or showing other forms of intellectual dishonesty. But the notion that the mass of the community accepted these high ethical standards was so strong that the mechanisms for enforcement depended on a kind of honor code, and the faith existed that even a cheat could be reached by an appeal to his ultimate commitment to the intellectual integrity of the institution. There was thus no necessity for much formalized expression of rules, virtually no enforcement mechanism, and certainly nothing that took into account the possibility that the accepted system would be challenged by persons inside the institution who found it expedient to defy it, or by forces outside who did not accept the notion that the university had a right to regulate itself. For these reasons, the ideal university was poorly prepared for the challenges that were to come from the young radicals. The faculties, which believed in and largely practiced the ethics described above, found it beyond belief that a group of persons who had no commitment to their ideals had come into the community and were not ready to abide by their version of the rules. The administrations, which were accustomed to the good faith dealings of the faculty and the mass of students, had neither the power, the mechanisms, the political position, nor, in many cases, the stomach to deal with destructive challenges to the institutions.

Whether such an ideal university ever really existed is beside the point. The important thing is that the faculties believed that it did. To them, it was a reality that all members of the community were honest, creative, seeking the truth, essentially altruistic, devoted to scholarship, accepting of the ethic; and that the community was an insulated sanctuary, influencing but not being influenced by the larger society, free of irrationality and emotionalism, nonpolitical, and idealistic. The faculties further assumed that their members would adhere to the truth, limit their public comments to the areas of their academic competence (drawing a sharp distinction, of course, between institutional roles and their rights as citizens), and adhere to the rules of scholarship at all times.

Beginning in connection with World War II and its aftermath, a series of developments began to diminish whatever reality this ideal concept of the university ever actually had. The pressure for mass education brought thousands and thousands of additional students into the institutions, with resulting changes in the personal relationship between students and professors, emphasis on mass production and efficiency, consequent loss of the individual equation, and general depersonalization of the educational process. There was no longer time to develop carefully the individual student's devotion to the scholarly ethic and process, and no longer the psychological glue to cement loyalty to the institution. More importantly, the professor became more and more a participant in the society around him. He found, as the rest of America was finding, that the affluent society offered its own rewards, and he became an eager participant in the action. The solitary pursuit of truth within the ivy-covered walls might have rewards in the internal satisfaction of the scholar, but the application of the same skills to a sponsored research activity or a consultant relationship to government or industry had a much more tangible payoff. And rare indeed was the professor who resisted the material temptation and continued to pursue his insulated, protected, scholarly way. As the rest of society rushed pell-mell for bigger houses and flashier cars, the faculty members, with only slightly more dignity and altruistic soul-searching, walked hurriedly (not stampeded) in pursuit of bigger research contracts and flashier consultantships. As the larger society discovered that professors could do something of practical value in the real world, it also discovered that professors put their pants on one leg at a time like everyone else, were subject to human failings, could respond to expediency, and were not above criticism. Thus, along with the material gain that accrued to faculty members in this development, there was a consequent loss of the aura of infallibility, the mystique of insulation, and the special respect accorded those who labor for principle rather than personal reward. While these consequences were quite apparent to the students, they were not fully realized by the professors, who persisted in believing that their role, prestige, and ethical system remained intact as in the ideal days of the university as sanctuary.

Institutionally too, there was a loss of distance and insulation. Partly as a result of the professors' interest in having a piece of the affluent action, and partly as a means of coping with their growing financial problems, the universities became much more directly a part of the general national system. They eagerly grasped for research contracts with the federal government and private industry, the overhead charges of which often made the difference between a comfortable and a tight annual budget. It mattered little whether the research was for the Department of Health, Education and Welfare or the Department of Defense. With equal eagerness, they sought money from any agency, public or private, which seemed to have promise of solving the problem of how to finance their rapid growth. The fact that this money might have strings attached, which would open the university to external regulation or control, either was not recognized, or did not seem to matter. The university, much more explicitly than ever before, became a reflection of and participant in the system. Previously, it had responded to and participated in the system in a much less explicit way—by gradual evolution of its programs to meet changing social and occupational needs, by grudgingly acceding to certain pressures of legislatures, alumni, or students—but always managing to retain its independence, regulating itself according to its own ethic and resisting the pressures of expediency, emotionalism and pragmatism. Now, the university was in and of the larger society, and its idealized ethic was largely eroded, even though the faculties seemed not to recognize that fact.

Into this changed and changing institution came the young radicals, set upon pursuing the course of self-indulgence, produced by and committed to an atmosphere of overpermissiveness, convinced of the validity of their own view of the world, superficially bright, verbally facile and expert at argumentation, hateful and contemptuous of authority, feeling a law unto themselves, intellectually undisciplined, arrogant, hostile and frustrated, and carrying the conviction that the great, oppressive, impersonal force which was the system was to blame for their frustration. The result of the confrontation between such individuals and an institution devoted to tolerance, freedom, good faith, peace, and mutual respect was predictably disastrous. The institution did not have the mechanisms to deal with a group that was not going to play by the rules of gentlemen and scholars. The faculties continued to assume that the radicals were only bright, sincere young people who rightly saw the evils in the world and only wanted to find a new and better way to solve our problems. The administrators vacillated among nervous compromise, efforts at reason, and arbitrary force, and nothing worked. The result was a long series of confrontations, disruptions of the educational process, weakening of the institutions, and loss of prestige and support—eventually the university lost effectiveness not only as a servant of the larger society, but, probably more important, in its allegiance to its own idealized ethic.

The initial attacks on the universities merely represented an extension of the radical's belief that he should be a law unto himself. On various campuses, this attack took varying forms, but the general theme was common: "We must have control over our own lives." Conduct regulations of any kind were impossible to accept, for they represented oppression, fascism, and an infringement on individual freedom. Requirements for the maintenance of hours were attacked early, and were generally quickly disposed of. Expectations of any standards for sexual conduct, personal habits, or appearance were similarly handled, and with equal ease. Matters pertaining to the operation of motor vehicles, mandatory residence in university housing, relationships to the community, responsibilities to landlords or other commercial operators, and even personal assaults upon other students, it was contended, were solely the concern of the students, and the university as an institution should not interest itself in them. Since a student was a citizen first and a student second, they said, such matters, if they represented problems at all, should be taken care of by the civil authorities and not as a matter of university discipline. In these struggles, the faculty, which had come to feel that their responsibility ended in the hall outside the classroom, and which had more important occupations in contract research or consultation, either took little interest or sided with the students, in a general libertarian spirit born of the days of good faith and trust in the responsible exercise of freedom. What an irony, in the context of the old ideal, to which the faculty continued to provide lip service, that the university community was self-contained and self-regulating, and therefore a special sanctuary from the real world.

The free speech issue, which had been born at Berkeley, also came in for its share of attention. Students, as citizens, had the same rights as everyone else, and were thus free to say what they wanted when and where they wanted to say it. Campus newspapers became organs for the most vituperative attacks, personal vindictiveness, and distorted political propaganda imaginable. Most efforts by faculty members and administrators to restore a semblance of journalistic responsibility failed because there was no general support for limiting a "free press," and when standards of responsible journalism were enforced, the vehicle of the underground newspaper, replete with four-letter words as well as distortion, took its place, usually produced at the expense of some poorly audited university budget account, and run off on university paper and mimeograph equipment and in a university-owned building. The radicals' success in these matters was usually a result of three factors: first, the university community's belief in the idea of free speech, supported by the earlier experience that no member of the community would deliberately lie or otherwise fail to play the game according to the accepted ethic; second, the radicals were regarded as idealistic, altruistic critics of the evils of the system, trying to improve things, whose "sometimes questionable" means were justified by their laudable ends; and third, a devoted and determined group of any kind, using tactics of intimidation, ridicule, and ostracism, can gain control of limited, but key, segments of the university apparatus, such as the student press, and turn it to their own autistic purposes. It is the old story—the minority can dominate when the majority is busy with other things, such as going quietly about the business of pursuing the educational opportunity offered by the university.

Another aspect of the radicals' campaign was reflected in their efforts to gain control over decisions concerning educational programs. "Since," the argument went, "it is the students who are affected by the kind of education they get, it must be the students who decide what that education will be." Here, the slogans concerning "relevance" came fully into play, and for the same reasons indicated in the preceding chapter. "Relevance" means that what is offered in the curriculum should be easy, have a grand conceptual sweep, lean heavily on "experience" (which generally means walking around and looking at things rather than applying oneself to rigorous study), and not challenge ideas the radical already believes to be true. And, of course, the students themselves should decide what is relevant. To some degree, the traditional belief of faculty members that *they* and not the students know what constitutes good education has thrown up a barrier to this totally permissive approach to higher education. Even so, its success is reflected in a growing tendency to relax requirements, modify standards, eliminate evaluations of the work a student does, and offer more and more opportunity for easier and easier access to the baccalaureate degree. And again, the delusion that the radicals really only want to improve things, and are sincerely interested in finding a better kind of education, has played an important part. Interestingly, however, when the radicals' proposals for greater control over their own educational lives have intruded on the really important prerogatives of the faculty, as in the areas of evaluating faculty performance, deciding on raises and promotions, setting other conditions of work, or demanding that the faculty lay aside some of its commitment to contract research and consultation in the interest of giving more time to the teaching of students, reform has been somewhat slower in coming.

The radicals have also attempted to gain greater influence over the general processes of decision-making in the universities. Demands for student participation in shaping long-range priorities are frequent. It is now a common expectation that universities will soon be run by a tripartite committee composed of students, faculty, and administrators, each with equal voting power. Control over budget decisions, personnel matters, the appointment of administrative offiiials, and so on, is an integral part of the effort to make things move in a direction personally satisfying to the radical minority, irrespective of whether it is consistent with the common good or the ultimate purposes of the institution. To some, this merely suggests a long overdue democratization of an overcentralized process. Keeping in mind the real motives of the radical personality, it is more correctly interpreted as one more evidence of his omnipotent conviction that he is right, that the world must not frustrate or control him in any way, and that he must have total freedom and total power, in order to remove his insecurity and the stress of his existence. Really at stake is the idea that the institution should be turned over to the radical for his own personal use, and that it should become his ally and extension in gaining whatever ends his "conscience," as already discussed, tells him are right.

From their concern over "freedom to control their own lives," which resulted in the radicals' attack on the inner processes of the university, the radicals soon moved to an attack on the university itself, as it reflected and symbolized the supposed evils of the system. Recalling what has already been said about why the system came to be a focus for the radicals' rage, it is easy to understand how the university came in for its share of the attack. Obviously, the university exists in and cooperates with the larger society, which nurtures and supports it. If it did not do this to some degree, it would soon cease to exist. Historically, as I have said, the university through its devotion to and practice of a unique, internally regulating ethical system, earned a position of special trust and responsibility in society. It has been a kind of isolated sanctuary, and this arrangement has paid off not only for members of the university community but also for society. Recently, as I have also noted, this position of isolation has been somewhat eroded, and the university is now more closely intertwined with the larger society than it was for a long time. This, as I have observed, has had mutual benefits.

Whatever the nature of the implicit arrangement between the university and society, the university came to be seen by the radicals as a particularly evil aspect of a generally evil system. The reasons for this are not hard to understand. Accustomed to great personal attention, the radicals found in the universities an IBM-ized, impersonal, mass operation. Led by their earlier academic success to believe that they would be as adulated and overindulged at the university as they had been throughout their lives, the realities of the universities' treatment of them came as a special blow to their omnipotence. Believing also that the superficial, position-paper approach to problems, which had been rewarded at home and in the public schools, would lead them to even greater heights at the university, they must have been especially disappointed when they found little opportunity for uniqueness, and even less for bending the world to their own image. Finally, the implicit expectation existed, as it always had, that something

191

would happen to remove their basic frustration and reestablish the sense of total comfort and indulgence that had characterized their earlier lives. And of course they were disappointed. The great promise once again did not materialize. Rather than accept their omnipotence, their professors had the effrontery to challenge it. And rather than provide them with the substantive tools to restore a sense of personal competence and strength, the universities offered further irrelevant exercise. Thus, psychologically, the university was perfectly positioned in their expectations to play the role of indulgent, overaggrandizing parent, and instead it only provided a situation in which they felt even more frustrated, hemmed in, and helpless.

Thus, as the antagonism of the radicals focused on the system for one set of reasons, it focused on the universities for another. The easy equating of the university, which was in fact a part of the system, with the system itself, occurred, and the university felt the full impact of radical anger and of the insistent demand for change, which was supposed to produce the long-lost infantile nirvana of the perfect world of peace, comfort, and freedom. The university was really approached in precisely the same way that an indulgent, overprotective parent would be. In the area of their personal lives, it was to provide no restrictions, no frustrations, and no demands but only indulgence, security, and the missing sense of individual competence. In the area of the radicals' relationship to the world outside, it was to be an advocate, an ally, and a source of sanctuary if things got tough. This latter expectation is seen in many aspects of the radicals' behavior. "The university *has to* take a stand on this issue," meaning that it must ally itself as an institution with *his* position on some political question. "It is long past time that the university *confront* the evils in this lousy system of ours," which means that the president of the university should make a public statement, preferably written by the radicals, that he thinks the free enterprise system has no benefits to our society. The real possibility that substantial segments of the university community might disagree, or that the university cannot speak with one voice, or that the system may have some substantial benefits, or that the university might well suffer a long-run destructive effect, or that, most importantly, the university,

192

once politicized in this fashion, would lose all its standing, credibility, and independence, simply does not occur to him. The insistent internal pressure he feels, that he is right, that he must not be frustrated, that he must have his way in order to feel comfortable, overrides any rational considerations concerning the welfare of the institution. And yet, incredibly, we find many faculty members, and even an occasional insipid or cowardly university president, acceding to such infantile demands by allowing themselves to be drawn publicly into making value judgments on highly complex political matters. Liberals in the academic community must wince occasionally when they realize that a university politicized for liberal purposes may as easily be turned into the tool and ally of reaction and repression.

The tactics of the radicals in the universities are very simple. First, an issue, preferably one that will rally some public support, is found. Previously, certain established mechanisms of the institution, such as the student government, the student newspaper, or a faculty body, have been seized or co-opted by the methods described in Chapter II. If that has not been done, an ad hoc group with a name that includes some good word like "peace," "freedom," or "concern," and lends itself to translation into a pithy acronym, will do as well. Out of the proceedings of this group, or as a part of a combined news and editorial program in the publication, comes a statement calling the attention of the community to the issue. Ideally, the issue appeals to one of the traditional values of the university community, such as academic freedom, but if this is not available, one of the newer radical concerns, such as freedom to decide on matters that affect our lives, will do. The propaganda build-up then proceeds for a time, and organizational meetings are held, in the hope of attracting a sizable constituency. However high or low the level of initial interest, there soon emerges a demand that immediate action be taken to remedy the situation. Meetings with university officials may be scheduled, under the guise of seeking rational discussion and solution. Invariably, if the demand is not met, there will be accusations of poor faith, stupidity, or lack of appreciation of the seriousness of the problem. It will then be made to appear that since nothing is being done to respond to a perfectly reasonable demand for the solution of the problem, or to provide redress of grievances, that it is necessary to show more insistence. At this point, rallies are held, and broader support is sought, either under some umbrella issue like justice or free speech, or as an expression of popular outrage at the recalcitrance of university officials. If even a small group can be persuaded, there will be a demonstration, usually involving a sit-in, or, ideally, some marginal interference with the operation of the university, or some minor destruction of university property. If the university responds by attempting to impede or punish the demonstrators, the issue is then further escalated to include accusations of arbitrary action, interference with basic rights, and so on. Sooner or later, enough provocation occurs to make the university authorities act, and the police are called. At this point, there is a shift to such issues as oppression and fascist tactics. Hopefully, a number of otherwise innocent sympathizers can be involved. Finally, if the police are forced to act to protect lives, the general peace, or property, and especially if there is any scuffling or violence, the university administrators are accused of violating the most sacred rights of the academic community, brutalizing the students, and generally behaving like inhuman beasts. The outcome hoped for is the alienation of large numbers of students from the university and from the system as a whole.

It is amazing how successful this tactic has been. On campus after campus, large numbers of unsuspecting students have been manipulated and used in this fashion, and come out of the experience feeling that an injustice has been done to them. Seldom is the responsibility traced back to the radicals, who are masters of avoiding accountability, a lesson they learned well in their relationships with their parents. Again, the tactics and the outcome are totally consistent with the radical's notion that the world is wrong, that someone outside himself is to blame for his distress, and that he is free from any responsibility if anything unpleasant results from his actions.

At many universities, there has long been a subtle but widespread sympathy for anyone who would attack the free enterprise system in any of its manifestations. In many liberal arts colleges, the faculties are so preponderantly left-leaning in their political views that it is amazing. In several departments with which I am intimately familiar, of a hundred or more faculty members, only a single one, or a few at the most, admit being to the right of the Democratic party on the political spectrum, but many are to its left. Whether this is by accident, design, or incidental self-selection, the result is that radical students are often supported and encouraged, not only in their beliefs, but in their demands and violent actions. Students with opposing beliefs are subtly discouraged or derogated, not only in public debate or discussion, but even in the supposedly objective atmosphere of the classroom. Sometimes this is done under the persuasive guise of academic sanctity, sometimes flagrantly. But it is done nevertheless, and its influence is heavy. It is hard for a moderate student to stand up under the emotional bludgeoning of his radical contemporaries, especially in the face of subtle intimidation by a faculty member. While this degree of total loss of scholarly integrity is typical of only a few faculty members, the pressures within many liberal arts departments for hewing to a liberal or radical party-line is immense. By accepting it one gains popularity, acceptance, and even academic reward. By resisting it, one can be made to appear stupid, naive, or uninformed. Thus the radicals find fellow-traveling encouragement, and the moderates are ridiculed for their efforts to resist.

By and large, the traditional university discouraged its members from asserting expertise in areas outside their personal competence. This was politically reasonable, and it was an expression of respect for the special competence of one's colleagues, into whose areas one did not intrude. This custom has now largely disappeared, and a good many of my academic brothers use their competence in one area as a justification for heavy opinionating in others. One finds sociologists who claim to be experts on the clinical effects of LSD, and political scientists who are familiar with the deeper moral issues surrounding promiscuous sex. Worse yet, one sees increasing evidence of a willingness to interpret data from the framework of emotional convictions, rather than attempts at objectivity, and all of this is carried on under the pompous mask of academic purity and sophistication.

The radicals' greatest successes have come at universities that pride themselves on being progressive institutions of high academic quality. It has been suggested that this is so because such institutions attract a higher proportion of bright, sincere, altruistic students who are alert to and concerned about the problems of the time. This may well be true, but to identify the motives of the radicals with those of the mass of bright, sincere, motivated students is a sad error. A somewhat more accurate analysis suggests it is at the Berkeleys, the Madisons, the Michigans, and the Columbias that the ideal conditions exist to nurture both the radical personality and radical tactics. These institutions have all been characterized by heavy involvement of their faculties in research, to the neglect of the teaching process. They have all grown into giant, impersonal, almost unmanageable operations, where even the stable student is hard put to find much individual attention or identity. They are all fragmented into a multitude of administrative units, so that it is hard to develop a sense of identity with the institution, and a consequent loyalty to it. They all have faculties who believe strongly in the traditional ethic of the university, including the self-regulating responsibility of its members and its immunity from outside influence. And they all have a long-standing reputation for permissiveness, or neglect, in their dealings with the behavior of students outside the classroom. In short, the institutions that have been most successfully attacked by the radicals are the ones that provide the ideal incubation place for the destructive aspects of the radical personality. By contrast, institutions that have stayed with their teaching responsibility, maintained standards of rigor and intellectual discipline, dealt forthrightly with unreasonableness as it began to occur, and recognized the reality that they cannot be the allies of every infantile or noxious demand, have had much less difficulty.

One final note about university life is in order before concluding this chapter. It is remarkable that the occurrence of violent radicalism is extremely rare in divisions of the university oriented to technical and professional training. Among engineers, dentists, physicians, and architects, the radical personality is much less frequently seen. Campus radicals are concentrated in the colleges of liberal arts, and particularly in the social sciences—sociology, psychology, economics, political science. Some speculations about this phenomenon are in order.

196

It is obvious that engineering, for example, demands a level of intellectual rigor and discipline inconsistent with the position-paper mentality of the radical. The same may be said for the hard sciences, and the professions based on them. Apologists for the radicals contend, of course, that an interest in social science merely reflects the radicals' more acute interest in social problems, and that a natural selection process, based on his special social conscience, leads him into these fields. Perhaps so, but we have known for a long time that the selection of one's field of study is a reflection not only of his rational choice, but also of his personality and his unconscious. And does not social science, however much it strives for rigor and the scientific method, offer the best possible intellectual area for the person who cannot discipline himself to be rigorous, and who wants to rely upon verbal cleverness, superficial understanding, and position-paper solutions? Of course, in order to be really successful in the social sciences, one must eventually develop the same attributes needed by a scholar in any field. But at the same time, the student who is looking for the easy way, the sweeping concept, the vague generalization, and impressive but superficial understanding hidden behind jargon and slogans, has an excellent opportunity for expressing his personality in these fields. The student who goes into engineering or dentistry must bring a greater discipline with him, and in the process of his training, he is given the practical tools for solving problems, which adds to his sense of personal competence. In seeing that he is able to do something, he comes to believe that he will be able to deal with other problems. As his competence grows, his confidence in himself as an individual grows as well, and he faces even the most dire problems with assurance in his power as an individual to do something about them. But if a student comes to his field of study already frustrated and insecure, already alarmed about the complexities of the problems he faces, and then realizes that the field he has chosen to pursue has no, or few, practical tools to offer him in the solution of these problems, is not his insecurity and frustration magnified? It is unfortunately true that the social sciences have not yet given us the means to attack complex social problems with the same assurance and degree of expectation of success

197

with which the technological disciplines allow us to approach a trip to the moon or the transplanting of the human heart. This is not to their discredit, but it may well be an important contributor to the continuing sense of helplessness and frustration that plagues the radical personality, leading him to assault both the university and the system, although in the long run these offer him the best chance of personal freedom and survival.

XI

HOW TO SUBVERT A CULTURE WITHOUT REALLY TRYING

The attempt of the young radicals to destroy the American system of government and revolutionize our society has had very few direct effects. Its most notable success has been in the weakening of some of our great universities, both internally and in the eyes of society. Beyond that, the legacy of the young radicals has been a few draft files burned or bloodied, a few people injured, a townhouse blown up, a few buildings bombed or burned, and the tragic deaths of four young people at Kent State. All in all, the movement has been characterized by empty rhetoric, infantile ranting and raving, the disgusting spectacle of the Chicago trial, and sensational claims and spectacular threats. If the young radicals were to disappear from the scene tomorrow, they would leave scant evidence that they had ever walked among us. The political revolution they sought has not materialized, not merely because it was a revolution that did not offer viable alternatives to what we have, but also because it lacked a coherent philosophical or ideological base and an effective set of tactics. Certainly the small amount of political thought evident in the idealistic early days of the New Left has not been translated into operation. The "participatory democracy" notion, which was supposed to provide for a new infusion of individual participation and power into the system, has found expression only in a few scattered meetings of the SDS, and in the hands of the radical personalities comprising that group, it has meant chaos and anarchy rather than effective individualism.

The student syndicalist movement, which was supposed to weld students and other members of the "underclasses" into a broadly based foundation for political action, has never found acceptance among more than a handful of super-frustrated misfits, and now appears only occasionally in the form of efforts by a few maladjusted junior high school students trying to form a union for power confrontations with their teachers and principals. Thus, the radical movement has been anything but a stunning success, not only because of the inherent weaknesses of its approach, but also because the radicals have been unable to persuade anyone who has enough logic, sense of organization, and personal discipline to make even a good set of propositions work. The very characteristics that make the radicals feel intolerable frustration, demand total freedom, and advocate the destruction of our system, also make them so disorganized and autistic that they cannot possibly succeed.

Nevertheless, some of the social and interpersonal forces that have produced the radicals are widely enough at work in our society to cause concern. When even a small number of our youth are raised in such a way as to produce the kind of personality described in this book, we should recognize that we are doing something seriously wrong. But when a much larger number of young people are chronically exposed to a set of values and conditions that make them want to drop out, turn off, and pursue lives of general aimlessness and decadence, we should push the alarm button with haste, and not turn it off until things are set straight. The primary danger to American society is not the political radical, but the much more frequently seen phenomenon of the young person who has no direction or purpose, who seeks the easy way to comfort and escape through drugs, alcohol, or pointless activity, and who ends up destroying himself, significantly weakening the entire society at the same time. And while political radicals comprise such a tiny minority as to be insignificant, a much larger number of young people, perhaps as high as 10 or 15 percent, are embarked on a course of hapless inaction and supposed comfort-seeking that bodes a serious threat to our society. These young people, like those who comprise the radical minority, suffer from deep psychological problems involving needs for instant gratification, a lack of a sense of individual worth and purpose, unsatisfying interpersonal relationships, and other problems causing withdrawal from effective participation in society to pursue a life of escape, alienation, and muted hostility to the system. In their omnipotence, the radicals claim that these young people are being produced by the effective spread of radicalism, and that every child who becomes alienated from his parents, ineffective in school, or unsuccessful in his life represents a victory for the radical ideology. And indeed there may be some truth in interpreting such losses to the individual and society as a victory for radicalism, if that victory is defined as the eventual erosion of an organized, purposive, ordered, civilized society. But to say that the radicals have succeeded in their purposes, and that their point of view has directly persuaded this larger minority to give up participation in the system, is both crediting them with more influence than they have actually had, and putting on them a responsibility that rightly falls on society as a whole. For what we, not the radicals, have done, is to permit the condition of our society to become such that alienation is popularized and rewarded, irrationality and indolence are an accepted way of life, and general decadence and chaos threaten to overtake us. How this has come about, and the dangers it poses for us as a nation and a people, is the subject of this chapter.

One aspect of the young radicals' approach to life and problems, which we have touched upon by implication but not directly, is a basic antiintellectual and antirational attitude. In the last chapter, I briefly discussed how the radical approach is basically incompatible with the traditional ethic of the university, where the reasoned, logical pursuit of solutions epitomizes the highest expression of man's intellectual powers. Methods or tactics relying on uncontrolled emotion and the gaining of immediate gratification of impulses, and representing the expression of panic, an autistic view of the world, or general infantilism, are intrinsically antirational and antiintellectual. Yet, as I have shown in the earlier chapters of this book, such attitudes and methods of procedure are not confined to the flailing rhetoric of the radical left. In fact, one of the most amazing paradoxes of our current situation is the willingness of supposed intellectuals of the liberal persuasion to be sucked in by the flagrant emotionalism of the radicals, as it directed toward one or another supposedly catastrophic issue. It is an insult to a commitment to reason, and a betrayal of belief in the intellectual process, to arrive at, or be drawn into, a position on an issue on the basis of emotion, and then piously to develop justifications and rationalizations for that position under the guise of being an intellectual. Further, this tendency is not confined to liberals who fellow-travel with the radicals. It is increasingly evident among segments of the general public. More and more we are taken in by the emotional flavor of issues confronting us, tantalized by the demagogic promise of instant solutions, and prone to decide on the basis of gut reaction rather than in terms of the facts and the long-term implications. Thus, on both sides of the racial barrier there are blatant appeals to underlying fear and hostility. We are asked to vote for political candidates because they are lovable, or to vote against them because they are not charming. We are exposed to constant appeals to act instantly and without deliberation because some emotion-laden words are associated with one or the other side of the question. The result is that we are less reasoned in our considerations, less cautious in our judgments, and more prone to act like the proverbial chicken with his head cut off when making important decisions. A society that allows itself to be led around by the seat of its emotional pants, whether by the radicals, Madison Avenue, or some opportunist or demagogue, will not fall into decisions to its ultimate advantage.

In totalitarian societies, the diet of information fed to the people is carefully manipulated and regulated. Those of us who lived through the era of Nazi Germany can recall how Dr. Goebbels, the Reichsminister for Information, built the art of information control to a fine science. In a more current vein, we see how, in China and the Soviet Union, virtually complete government control of the channels of communication insures that the people will hear only what the regime thinks is good for them. The events of their own country and the world are carefully interpreted, with no concern for truth or objectivity, in a way designed to create opinions and attitudes required by the interests of the dictatorship. In our own country, fortunately, we have a much freer access to information and thus a much better basis for making intelligent judgments about issues. Government control of the news and of communication channels is generally limited to regulating radio and television in the interest of fairness, and there is virtually no governmental influence on the printed media, such as newspapers and magazines. Such government control of information as does occasionally occur is rationalized or justified on the grounds of immediate considerations of national security, and while certain government agencies occasionally stretch this definition to an uneasy point, the court system ultimately limits this abuse to insure that the public is not denied general access to matters about which it should be informed. In the final analysis, the separate operations of the branches of government, the free press, the conscience of individuals, and the everyday judgment of citizens serves as an effective deterrent to flagrant governmental control of the news. Under this system, the American citizen should be assured that he will have a fair and sufficient exposure to the facts to provide him with a basis for intelligent judgment.

Unfortunately, this is not entirely the case. There are other ways of manipulating information and interfering with the public's ability to make rational decisions. We have long been accustomed to dealing with some of these methods as they are practiced by politicians, and we have come to expect that political figures will shade the facts slightly, present a one-sided view of the issue, or otherwise engage in recognized techniques of propaganda to make their point of view appear to be the only logical one. Familiar as we are with these tactics, we apply a proper discount to the value of arguments and implied promises in the area of political behavior. We also have come to understand that such techniques are applied in the editorial pages of newspapers, we take into account the existence of bias in such items, and we have learned to separate the opinion of the editorial page from the straight, objective reporting of information that we expect on the news pages. We are also conditioned to expect a similar separation of "straight news" from propaganda, opinion, and other non-rational influence techniques in our other communications media, such as magazines, radio, and TV.

For a variety of reasons, this separation is becoming blurred. Television reporting represents the most obvious example. Most national television news reporters also engage in news commentary, the expression of opinion, and other

203

forms of editorializing. It is common to see a national TV personality reporting the news at 6:30 P.M., and to hear him on a radio commentary at 7:45, or to see him again narrating a "News Special" at 10:30. Thus, however scrupulously he tries to objectify his reporting on the national news, we become aware a short time later of his personal position on the items he has earlier reported. And if we are too busy to pay close attention to the distinction between the two roles, it is easy to conclude that he is still the objective reporter when we hear or see him while he is frankly committed to influencing opinion by whatever subtle or clever techniques of propaganda he decides to use. In this way, possibly because the confusion of roles is deliberately fostered, or, more charitably, because the individual concerned fails to see the implications of what he is up to, public opinion is subtly led in the direction of the personal position of the TV reporter. And the public is usually not sufficiently alerted to the process to avoid being duped.

In some instances, antirational techniques are even more obvious. No intelligent citizen believes that he gets all the news, and he recognizes that there has to be a process of selection. However, he does have a right to expect that he will be given a fair, representative sample, and allowed to draw his own conclusions therefrom. The question is whether the American public is getting such a balanced view of the facts and issues. At every stage of the news gathering and news presenting process, judgments influence what the public finally sees. What story is going to be covered at all? Who is going to cover it? If interviews are conducted, who will be questioned? What questions will be asked and how will they be phrased? How much of each respondent's answers will be reported? At the editorial level, other questions: Which of the stories covered will appear on the program or in the paper? Where or when, that is, how prominently, will they be presented? How many of them will be repeated, or shown on prime time, or later commented on, or made the subject of a special program. At each and every one of these stages, individual judgments are made, and these judgments may be as easily conditioned by prejudice, emotion, or a ready-made commitment to one or another point of view as by objectivity, integrity, or commitment to reason and to faith in the people's wisdom. Thus, it is an easy matter for bias to be introduced, and for the public to receive slanted, one-sided coverage as limiting on their ability to make good judgments as news rigidly controlled by a government propaganda bureau.

The reader should take special notice, over the next few days, of instances of this process of selection and distortion in operation. It makes no difference whether he gets his information from the local news, national news, radio, TV, or newspapers, since examples can be seen in all the media. Can you tell from the questions a reporter asks, or the way he asks them, where he personally stands on the issue, or how he personally reacts to the respondent? Is he sympathetic or antagonistic? Does he try to pin the respondent down, or does he let him off easily? What kind of comments does he make after the interview is over? Examine the look on his face and the tone of his voice, for therein lie clues to his personal bias and to the direction you are being pushed in. Suppose that a series of interviews is being conducted on a campus issue, or a matter of broader public concern. On campus, during the days of major disturbances, it was common to see interviews with members of the angry, disruptive minority, and no suggestion whatsoever that the vast majority of students might feel quite differently. In this way, the position held by only a fragment of the people involved can seem to represent an overpowering consensus, and, depending on how the interviews are handled, to be just and reasonable. In another vein, examine how the various news media, through the selection of their stories, the point of view that is subtly expressed, or other means, manage to give a one-sided emphasis, an appealing emotional flavor, or a cynical cast. Dishonest and deceitful? Perhaps not. But productive of a less than objective view, and not supportive of the basic idea that the fully informed citizen can be trusted to make an intelligent decision. The entire operation smacks of the old notion that somebody else knows best, that the self-styled intelligentsia somehow has a special insight and competence. The fact is, of course, that many such persons have no special claim to either objectivity or wisdom, and in the present climate, are at least as likely as anyone else to arrive at conclusions on the basis of emotion and then justify them with contrived arguments. The citizen might well demand, "Just give me the facts and let me make up my own mind."

The extent to which the American public is fed a well-regulated diet of prejudiced viewpoint and distortion ultimately depends on the balance and integrity of the news-processing organizations. No one individual can claim or assure perfect balance or objectivity. However, it has been our faith that a fairness is insured when an organization is made up of people of widely diverse views, since these views will interact in a healthy way to protect the public from one-sidedness. Certainly this protection would seem to operate in some areas—any newspaper that carries both William Buckley and James Reston as syndicated columnists can hardly be accused of one-sidedness. In radio and TV, the same balance seems to exist—if we confine our examination to those whose exclusive job is commentary or editorializing. But are we equally well protected when it comes to the views and influence of the celebrities who run the national talk shows, and of the featured personalities who double as commentators on the national news shows? One might ask: Where do Walter Cronkite, Harry Reasoner, David Brinkley and John Chancellor (and his predecessor, Chet Huntley), Eric Sevareid, Dan Schorr, Roger Mudd, and Dan Rather fall on the liberal-conservative spectrum; that is, where do they stand on the key issues? Or the reporters on their news programs who provide field coverage of events? Do they lean noticeably to one side or the other, or do they represent a balanced view? What about Dick Cavett and Lou Gordon? Are they merely trying to draw out opinion, or do they convey a clear editorial message, and if they do, does the "equal time" doctrine apply to their political commentary? I don't have to answer these questions for you—make your own observations and come to your own conclusions.

Human nature being what it is, there is no need to suspect the news purveyors of malice, dishonesty, or deliberate wish to deceive. In order for the people to be subtly led in one direction or the other, it is only necessary that the men involved share a general point of view, and for that point of view to be reflected in the judgments made at various stages in the process, or for the public to be confused about what

206

is straight reporting and what is commentary, or for personal opinion to be expressed subtly through an unconscious choice of words, point of emphasis, or facial expression. We may credit our national newsmen with sufficient integrity to avoid deliberate deception, but we need not assume that they are always sufficiently self-aware to avoid the other dangers inherent in their position of heavy responsibility. It is quite possible that group pressures operate on them just as they do on members of departments of social science in our universities, and that a kind of "party-line" comes to operate within the news media subculture. It may be that Vice President Agnew is not so paranoid, after all, when he accuses the media of bias, but is only expressing less gently a concern that would be voiced by anyone seeking objectivity and balance on the basis of a commitment to true intellectualism and liberalism.

If there is a danger of one-sidedness in the responsible sector of the communications media, the condition is much worse among those who make no pretense of objectivity. Examples of blatant editorializing occur daily, and in every area of public communications. For example, a local newsman, who has projected a generally cynical view of the present national administration, repeatedly finds ways to suggest that the President's visit to China has little value. Recently, in introducing the evening news, this man took pains to point out that four hours of discussion between Mr. Nixon and Mr. Chou represents a lot of talking—"Or," he asks, "does it really?" He then noted the perfectly correct fact that nearly half the discussion time was given over to translation, so that Mr. Nixon's seven days in China really only amounted to three and one-half days, and the tone of his voice, while not quite sneering, left no doubt that he thought the whole thing pretty much a pointless exercise. Or a local newspaper runs a news story on the Chinese ballet, which was attended by Mrs. Nixon, and concludes the article by referring to the leading dancer's look of piety and reverence as she pressed her face into the folds of the red flag of revolution. Perhaps the reporter was only lifting her story from the propaganda statement issued by the Chinese information ministry. Perhaps she was simply moved by the beauty of the ballet. But perhaps her story reflected her own emotional commitment to the concept of the "people's revolution," which she was trying, either

207

deliberately or unconsciously, to persuade her readers was the way, the truth, and the life not only for the Chinese but for the American people as well. This kind of thing is seen constantly in various organs of our country's supposedly free press. In the feature section of a Sunday paper in recent weeks, there has appeared a series of articles heroizing a person who has a stated goal of turning as many young people as possible on to drugs, glorifying the supposed humanity and beauty of a commune, and otherwise supporting the ideas and patently destructive behavior of the counterculture. Over and over again, the bizarre is aggrandized, the conventional is derogated, and the reader, either openly or subtly, is urged to believe that our accepted way of life is the path of fools, exploiters, and mossbacks. The total impact of these antirational appeals is tremendous, and particularly so on younger people, who have neither the experience nor the internal discipline to discern what is being done to them. For the young person already in psychological difficulty, the idea that escape from tension is promised by drugs, communal living, or the destruction of the existing culture is particularly devastating, not only to his own future, but also to society as a whole. Thus the total effect of the operation of emotionalism, bias, and flagrant propaganda in our supposedly free press is to detract from a rational solution to our problems, again promising the easy way out, and introducing a major antiintellectual element into a system that depends on all its members to use their reasoned judgment in coming to decisions about their own lives and the general good.

The destructive influence of emotion and propaganda on our ability to arrive at reasoned decisions, and hence on the strength of our society, is at work not only in our public communications media. Such tactics are very frequently seen in face-to-face relationships, small groups, and in both public and private settings. Here, the pressure on the individual who tries to take a reasoned stand is immense. One of the favorite tactics of young radicals is to confront an individual, or a small group of responsible officials, with a large group of their own, and in these circumstances the atmosphere is charged with personal threat and intimidation. It takes a very strong person, or a very resolute small group, to stand up to their responsibilities in the face of what may be interpreted as a threat to their physical safety. Other sorts of emotional pressure may be applied to produce a sense of guilt—suggestions that one is rigid, intolerant, reactionary, or racist, made in an atmosphere of righteous indignation over some supposed injustice or indignity, or in the name of peace, freedom, or whatever, are also difficult to deal with, particularly if one is made to feel that he is the only holdout against the wave of emotion. A chronic pressure is applied in the name of liberalism, based on the idea that the liberal, permissive, or indulgent approach is the only one justified in the name of decency and humanity. Thus, those who counsel reason or patience are castigated as having no respect for their fellow man, or are isolated and rendered helpless by the accusation that they have no sympathy for the pressing issue of the moment.

Every human being has a basic urge for comfort, for the release of tension, and for the gratification of his impulses to enjoy the fundamental pleasures of sex, nourishment, personal contact, warmth, and physical safety and security. A society that gives no opportunity for such gratification becomes drab and morose, as in a totalitarianism where the individual is submerged to the interests of the state, or hypocritical and repressive, as in a Victorian environment. On the other hand, a society that permits the uncontrolled expression of such urges, without consideration of the consequences to its individual members or itself, gradually moves through stages of self-indulgence, license, anarchy, and finally back to the jungle. In our own society, the level of comfort-seeking, self-indulgence, and demands for unrestricted gratification of impulses is such as to give cause for alarm. Our devotion to the easy life and the easy way may well be moving us past reasonable pleasure-seeking in the direction of license and social disorganization. In the next several pages, we will look at various ways in which this condition appears in our society, and some of its possible consequences.

One of the reasons Americans have worked so hard is that they have looked forward to the leisure which hard work produces. Now, in the affluent society, many of the age-old dreams of leisure and freedom from toil seem to be coming true. The four-day week, several long weekends a year, and a full month's vacation for everybody seem within reach. Earlier retirement and lessened need for great productivity during their working years are rapidly becoming realities for the mass of people. The productive capacity of the technological-industrial system urges all of us to think in terms of less demanding, less tedious work, and the average fifty-year-old workingman has a standard of living beyond the wildest fantasy he may have had during the depression years. Yet the very success of the system in materialistic and comfort-producing terms seems to be a force that may undermine it. With the image of affluence present in the minds of all, and (for the moment, at least) enough reserve available to insure the nonproductive a survival level of economic support, the idea is easily developed that affluence and leisure are automatic. For the child who has grown up in a middle-class home, the possibility of economic distress is so remote as to be unreal. The average family simply does not experience enough significant personal consequences of the nonproductivity of the rest of society to cause it to bring home to the growing child the hard fact that economic security is not guaranteed, either to the family itself or to the system as a whole, although there is some indirect indication that more and more families are beginning to chafe under the pressure of high taxes, which to some degree reflects the declining productivity of larger and larger segments of society. Most subversive of the strength of society in the long run, however, is the fact that growing numbers of young people see no purpose in work, or in preparing themselves for productive participation in society. This is one of a complex of factors that make school seem irrelevant in the experience of some young people, which indeed it may be if they personally expect to survive without having to work. So long as such attitudes exist only among a small minority of the population, the rest of society will likely accept the burden of carrying the nonproductive. Unfortunately, if the proportion rises, one of two things will happen. Either the productive segment of society will eventually require that the work associated with productivity, as well as the benefits, be equally spread, or the nonproductive minority will come to dominate and the entire system will gradually lose its strength and its competitive position in the world. Thus we can see that the lessening of the emphasis placed on work, growing out of our present affluence and self-indulgence, may in the end cause both our standard of living and our general culture to

210

decline. Perhaps there is some justice in the consideration that when it does, if it does, those who advocate one or another form of nonproductivity as a way of life will be among the first to feel the effects of the crunch or the general decline.

Another aspect of the general attitude of self-indulgence and permissiveness is the frequently advocated idea of "do your own thing." This notion is sometimes supported by the idea that doing one's own thing is one way to reassert our lost individualism, or a normal expression of our urge and our right to personal freedom. Perhaps, properly and reasonably practiced, doing one's own thing could reflect both of these perfectly laudable goals. Too often, however, it has come to mean doing precisely what one wants to do, when one wants to do it, without respect for the destructive effects on the person or society, and without consideration for the rights of others. Instead of freedom and self-realization, it implies a total laying aside of responsibility, an immediate and complete gratification of any urges, and license rather than freedom. The ultimate extension of the do-your-own-thing philosophy carries us back to the edge of the jungle, rather than toward a new era of human freedom. The invitation to do your own thing, which is freely extended to our young people in a myriad of versions, may easily become an enticement to engage in activities they are not emotionally prepared to handle, with ultimately destructive effects. To a youngster already plagued with psychological problems, as a result of parental mishandling or the general conditions in society, doing his own thing may mean taking part in any impulsive action whatsoever, so long as it promises instant gratification or relief from tension. Children and adolescents in a complex, problem-ridden society have a difficult enough time without being seduced into activities that only accentuate their uncertainties. In their efforts to learn who and what they are, laying the base for satisfying emotional relationships, preparing for a productive life, and keeping themselves safe and healthy, they are not assisted by being led into promiscuous sex, drugs, the street life, alienation from their parents, dropping out, or other expressions of the promised land offered by the counterculture. Because of a need for immediate gratification, an urge to escape responsibility, a new and often uncontrolled strength of sexual or aggressive impulses, and a lack of inter-

211

nal discipline, the young person may experience the idea of doing his own thing as a powerful exhortation to say "To hell with everything except what I want now"; if so, he will pay a harsh price later on.

Messages appealing to and encouraging impulses toward instant gratification, irresponsibility, and alienation are epidemic in our society. The music of the youth culture is filled with lyrics that play on fear, loneliness, hostility, or other negative feelings, and subtly encourage running away, cynicism, distrust of parents, dropping out, or the search for some vacuous deeper meaning in the stream-of-consciousness blathering of a passing hero of the rock scene. As an exercise, readers who have teen-age children with record albums are invited to read the lyrics, or better yet, listen to the messages conveyed by the music, and to keep a tally of the frequency of mention of escape, irresponsibility, the aggrandizing of drugs, revolution, and similar concepts, and of suggestions of hope, solutions, the strength of the individual, or other positive or optimistic attitudes. Some may argue that these lyrics only express the deep despair and pessimism of the younger generation, and that they would not sell as they do unless they struck some meaningful note in the mass of our youth. I grant that they do reflect the attitudes of *some* of our young people, but would point out in turn that they are designed to appeal more broadly by suggesting a way of life in which impulses are instantly gratified, troubles are whisked away by the dulling effect of drugs, and freedom is absolute. Powerful incentives these are to adolescents, who are normally plagued by developmental problems, and are encouraged in the pursuit of instant ease, quick solutions, and total comfort without responsibility by the behavior of some of their noisy contemporaries and in many instances by their parents. Thus, the general conditions of society produce, contribute to, and interact with the irresponsibility of the minority to encourage the stable child to doubt, and the marginal one to adopt one or more of the destructive escapist patterns offered him by the "new culture."

The same pattern, or a very similar one, is seen in many other areas of activity pointed toward our young people. We are constantly bombarded by antisociety propaganda, pretending to be entertainment, which extols the virtues of drugs,

212

revolution, defiance of authority, and the destruction of the existing system. As an example, let me cite a recent experience. A fourteen-year-old girl, suffering from deep feelings of self-doubt and chronic worry about her popularity, obtained a book on drugs from her school library. The book, ostensibly a diary kept by an adolescent girl, was a chronicle of how the principal figure had found happiness, new insight, a circle of beautiful friends who accepted her, independence from her parents, self-realization, and contact with the infinite, by getting deeply into a variety of drugs. The naivete, hollowness, and underlying despair of the diarist were apparent only if the book were read carefully and with sophisticated attention to clinical signs. The fourteen-year-old did not read the book carefully, and completely lacked any clinical sensitivity to the diarist's deeper feelings. Nor did she read the brief epilogue, which told of the girl's death from an overdose; as a result, she was left with the feeling that drugs were the greatest thing going, and all but came to the conclusion that they would solve her problems. Admittedly, the girl already had problems, without which the book's seductive message might not have been as effective. But if there had been no seductive message to begin with, would the possibility of solving her problems through taking drugs have occurred to her at all? And if drugs had not invaded the youth culture at all, would children be worse off, or would other, less destructive options for the solution of their problems be more attractive to them? Certainly no one book tips the scales for any one child, but when the use of drugs is chronically advocated, either directly or in subtle ways, the total set of messages and conditions *does* make a difference in the lives of a great number of children.

Not only drugs are thus promoted. A whole range of impulses, disguised as entertainment or education, press for immediate gratification. Promiscuous sex, without depth of emotional experience or commitment to the other person, is promoted by appeals to total freedom, and supported by ugly pornography, underground films, and word-of-mouth smut. Total instant comfort is promised in the guise of freedom. Anger and alienation are encouraged in the name of justified resistance to the oppression of parents, schools, the system. Perhaps the best way to illustrate the means and ends of those who advocate the counterculture is to quote from their own statements of purpose and tactics. The following, from a mimeographed handout distributed widely to young people, was signed by the Minister of Information of the White Panther Party, more recently called the Rainbow People's Party.

First I must say that this statement, like all statements is bullsh—— without an active program to back it up. We have a program which is on-going and total and which must not be confused with anything that is said or written about it.

Our program is cultural revolution through a total assault on the culture, which makes use of every tool, every energy and every media we can get our collective hands on. We take our program with us everywhere we go and use any means necessary to expose people to it.

Our culture, our art, the music, newspapers, books, posters, our clothing, our homes, the way we walk and talk, the way our hair grows, the way we smoke dope and f—— and eat and sleep—it is all one message, and the message is FREEDOM!

We are free mother country madmen in charge of our own lives and we are taking this freedom to the peoples of America in the streets, in ballrooms and teen-clubs, in their front rooms watching tv, in their bedrooms reading the Fifth Estate or the Sun, or jacking off or smoking secret dope, in their schools where we come and talk to them or make our music in their weird gymnasiums—they love it—we represent the only contemporary life-style in America for its kids and it should be known that these kids are READY!

They're ready to move but they don't know how, and all we do is show them that they can get away with it. BE FREE, goddamnit, and f—— all them old dudes, is what we tell them, and they can see that we mean it. The only influence we have, the only thing that touches them, is that we are for real. We are FREE, we are a bunch of arrogant motherf——ers and we don't give a damn for any cop or any phony-ass authority control-addict creep who wants to put us down. I heard Stokely Carmichael in 1966 call for "20 million arrogant black men" as America's salvation, and there are a lot of arrogant black motherf——ers in the streets today—for the first time in America—and for the first time in America there are a generation of visionary maniac white mother country dope fiend rock and roll freeks [*sic*] who are ready to get down and kick out the jams—ALL THE JAMS— break everything loose and free everybody from their very real and imaginary prisons—even the chumps and punks and hunkies who are always f——ing with us. We demand total freedom for everybody!

And we will not be stopped until we get it. We are bad. We will not be f——ed with. Like Hassan I Sabbah The Old Man of the Mountain we initiate no hostile moves, but when moved against we will mobilize our forces for a total assault. We have been moved against every day of our lives in this weirdo country, and we are moving now to overturn this motherf——er, scrape the sh—— off it and turn it back over to all the people. All power to the people! Black power to black people! As Brother Eldridge Cleaver says, the sh—— is going down and there's only two kinds of people on the planet: those who make up the problem, and those who make up the solution.

WE ARE THE SOLUTION. We have no "problems." Everything is free for everybody. Money sucks. Leaders suck. Underwear sucks. School sucks. The white honkie culture that has been handed to us on a silver plastic platter is meaningless to us! We don't want it! *F—— God in the ass. F—— everybody you can get your hands on.*

Our program of rock and roll, dope and f——ing in the streets is a program of total freedom for everyone. And we are totally committed to carrying out our program. We breathe revolution. We are LSD-driven total maniacs in the universe. We will do anything we can to drive people crazy out of their heads and into their bodies.

Rock and roll music is the spearhead of our attack because it's so effective and so much fun. We have developed organic high-energy guerrilla bands who are infiltrating the popular culture and destroying millions of minds in the process. The MC5 is the most beautiful example.

The MC5 is totally committed to the revolution. With our music and our economic genius we plunder the unsuspecting straight world for money and the means to carry out our program, and revolutionize its children at the same time.

And with our entrance into the straight media we have demonstrated to the honkies that anything they do to f—— with us will be exposed to their children. You don't need to get rid of all the honkies, you just rob them of their replacements and let the breed atrophy and die out, with its heirs cheering triumphantly all around it.

We don't have guns yet—not all of us anyway—because *we have more powerful weapons—direct access to millions of teenagers is one of our most potent,* and their belief in us is another. But we will use guns if we have to—we will do anything—if we have to.

We have no illusions. Knowing the power of symbols in the abstract world of Americans we have taken the White Panther as our mark to symbolize in our strength and arrogance and to demonstrate our commitment to the program of the Black Panther Party as well as to our own—indeed, the two programs are the same.

The actions of the Black Panthers in America have inspired us and given us strength, as has the music of black America, and we are moving to reflect that strength in our daily activity just as our music contains and extends the power and feeling of the black magic music that originally informed our bodies and told us that we could be free.

I might mention Brother James Brown in this connection, as well as John Coltrane and Archie Shepp. Sun-Ra. LeRoi Jones. Malcome [*sic*] X. Huey P. Newton, Bobby Seale, Eldridge Cleaver, these are magic names to us. These are men in America. And we're as crazy as they are, and as pure. We're bad.

WHITE PANTHER PARTY 10-POINT PROGRAM
1. Full endorsement and support of Black Panther Party's 10-Point Program.

2. Total assault on the culture by any means necessary, including rock and roll, dope, and f——ing in the streets;
3. Free exchange of energy and materials—we demand the end of money!
4. Free food, clothes, housing, dope, music, bodies, medical care—everything! free for everybody;
5. Free access to information media—free the technology from the greed creeps!
6. Free time & space for all humans—dissolve all unnatural boundaries;
7. Free all schools and all structures from corporate rule—turn the buildings over to the people at once!
8. Free all prisoners everywhere—they are our brothers;
9. Free all soldiers at once—no more conscripted armies;
10. Free the people from their "leaders"—leaders suck—all power to all the people—freedom means free everyone!

Can this nauseating rot be real? Can anything so steeped in hatred, obscenity, and abject degradation be anything but the rantings of a sick mind, to be regarded with the compassion due a person so deeply troubled that his delusions of power and grandeur become translated into such a degree of irrationality and destructiveness? Yet it is real, and not only to the mind that spews this vile message into society. It is real to young people who are prompted thereby into lives of total alienation and uselessness. It is real to heartsick parents who see their children drawn into it, and whose efforts to salvage them are met with the paranoid belief that whatever parents try to do is a hypocritical fraud designed to oppress. And it is real to those of us who offer our professional energies to repair the broken lives and the lost minds, only to find our efforts rebuffed because such tripe has led the victims to believe that our goal is to turn them into political prisoners. And the man whose name appears under these writings was recently heroized in the Sunday magazine section of a major newspaper as representing the glorious freedom of the new culture.

How can this offal appeal to anyone? The tactic amounts to nothing more than trying to call into action the basest hostilities, sexual desires, viciousness, and urges toward complete irresponsibility that can develop in a troubled young person. It is an appeal of the disturbed to the troubled, the vicious to the hostile, and the licentious to the frustrated. And while the form of this appeal quoted above is particularly stagnant, milder but unmistakable evidences of it are found in the music, movies, books, and even newspapers of the entire society. Senseless, mindless, irrational, and subversive of any civilization, no matter what its political complexion, it is peddled in the name of peace, freedom, escape, and promise of contact with the mysteries of the infinite. As a political program or a way of life, it contains nothing even the most radical leftist with a trace of intellect would claim as his own. But as a means of destroying individual lives and thereby eventually of subverting a civilization, it has an effect. Every young person in whom parents or society have failed to develop a sense of decency, discipline, and competence is a ripe target for the attack of such slime-mold philosophizing. Every child thus lost represents a loss to all of us and to all of civilized society. It is impossible to believe that even our worst enemies in the world would deliberately conspire to inflict such degradation on us, but the effect is as successful a subversion of our national system as anything they might have planned. Even worse, our own attitudes implicitly encourage this way of life, by allowing conditions to exist in which personal problems or inadequacies are blamed on the system, personality accountability is nowhere demanded, and total self-indulgence is a credible alternative to productive effort and discipline.

What are the realities of life in the counterculture? Does such an existence really bring the peace, love, and beauty its adherents claim to believe in? Is there in fact a new birth of freedom, a deeper meaning, and a more satisfying sort of relationship with other human beings, marked by respect and altruism? Certain scattered hippie groups are sincerely trying to find these values in communal arrangements, where they strive for a simple life in pastoral conditions, trying to make a living through craft work or primitive agriculture. Some of

218

these may be succeeding, although in a world of competitive technology, they have to be most committed and willing to sacrifice much of the guaranteed security of the affluent society. Again, a large-scale commitment to such activity would appear highly impractical in a world where many other peoples are striving mightily to lift themselves out of just such an existence. A couple of billion people already living at the level the hippies seek, would gladly trade places and enjoy the benefits of our productivity. Moreover, if a substantial portion of our people decided to drop out of the system, there are other nations eager to take over both the work and the responsibility of a powerful industrial-technological complex. Thus, the hippie life may be a valid and successful escape for a tiny minority who cannot tolerate the demands of our modern society, but it is not a very practical solution to our problems.

In the more typical situation, however, even that much of an ideal of a more humane life is not found. Time and time again, both clinically and socially, one sees that those who participate in such excursions into the counterculture eventually express in those settings the same deeply defective qualities of personality that led them there in the first place. Whatever the dream, the street life and the counterculture, in reality, are gathering grounds for human despair, marked by anger, alienation, hatred, emptiness, and loneliness. Under the banner of love, sex takes on a loveless, dehumanized quality, without depth or commitment. People are simply used, in a hopeless effort by the unsatisfiable to gain instant satisfaction. Indolence and indifference are everywhere, fed by psychological withdrawal, a basic inability to deal with deep relationships, and the blurring effect of drugs. Freedom means aimless wandering on the streets, with no purpose and no real satisfaction, or languishing in a dirty pad, where the level of personal hygiene and sense of competence is so low as to further degrade self-respect. Selfishness and greed are practiced under the pretext of a commitment to sharing in the common good. Altogether, this life style turns out to be an unappetizing, unsatisfying, destructive exercise in hatred and futility, although many young people do not awaken to this fact until their lives are seriously damaged, often beyond repair. The price of momentary escape into the counterculture is either a lifelong handicap of wasted years, blown minds, permanent damage to vital relationships, and lost potential, or a hard way back by learning about the realities of the world through bitter experience.

Drug use among young people is rapidly becoming a national calamity. Because of easy access and permissive attitudes, it is a rare child who does not feel the temptation to get into the drug scene. The reasons why young people get into drugs are very complex, and again relate to conditions that permeate society as a whole. A recapitulation of these conditions would be tedious for the reader, and in fact is not needed. It is merely necessary to recognize two things: first, that the drug culture offers the psychologically disturbed young person a very enticing promise of easy solutions to problems; and second, that the effect of the widespread use of drugs is both destructive of individual lives and completely subversive of a society based on reason, discipline, and productivity.

The drug scene has a tremendous psychological appeal to children who suffer from a variety of disturbances growing out of the defects of our society. I have never seen a young person get into drugs who did not already have a serious problem in his relationships with his parents or peers, suffer from a sense of personal inadequacy, or have difficulty in dealing with discipline and authority. Basically, the adoption of drugs by children as a means of dealing with personal problems (an analogy to the use of alcohol by their elders) is a neurotic solution characterized by escape, self-destructive acting out, and symptomatic expression of deep personal conflict. Like all other neurotic solutions, drug use is no solution at all, since it provides only temporary escape from the conflict without offering any real or permanent resolution of the underlying difficulty. In fact, it is worse than many of the familiar neurotic patterns, because the psychological and physical effects of most, it not all, the drugs in common use actually destroy or gravely interfere with the person's abilities to develop a more appropriate and satisfying solution. In any case, the drug scene is an enticing alternative for the disturbed child, both in its immediate effects on the functioning of his mind, and also in the sense of offering a subculture where he is able to hide from his personal problems.

The general effect of many of the common drugs, including marijuana, on mental functions is to create an artificial sense of well-being, loss of inhibition, excitement, and euphoria. The user is enabled to forget, his awareness is blurred and he is taken away from his worries, and generally he escapes from frustration. Many people use alcohol for the same purposes, without suffering any permanent ill effects so long as moderation is practiced. Of course, the long-term effects of alcohol on the nervous system and other vital parts of the body are not such as to recommend its intensive or frequent use. Unlike alcohol, however, some drugs, such as LSD and mescaline in particular, but also marijuana, create the illusion that the fantasies and supposed insights experienced have a validity in the *real* world, so that their continued and repeated use is encouraged. While there is no comprehensive research to prove this to the satisfaction of those who are into the drug scene, the clinical evidence is unmistakable. In addition, many of the drugs in general use are frequently laced with frank poisons, such as strychnine, or physiologically addicting substances such as cocaine, heroin, or other opiates.

Such drugs serve as a means of escape from tension by dulling consciousness, providing a high, and seeming to make the world—at least momentarily—a more simple and pleasant place. If this were their only appeal, we would not be facing such a calamitous problem. Beyond its immediate effect on acute consciousness, however, the drug scene meets a series of pressing, albeit neurotic, psychological and social needs. For the child lacking confidence in himself and in his ability to make friends, it provides a group of associates who are themselves so dissatisfied that they make no demands for standards, performance, or even basic integrity. In this sense, the drug subculture is a peculiar society of the damned, the inadequate, and the irresolute, bound together not in any positive relationship, but by a mutual haplessness. For the affection-starved, it offers the initial appearance of acceptance and love, about which much is made, although the capacity for love based on intense commitment is seldom seen among devotees of the drug scene. For the frustrated and hostile, it offers a way of escaping from and defying parents and the larger society. For the overindulged, it offers the promise of undisturbed comfort and freedom from responsibility. For the marginal psychotic, it offers validation of his delusions by suggesting that everyone is as crazy as he is. For those lacking in a sense of personal identity, it offers group membership, a sense of importance, a reward for being cool, and a special experience of being "in," which is enhanced by its special vocabulary, ritual, and mystique. For the adolescent looking for excitement or risk, it offers the titillation of doing the forbidden and the dangerous. For the sexually deviant, it offers an opportunity for gratification without judgment, sanctions, human investment, or accountability. In short, the drug scene offers a self-defined subculture in which neurotic emptiness and social alienation are encouraged as a legitimate way of life.

Beyond this, based on extensive clinical experience with several score young people who are or have been into the drug scene, I am convinced that the use of hallucinogenic drugs *or marijuana* results in long-lasting and perhaps permanent effects on attitudes and intellectual functioning, and it will take more than the flaccid testimony of drug advocates to unconvince me. The syndrome and progression of symptoms are very clear. At the first level, the typical effects of intoxication, listed earlier, are seen. Next the user develops a longer-lasting attitude of indifference and noninvolvement in the affairs of his own life. He becomes complacent and somewhat detached, and his motivation for school or work slackens. He presents the appearance of simply not caring about himself, his human relationships, or his future. Next, there is an increasing abstractness and superficiality in the way he thinks about things, to the point where his logical ability is interfered with. Associated with this is a lessening of his ability to delve deeply or rigorously into problems, or to maintain mental discipline. It becomes too much of an effort to organize himself, or to attack a problem of any complexity. Next, there is an increasing belief that he has found some mystical new insight, road to truth, or spiritual contact with the infinite, although whatever content there is in this truth or insight cannot be communicated to another person. At the same time, he rapidly loses the ability to examine himself or his ideas critically, either becoming completely vague and circumstantial, or defensive and antagonistic at the raising of questions about his idea. Finally, he becomes confused, totally detached, incapable of reasoned discussion, and often shows a distinctly paranoid outlook.

Thus, both in its social and its psychological effects, the drug scene is a very bad scene. It supports maladaptive solutions, and it gradually robs the individual of the motivation and mental tools to help himself or to be helped. And drugs pose a particularly serious threat to everyone, not only to young people, for they and the subculture surrounding them are an expression of some very basic weaknesses in society—the loss of discipline, the waning sense of individual importance, the search for total comfort, permissiveness, and a decline in our devotion to rational processes, as opposed to emotion, in the solution of problems. Rather than offering a basis for overcoming these weaknesses and solving our problems, the drug scene multiplies them by seeming to be an answer, or a plausible way of life, to many young people. Thus a downward and self-perpetuating cycle is established, the breaking of which does not seem in sight at the moment.

Further, the basic institutions of society, which we would ordinarily expect to serve as a counterforce to the growing decadence, are themselves being weakened. Starting with an example of prime importance, it is clear that the family, as a social institution, is far less effective now than it was only a few years ago in providing a base for the development of children with the necessary strength and discipline to resist the spreading decadence. The reasons for this are complex, but many of them revolve around the fact that parents, as well as children, are caught up in the comfort-seeking orgy of the affluent society. In many liberal middle-class families, so much money and leisure time is available that satisfaction and relaxation are habitually sought outside the home. Getting out of the home is looked forward to as a release from pressure. Spending nights or weekends away has come to be the primary way of having "fun" in many such families. While the children may occasionally accompany the parents on these jaunts into the glittering world of fun, the message to them is clear nonetheless—home is a place to eat and sleep, but not a central source of gratification. In this way, the close ties of the family, which provide a basis for later loyalty and influence, are subtly weakened. In extreme cases, the children are regarded as impediments to the freedom of the parents, and are tucked in early, left with a babysitter, or otherwise disposed of while the parents turn their attention to the "real" fun offered by their affluence. In this way, the implicit notion that the child is of little real importance is conveyed, and it is not surprising that some of the psychological glue sticking families together gradually dries and breaks away. Another variation on this theme is the condition of the overworked, overbusy father, and the harassed, irritable, demanding mother. The father is so busy with the pursuit of even greater affluence that he has no time to be a father in the traditional sense of the word. As a result, the combined responsibilities of nursemaid, housewife, taxi driver, and disciplinarian fall on the mother, and she feels overpowered and irritated. When the father does come home, the mother feels that he should meet her needs, and the kids too often take a back seat. Following the pattern set by the parents, the kids either program themselves into a frantic round of organized activities, or gradually drift out of the family circle to find their gratifications in the streets, with peers who are similarly handled at home, and in a variety of other activities offering little real psychological gratification. In the meantime, the parents try to make up for their lack of real commitment to the children by supplying a never-ending stream of "things" as assurances that they really love them, and the pattern of material indulgence, permissiveness, and lack of discipline, which I have commented on at length, gets established. Small wonder that such parents lose control of their children, and that the children begin to feel alienated and to detest the materialism their parents use as a substitute for not meeting their real responsibilities to the kids. Perhaps we must once again recognize that being a parent is a full-time responsibility, and that the adequate discharge of that responsibility may not be compatible with full-time indulgence of oneself in the affluent society.

Not only is the family losing its influence as a point of reference and satisfaction in the society, it is also losing its moral and educational force as well. More and more of the responsibilities for raising children are being turned over to outside agencies. More and more, the temptations of the affluent society are producing unethical or morally destructive actions on the part of parents. Too many parents are caught up in alcohol and cigarettes to be in a position of strength when arguing about promiscuous sex or drugs. It does not surprise me in the least to hear accusations of hypocrisy and immorality flow out of the mouths of young radicals, since these are facts of life to which many of them are exposed in their own homes. And if not in their homes, then in the surrounding society, where the exploitative sexual gymnastics of public figures become a reason for amusement or applause, and where the easy way to affluence through cheating on your income tax is admired. Morality, like love, peace, charity, and respect for other human beings, begins at home, and if we want clean, strong, purposive, disciplined children, we ought to set a constant example of these things in ourselves and our neighborhoods.

Many secondary social institutions are also being weakened as a constructive influence upon young people. The neighborhood, rather than representing a unified common base for small groups with common values and common interests, is now more often a place to park the car, mow the lawn, or attend a monthly social blast. People do not find an identity or a base in the neighborhood, and the mutually strengthening interpersonal relationships of a former day have given way to a sense of isolation within which everyone goes off in all directions, doing their own things. This is reflected in the lives of the children, who at an early age begin to go somewhere else to find support and satisfaction. The community rarely demonstrates a common purpose, with the result that no one takes any responsibility for anyone else, and particularly not for anyone else's children. There is little reinforcement of standards and limits on children, even when they are still small enough to confine their activities to the nearby area, and an important element of community participation in the process of developing discipline is lost.

I have already discussed the schools; it is only necessary here to add that they too, for a variety of reasons, no longer have much real influence on children, at least insofar as setting common standards and expectations is concerned. The semblance of community participation in the affairs of the school, and the immediate collaboration of schools and parents when it comes to dealing with a difficult problem in a child's behavior, seems destined to be lost, sacrificed to the social manipulators' belief that it is more important to assign

225

children to schools by racial quota than it is to keep parents directly involved in the control of their own neighborhood schools.

As far as society's other institutions are concerned, the pattern of declining influence on children, with a consequent loss of standards, mutually supportive expectations, and gratification of the child's needs for points of reference and reliable social groups within which to define himself and find security, is seen everywhere. The traditional activity groups, such as the scouts, are hard put to compete in immediate excitement and impulse gratification with the glitter of neon-lighted rock bands and juvenile nightclubs, even though such programs offer many gratifications that are needed but lacking in the life of the middle-class suburban child. The youth programs of some religious institutions have deteriorated to the point that they offer the young person the same kind of vacuous search for "experience" and "deeper philosophical meaning" that is offered, only slightly modified, in the alien-ated ramblings of the counterculture. Some religious institutions, rather than serving in their appropriate role as exemplars of moral and ethical standards, have become so preoccupied with political action and social do-gooding that they seem more concerned with social welfare than with God. Those which have not are subject to attack because their more traditional devotions are not viewed as relevant by liberal critics. Nationality groups, social clubs, lodges, fraternal organizations, and other examples of the "square" life have either fallen victim to the instant pleasure of the affluent society, or have declined because they require long-term commitment of their members. Indeed, all of society's secondary institutions have been subverted in one way or another by the rising tide of cynicism, supposed sophistication, and sneering negativism toward anything that smacks of tradition or conventionality.

As a final comment on the role of social institutions in American life, it is worth taking a brief look at the law, for it is the ultimate force standing between an ordered, civilized society on the one hand, and chaos, anarchy, and the jungle on the other. I have already mentioned the characteristic antagonism of the radicals for the police, and have shown its sources. Belabored by such hateful attacks, and handicapped by the occasional intemperate use of authority, society's law enforcement agencies are the subject of declining respect. Police contact with the public is as impersonal and bureaucratized as that of any other agency of government. As the symbol and literal expression of discipline and limits, the police come in for particular unpopularity in a society increasingly devoted to notions of total freedom and self-indulgence. In the police, the radicals and a great segment of the liberal-intellectual community see the threat of some degree of control over their personal wishes to define reality in their own way, and their attitude and influence is seen in campaigns to take away from law enforcement agencies the tools that might be used to impede this drive toward absolute self-determination. And while a small minority of those who chronically castigate the police might indeed be able to behave in a civilized fashion under conditions of anarchy, they are somewhat foolish to assume that everyone would act the same way. In any case, the police, like the other traditional institutions of society, have been substantially weakened in their efforts to maintain order, with damaging results to the processes of a civilized society. To paraphrase a bumper sticker that was current a few months ago, "If you hate the police, the next time you're in trouble you should call a liberal-intellectual or a hippie." Of course, to the extent that the police are criticized, the FBI is subject to even more vituperative attacks by the anarchy-seekers. In liberal-radical circles, the FBI is regarded as the oppressive arm of a police state, peeping in every keyhole, maintaining secret files on everyone, and generally attacking the individual's freedom and privacy. It is interesting to note that organized crime and the radical left have a common stake in discrediting or weakening the FBI. Both crime and chaos benefit from the subversion of the law enforcement process, one for illicit material gain and the other in the pursuit of anarchy.

In the meantime, the rest of society suffers. In large cities, hoodlums and criminals of every description create conditions in which the average citizen must fear for his life and property. Drug pushers operate openly, not only in the central cities, but increasingly in the suburbs. In the schools, children who are trying to mind their own business and go about the process of getting an education, are intimidated, harassed, or beaten. In some, children are unable to go to the bathroom for fear of being assaulted or robbed. Extortion and molestation are frequent, even in some elementary schools. And school authorities, law enforcement officials, and concerned parents and citizens seem powerless to interrupt this progression toward chaos.

In these developments, the courts have played a vital part. Following the example set by the United States Supreme Court, the judicial system has gradually circumscribed the activities of the police to the point where effective law enforcement is next to impossible. In certain jurisdictions, things have reached the point that a full adversary proceeding is necessary if parents wish to enforce their wishes that the child adhere to reasonable standards of conduct, such as coming in at a prescribed hour. It is not unusual for both parents and child to be represented by counsel, and some attorneys who thus represent children seem more interested in getting vicarious kicks from encouraging the child in his incorrigibility than in preserving the law or the general social order. At the national level, we have seen the gradual erosion of the rights of parents, communities, local and state governments, and law enforcement agencies to deal with their own affairs or to bring disciplinary influence to bear on disturbed children, who are acting out their problems against society, or on people whose general irresponsibility and defiance of the law poses a threat to the social order. All this has been done in the name of extending personal freedom, supposedly as guaranteed by the Constitution. But the Constitution has been stretched and warped in the hands of a court that is not guided by the principle of whether a matter is logically supported by a reasonable interpretation of the document, or by the intent of the framers of those inspired articles, but rather by a highly subjective interpretation based on some momentary concept of "right" or "social justice." Even stranger are the contradictions in the court's own actions. The court seems to assume that certain persons, or classes of persons, are guided by the highest considerations of decency and altruism, devoted to building a better society, and deeply concerned for the common good. Thus, loopholes are found in the law to permit convicted criminals to be freed on technicalities of the narrowest sort, the rights of the accused taking precedence over society's right to protection, and the wildest possible definitions of personal freedom dominating a concern for an ordered society. At the same time, and almost in the same breath, the court gives no credit to the general public, on either an altruistic or a pragmatic basis, to move freely to remove racial discrimination, to take individual action to deal with other social problems, or otherwise to behave as rational or decent human beings. In these areas, the rights of the individual to come to his own conclusions and to exercise his freedom of personal choice are more and more tightly limited, and the supremacy of government over the individual is vigorously asserted. It seems only reasonable that if the United States Supreme Court is going to base its actions on the concept of faith in the individual's ability to make the right choices in pursuit of the common good, as was contemplated by Jefferson and the other architects of the republic, the justices should apply that concept consistently, and should strive to reestablish social and psychological conditions in which the people have a right to make those choices, and general conditions of society encouraging disciplined participation in the decision-making process. But to foster at the same time a situation in which complete individual freedom is allowed in certain areas, and no effort is made to maintain individual responsibility for taking reasoned actions in other areas, seems at best inconsistent, and at worst totally shortsighted and destructive.

I have referred repeatedly in this book to the effects of uncontrolled comfort-seeking on society. In the family, the neighborhood, the schools, the communities, and even in the courts, the easy, expedient way has become dominant. This attitude also operates in other areas, with perhaps even greater implications for the breakdown of our society. In public life, in business, in the educational institutions, we see example after example of the individual who pursues his responsibilities with much greater attention to avoiding personal discomfort, inconvenience, or stress than to the principles involved or the long-run good. In their search for peace, or in an effort to avoid confrontation, such individuals chronically give in, compromise, or mediate because a forthright stand, which might cause them some loss of comfort or popularity, is not regarded as expedient. Their actions are easily rationalized as a means of keeping things quiet, responding to the legitimate complaints of vocal pressure groups, or playing the role of the detached peacemaker. When such behavior appears throughout society, and when supposedly responsible people constantly compromise and pass the buck, the system itself is the loser, and all of us with it.

Consider the following example, which I have invented for illustrative purposes. Suppose a child, at the age of six or seven, begins to insist on having his own way. His parents do not try to control him because they do not want him to be upset or angry with them; they give in. Next, the child begins to terrorize or intimidate his contemporaries in school. Partly because they don't want the struggle, partly because they don't know how, and partly because they are afraid of the parents, the school authorities do not attempt to correct the misbehavior either. Or, if they try, the parents accuse them of harming the child, either psychologically or physically, and with the help of a lawyer and/or the courts, make the school back off. In some cases the school treats the child not as a disciplinary problem but as a mental health problem, which indeed he may be. In any event, the child is taken to a psychologist or psychiatrist. While a growing number of my colleagues recognize the necessity for their being a party to and a participant in the process of setting and enforcing reasonable limits, too many still take the position that the child can do no wrong, or that it is their responsibility to "treat" the child and someone else's to set limits on his behavior. This abdication of responsibility is rationalized in terms of the need to maintain a "relationship" with the child, and they take it for granted that a relationship is impossible without continued indulgence and implicit approval of all of his behavior. In any case, the child's behavior is not controlled at this level, either. Next, the child moves to more overt antisocial actions, and encounters the police. The police are regarded as unsympathetic or brutal if they do not treat him with kid gloves. Next, the juvenile court, where the mental health exercise may be run through again, but where the application of effective limits on or sanctions against the child's misbehavior is rare. Soon the child is seventeen or eighteen—regarded as an adult in the eyes of the law. He then commits an act of major social destructiveness, and again the pattern of justification, excuse, and standing aside by the institutions of the society occurs. At each step, the youngster has learned an important lesson—that nothing is really *his* fault, that whatever happens to him can be blamed on society, and worst of all, that if he is clever enough or obnoxious enough, he can cause the threatened limits to crumble away. Finally, the child, now a young adult, stands face to face with a private citizen or a police officer on the street. The child wants something. The citizen resists, or the policeman tries to stop him. The child has a gun or a knife. The ultimate confrontation occurs, postponed since the day the child first said, "I will not," to his parents: in it the child, the policeman, or the citizen dies. Society's failure to bring home responsibility and discipline to the child at any of the previous steps finally results in tragedy. For no matter how many false messages we give the child about his own omnipotence, sooner or later he will confront the reality of civilized life: namely, that he cannot always have everything his own way.

The process just described occurs in many other forms and areas of our national life, and with parallel consequences. Every time a supposedly responsible person stands aside to let a tough question go by, the point of attack of the individual or group making the demand moves up a level or two in the system. This pattern is very familiar on college campuses, and its similarity to the previous example is easily seen. Suppose that a small group of students in one college of a major university decide that they want something; for instance, the abolition of all defense-related research at the university. At first, they approach a professor or two, who might meet their responsibility to the community by explaining the relationship and mutual interdependence of the university and the national security. But they do not, either because they do not see it, do not care about it, or basically sympathize with the students' position. The attack then moves up a step, perhaps to a dean. The dean doesn't stand up to the issue, because most of the defense research is done in a different college of the university, and besides, why should he be bothered with arguing with students? Then to a vice president, whose efforts to deal with the attack are swept away by intimidation and pressure tactics. Then to the president, who decides that the issue can be compromised in some way, since the entire community must have some common purpose and a way can certainly be found to harmonize any minor difference. Then to the governing board, which may try to take a stand, but is eventually persuaded by various political considerations that it is really better to give in. The process then moves outside the institution, and various sectors and levels of the national system are attacked. Finally, the demand may reach the President of the nation. And there, the buck stops. There the confrontation, which should have occurred a long time before, finally does occur, just as it did with the teen-ager pointing the gun at the policeman. There, finally, the ultimate requirement that the individual moderate his demands in the interests of the common social good is applied.

These are, perhaps, contrived examples, but the point is clear. Each time a supposedly responsible person or group stands aside instead of confronting an unreasonable demand, the demand moves somewhere else, gaining momentum as it does. Finally, the irrationality, finding no other foe, confronts the system, sometimes with very dire results. Thus, each time a supposedly responsible person, like a parent, a teacher, a juvenile judge, a university president, or a senator from the loyal opposition, buys himself a little peace, popularity, or precarious potency by compromising with unreason or mediating with madness, a little bit of the integrity of our civilization is lost. In the final analysis, it is not merely the President of the United States who has a stake in bringing home responsibility and discipline, it is every one of us. There is an old saying that a chain is as strong as its weakest link; where the chain of responsible action in the face of unreasonable demands is concerned, sad to say, we have a lot of very weak links.

To a great degree, however, we get what we ask for and want in those whom we put in positions of responsibility. The sort of behavior we see at various levels of our public life would not be long pursued if it did not meet with some approval from most of us. In the interest of immediate peace and comfort, we implicitly demand the compromise that quells the noise, the expedient act by a public figure that allows us to go undisturbed through another day of affluence, and the buck-passing that puts a little more distance between us and the problem. Perhaps we are not encouraging irresponsibility in a studied way, but the effect of our own not wanting to stand up and face issues squarely is the same. Do you believe that we would tolerate a national leader who told it like it is, who said that we are in deep trouble as a nation, that the mark of decadence is upon us, that we are soft and flabby and over-indulged, and that our children are the same, that other peoples are moving while we are resting, and that a national and personal sacrifice of immense proportion is going to be necessary if we are to save ourselves and our way of life? Do you believe that anyone who said that we had to trim our standard of living by 20 percent, or reduce government expenditures by 10 percent, or limit ourselves to a two-week vacation with no long weekends would have any chance at being elected to anything? Do you believe that Thomas Jefferson or James Monroe or Abraham Lincoln or Theodore Roosevelt could be elected President of the United States today? I doubt it, because men of this stripe would demand too much sacrifice, would expect too much of the individual, would not tolerate enough foolishness, or would in other ways be too tough or forthright or uncompromising to make us comfortable. At a time in our history when we should cry out for the kind of leadership that would restore to us a sense of dignity, decency, purpose, and individual strength, we seem satisfied to pursue pap, pablum, and pleasant propaganda. Rather than face the momentary stress of supporting a leader who might call us back to responsible action, we allow our general comfort-seeking to force our public men to present only the bright, the complimentary, and the optimistic, and thus we make it most difficult for them to take the needed strong stand, the responsible action, and the principled position. Until we understand and communicate to those seeking leadership that we are prepared to face things as they are, rather than as we would like them to be, we will get individuals in seats of responsibility who place the easy, short-run, expedient, pleasant, and comfortable action ahead of the ethical, principled, long-run, responsible, and disciplined. The price of saying no to a nonnegotiable demand may be immense personal pressure, castigation, and even terrorization, and any responsible person who tries to say no will find comfort and strength if he can feel that he is not alone.

The growing decadence in our society is nowhere clearer than in the area of human relationships. Respect for the dignity of other human beings is at a low ebb. With the general subversion of authority and the erosion of discipline, the notion that "it's all right—you don't have to" seems to apply to even the most basic consideration for manners, courtesy, and respect for the feelings of others. Many children feel no hesitation in cursing parents or teachers, physically abusing their peers, vandalizing property, or scrawling obscenities on the walls of public places. Vile epithets, crude personal insults, slanderous and irresponsible accusations flow freely in the vernacular of radicals, certain hippies, and some of the general adolescent population. "Nigger," "honkie," "racist" are hurled freely across the racial aisle at public meetings and private hate sessions. The sex act is degraded to the level of animalism in the speech and vernacular of the street people, the supposedly liberated, the deviant, and the purveyors of pornography. Simple kindness, loving respect, appreciation, and mutual consideration are increasingly rare elements in our treatment of one another, and even though many of us make a deliberate effort to communicate such attitudes toward those we are in contact with, cynicism and negativism are as much dominant attitudes in dealings among people as they are in the general outlook of the society. Part of the quality of a civilization is reflected in how its individual members treat one another, and it would appear that considerate expressions toward our fellow human beings are not regarded as being of very high priority.

In this chapter, I have examined some of the generally unnoticed forces that are eating away at the vitality of our national life and system. The evidence suggests strongly that much of the social glue sustaining our kind of civilization is coming unstuck. Such evidence exists in: 1) the growing tendency of both individuals and groups to reject reason and intellect as legitimate bases for solving problems; 2) the opportunity for emotion and bias to determine what information reaches the public; 3) the loss of commitment to productive work; 4) the "do your own thing" philosophy; 5) the influence of the alienated counterculture; 6) the spreading use of drugs; 7) the breakdown of our basic social institutions; 8) the loss of discipline in society; 9) the failure of those in positions of responsibility to stand up to tough decisions; and 10) the degradation of human relationships. No ten-point program could have been devised more effectively to subvert our culture and destroy our civilization. It is not the young radicals who endanger the American system, it is the decadence of a society which has forgotten the sources of its own strength—strength, which if mobilized and applied, is ample to flick away the effect of the radicals, crush out the malaise of the counterculture, restore discipline, responsibility, and order, solve the myriad of generally recognized problems, and bring back to ourselves and our nation a sense of pride, competence, and decency.

XII
QUO VADIS, AMERICA?

It is too early to predict with certainty whither America will go in the next few decades. However, it is apparent what is going to happen to our nation, and to us with it, if we keep to the path we are now on. The details cannot be foreseen, but that we will suffer a disastrous decline is inevitable. One of two things will happen. We may slide further and further into the decadence of undisciplined self-indulgence, gradually becoming weaker, more dissolute, more plagued by internal strife and disorder, and less able to sustain our competitive position in the world. More vigorous and more determined peoples, striving for conditions of life we have already attained, will assume power and responsibility in the world, and we will fall to them either by military conquest or by a gradual process of economic and ideological subversion. The alternative is almost equally drab. Those among us who retain their strength and discipline, almost no matter how few, will seize the tools of government and power and impose upon the rest of us the conditions necessary for national survival, but at catastrophic cost to our personal freedom and our democratic form of government. The first is the pattern of a decaying Rome. The second is that of any nation that allows itself to move into chaos and social disorganization, for whenever in history a group of people have been faced with a choice of freedom carried to anarchic license, or order carried to repression, repression has won. And it is patently clear why this is true—because a people who pursue freedom to the point of anarchy gradually lose the personal strength and the determination to defend themselves, while the attitudes associated with the wish to repress are consistent with the strength to do so. In a society whose members become preoccupied with the expression of their personal freedom, the sense of personal responsibility and accountability is lost. When that occurs, the delicate balance between freedom and responsibility, contemplated by the Jeffersonian philosophy and the single most important foundation stone of our democracy, falls away. And with it eventually fall our system of government, our ideals, and our way of life.

Is it already too late? Are we already so committed to the conditions of life that have developed in our country over the past few decades that we cannot mobilize the strength to turn us from this path? Indeed, the process of compromise and ease-seeking is deeply established among us. We have become accustomed to not taking a stand. Again and again we excuse irresponsibility. Again and again we call no one to account for actions that are patently destructive. We seem to care little, or hardly to note at all, as this process of not-taking-a-stand-until-it's-too-late weakens the institutions of society. We allow the most nauseating and irrational actions to go on under the mantle of free speech, and the destruction of property, interference with the rights of others, and attacks on our personal safety to be justified as reasonable expressions of "political" beliefs. We have schooled ourselves well in how not to take a stand on the small, day-to-day issues; is it already too late to take a stand on the fundamental ones?

Early in this book, the massive problems of our international and domestic life were reviewed, and their complexity and lack of susceptibility to quick or easy solutions was emphasized. It is clear that these problems will only succumb to the most careful, tireless, devoted, and rational effort. If, however, this kind of effort can be brought to bear, these problems stand an excellent chance of being solved. The economic potential, the technological base, and the productive capacity are all present. The basic motive of all men to survive provides a general incentive to solve world problems rather than destroy ourselves. Reasonably considered, our chances to solve our political and social problems are quite good. But there are two steps in the process of solving any problem—the first is assuring that the tools are available to do the job, and the second is picking up the tools and doing the job. The first step is basically technological and economic, but the second is essentially psychological. And as we have seen, the psychological preparation of a growing number of our children is such that we may reasonably doubt whether they will pick up those tools. And our own psychological condition may be such that we do not have the strength or resolve to make sure our children again get that preparation.

It is reasonable to examine in slightly different terms how well we are doing in preparing our young people, by precept and example, for participation in a free, democratic society. To review briefly what was discussed earlier, we may note that the strength of the democratic system, as conceived by Jefferson, rests upon some very basic qualities and attitudes of its members. These attributes, which are essentially psychological in their origin, although economic and political in their expression, must be broadly present among the citizenry if democracy as ideally conceived is to work. Taking these attributes in no particular order and with no effort to be comprehensive, the list would certainly include the following: the ability to exercise reason and logical judgment in pursuit of personal satisfaction balanced against the social interest and the long-run good; the capacity to conduct one's own affairs, to be competent and resourceful as an individual, and to gain a sense of satisfaction and worth therefrom; the willingness to give one's productive best to his work, and to be judged on the merits thereof; a trust in and attitude of charitable good faith toward one's fellows; sufficient denial of one's immediate satisfaction to harbor resources against the future; integrity and honesty as a requirement for the support of a reasoned approach to problems; and an appreciation of the delicate balance between freedom and responsibility.

In our own lives, in our society, and in our treatment of our children, how well are we securing and perpetuating these basic attitudes, which must be present if our democracy is to work? Since I have already discussed many of these matters, a brief look at each is sufficient for our present purpose. On the matter of reason and logical judgment, we see our lives and our decisions increasingly dominated by emotions of every kind, and our free access to facts objectively presented impeded by bias and more emotion. On the matter of personal interest and the long-run good, we are busily engaged in over-using our resources and taxing our personal and national budgets to the point or runaway inflation. Similar attitudes of selfishness and short-run interest are at work in the matter of immediate satisfaction versus harboring resources for the future. What about our sense of competence and resourceful-ness as individuals? We see it pushed aside by the mass society and crushed by the bureaucracies, which give the individual no credit for reason, energy, or competence. Where do we stand on the matter of individual productivity and a willing-ness to be judged on merit? We excuse the slipshod, reward and encourage the mediocre, and resist the suggestion that differential talent and motivation may have differential value to the society as a whole, mistaking the political proposition that "all men are created equal" for the psychological reality that some turn out to be more energetic and skillful, and thus of more general social value, than others. What of trust, good faith, integrity, and honesty? In their place we find suspicion, adversary confrontations even when a mutual goal is sought, deliberate deceit, compromise, expediency, and a general degradation of human relationships. And regarding the most crucial consideration of all, the recognition that individual responsibility is a sine qua non of personal freedom, we have instead the repeated example that anyone may do anything he wants, whenever he wants, without accountability or con-cern for the infringement of the freedom and rights of others. As an example to our children, and as a basis for developing the steadfast, purposive citizens who must carry the responsi-bility for the survival of our democracy, the present state of our society has precious little to recommend it.

Can we arrest this trend toward decadence and once more bring to bear on our problems the qualities of character that made us the greatest nation in the world? Is the great dream which is the American ideal to die in a despond of weakness, dissipation, and dirt? Are we to founder and eventually sink, glutted by the material luxury that reflects one aspect of the success of the system? Or can we rise above the temptation to rest on our past achievements and to play our plastic fiddles while the cities of the republic burn?

On these figurative but fundamental questions, as much

as on the issues of nuclear war, pollution, race relations, and the mass society, does our future rest. The answer to these questions lies in what we are willing to do, *now*, to repair ourselves. We are not powerless cogs in the mass society, and we should stop acting as if we were. We are not helpless victims of bureaucracy or the affluent economy. And we need not be weak, dissolute, incompetent, and decadent. There still lies within us the heritage of the Founding Fathers, with its matchless blend of idealism and horse sense. We have not yet lost the power to control our lives and to shape a society of decent, responsible, free men. The question is not whether we can, but whether we will.

How can we do it? Some of the steps are simple, and require only the efforts of each of us as individuals. Others will take more doing, and demand concerted political and social action. Let us start with a few simple things that every individual can do to restore a basic sense of competence and personal strength. First, each of us can begin to do more things for himself, to shed the fat of affluence and the powerlessness and dependence that grow as we further enmesh ourselves in the mass, bureaucratic society. Instead of feeling that we must ride or be taken everywhere, we can begin to walk. Who would be harmed by walking two miles to work, or painting his own house, or caring for his own yard? Why call someone to do something you can easily do for yourself, or can learn to do without much effort? "It would take too much time," you say, "and I have more important things to do." Is anything more important than learning to rely on ourselves, and is anything more vital than to demonstrate to our children that the individual, using his own wits and energies, can be less dependent on others? We can also set an example of less self-indulgence. Rather than basing our decision to buy something on whether we want it, we might begin to ask the question, "Do I need it?" What is the advantage of a power lawnmower over a hand mower, except that it makes it a bit easier and quicker to mow the lawn? The benefit of the power device must be weighed against the need for exercise, the added pollution of the atmosphere, and the using up of our natural resources. Beyond the fact that it goes fast, quickly taking one nowhere, what is the advantage of a snowmobile over a quiet walk through the fields and the snowy woods? If we were to walk, we might even have time to see and cherish the tiny beauties of the woods and fields, which we have waited all week to visit. As an experiment, it would be interesting and educational for any family of four that lives above the poverty level—that is, makes more than five thousand dollars a year—to decide to impose a 10 percent cut in their expenditures on themselves. Among those with higher incomes, the educational value of this experiment will multiply if the self-imposed cut is on the order of 20-30 percent, instead of 10 percent. What would this do? The economic effect to the consumer society might be troublesome at first, but two benefits might accrue. First, the effect of reduced demand might bring some pressure against inflation and restore a degree of consumer control over prices. Second, it would be a practical example to our children that harboring resources for the future is a value we truly believe in, that economic security is not guaranteed, and that we do not have to act like self-indulgent pigs just because we have the means to do so. "Well," you ask, "then why work so hard if we are not going to have the immediate material benefits of our work?" The reasons are several—because you are thinking of the future, because you are trying to set an example in self-discipline, and because you as an individual are thereby doing something that will add to the strength of the nation. The disciplined, rational life finally comes down to a matter of the individual; those of us not already corrupted by the conditions around us have a special obligation to maintain standards, first within ourselves, and then by influencing the rest of society to do the same.

At the level of the family, many things can be done. Of foremost importance, we must recognize that children cannot be raised effectively in our spare time. Those who do not want the responsibility of having children simply should not have them; but if they do, they had better stand up to the responsibility of making a life for themselves and their children in which the children are not relegated to the position of nuisances. The devaluation of the importance of children, the replacement of attention with indulgence and of our disciplinary responsibilities as parents with a kind of detached permissiveness, contribute most significantly to the breakdown of family life and eventually of civilization. Doing an adequate

241

job as a parent and trying to take full advantage of the glittering pleasures of the affluent society may simply not be consistent with each other. We must pay much more attention than we have to the process of offering interpersonal satisfaction to our children and gaining it for ourselves in a solid family life. As another educational exercise, I suggest that you program the next two weeks of your life in such a way that all your leisure time, and all your pleasure-seeking, is limited to family activities. For two short weeks, try to see what you can find to do with your spouse and your children that does not require you to spend any money. See what things in your life already offer the opportunity for satisfaction, including simple conversation, walking around your neighborhood or your community, or playing some game that all can enjoy. In this experiment, you are allowed to use the car for family purposes once each weekend, providing you do not drive it more than twenty miles in toto. You may invite friends in to visit, so long as you do not spend extra money for the entertainment. You are allowed to visit friends or neighbors, if the same restrictions are understood to apply. But no movies, no bowling, no eating out, no spending on toys or other goodies. And if you want the test really to be a stringent one, pull the plug on your television set for the entire two weeks. "I would go completely up the wall," said one of my neighbors when I suggested this to him. If this is your reaction, please ask yourself why. Are your spouse and your children not adequate competition for the "things" of the affluent society? Is there not sufficient love and order and devotion among you to support your psychological needs for even so brief a period? Have you lost the interpersonal glue that holds people together in the common pursuit of goodness and decency? I hope not, but if you have, there is no time like the present to begin to stick things back together again. And who knows, you may even find strength, love, satisfaction, and mutual trust and respect in the process. I guarantee that if you can manage to complete this experiment successfully, and do not turn into an irritated bully in the process, you will find that you have a better basis for setting limits, maintaining standards, and establishing self-discipline in the children than you have now. Children do not need or even want the material gimcracks so many parents provide as a substitute for close family relationships. Rather, they need a sense of importance as individuals and a basis for seeing themselves as competent human beings who are secure enough to deal with difficult problems. There is no better way to develop these attitudes than with a stable family life, and with the example of parents functioning as such persons themselves.

The family also offers the opportunity to develop in our children characteristics necessary to their successful functioning in a free, democratic society. In the family, reason and logical judgment, as opposed to emotion, can first be demonstrated as a means for dealing with difficult problems. It is in the family also that personal satisfaction is first balanced against the common good, and that one experiences the concept that there are standards of acceptable performance, learning that he will be judged fairly on his merits. Moreover, in the family the child first learns the value of honesty, integrity, and good faith in dealings among human beings. Finally, in the family the child may be taught that freedom implies responsibility, and that internal limits must be developed so that more oppressive external controls will not be imposed. The benefits of this kind of family life include the production of children who are comfortable and effective as citizens in a democratic society, as well as the development of a deeper, more satisfying set of human relationships, far outweighing in their reward to the individual all the material indulgences of the affluent society.

The family's responsibility for its children does not end at the front door. In its relationships with the neighborhood and the school, the family has an obligation to pursue the same basic values mentioned above. While it is necessary sometimes to insure that the child is not exploited or brutalized by some agent of society, it is also mandatory that the parents make common purpose with neighbors and school authorities in setting and enforcing standards of behavior and performance. It serves no purpose to give the child the impression that he is not accountable to others, for to do so only adds to the difficulties discussed in this book. The family must extend its protection when the child needs it, but it must also support other persons and social institutions in their attempts to develop responsible independence in the child.

At the level of the neighborhood, there are also many

missed opportunities to establish conditions encouraging a sense of belonging, loyalty, and personal competence in the child. Neighbors, no matter how diverse their occupational pursuits, have a natural common purpose and common interest. There is no reason why the neighborhood cannot offer a reliable, satisfying base for mutual pursuits, support, and recreation. If the child has the experience of seeing his family functioning within and gaining satisfaction from relationships in this extended community, he gets a much more solid basis for personal security in larger, more remote groups. Thus, neighborhood organizations of various kinds, designed to promote a feeling of identity and personal worth, can offer the child an excellent foundation for the development of his individuality within a framework of responsible group membership. For example, nearly all the things for which children now rely on larger and less personal groups might as easily be conducted in the neighborhood. Activity groups, music groups, dramatic groups, sports groups, and the like are all within the capacity of the neighborhood, not only for the benefit of the children, but also as a way of providing satisfying and disciplined outlets for the adult members of the family. Enmeshed as we are in the impersonality of the mass society, it would be quite natural and salutary to return to a smaller group base such as the neighborhood, to remove the impersonality and lack of direct interpersonal satisfaction. Smaller, closer, more reliable units of social organization are vital in reconstructing the social fabric of the democratic ideal, and the neighborhood seems an excellent place to start.

With a neighborhood social unit as a base, small groups of citizens can be extremely effective in bringing their influence to bear on other social institutions influencing the lives of our children and the values to which they are exposed. While the opportunity still remains—that is, before we let centralization and social manipulation take them away from us—both individuals and small groups can successfully insist on an educational program in our local schools that will again prepare our children for responsible participation in our democracy. It is in the power of neighborhoods to demand and get an educational program, at least at the elementary school level, that combines humanity, creativity, and broad opportunity with discipline, rigor, and fundamentals. Without the former, education can be narrow and oppressive, but without the latter, the process is not education at all. What a remarkable experiment it would be to turn over to the citizens of a city block, or a small neighborhood, the complete control of an elementary school designed for no more than fifty children aged five to thirteen, and no more than two teachers. Give the neighborhood the power to hire and dismiss the teachers, to determine the curriculum and the standards for behavior. To make the experiment even more dramatic, give this responsibility to forty or fifty families in a close-knit neighborhood in a black ghetto in the central city. Put as many dollars of support per child into the program as are now going into the average school program in the state. What kind of elementary school program would you get? I am completely confident it would be one that is able to produce kids who can read, write, do arithmetic, and have the other preparation necessary for competent high school work. They would also be disciplined and have a sense of individual accomplishment and self-respect, and in general would be better fitted to face the problems of the world than the same children passing through our present bureaucratized, overspecialized, overcrowded, permissive system. Might we not once more trust parents to insure the kind of education they believe their children need—at least sufficiently to release a few, on an experimental basis, from the chains of the mass society? The public school system is part of a total system of government supposedly designed to serve us, not to master us; what better place to try our strength and individual power than upon the unit of government closest to most of us, the elementary school.

"Not practical," you may say. "Inefficient." "Try it and see," I respond. And consider whether twenty-five elementary school children can be educated by one teacher, in one self-contained freestanding classroom, under the control of their own parents. My budget for the operation would look like this: Teacher's salary: twelve thousand dollars; prorated annual cost of building and permanent equipment: three thousand dollars; utilities: twelve hundred dollars; books and supplies: twelve hundred and fifty dollars; lease of nearby lot for playground: twelve hundred dollars; transportation: zero; administrative costs: zero; bureaucratic costs: zero. Total outlay per child: approximately seven hundred and fifty dollars. Add whatever options your neighborhood might desire, add or subtract variables depending on local conditions, then compare your total with the amount it now costs to educate one child for one year in your school system. Make sure you know something about teachers' salaries and building costs, then do your own arithmetic and decide whether you might prefer a locally controlled system. Be prepared to face the responsibilities, because you may have to serve your term on the school board or be asked to support the teacher's attempt to discipline your child, or you may have to get used to having your child home for lunch, since the school no longer will attempt to do all these things alone. But you might like to do your own cost-benefit analysis, and see how well satisfied you would be with the total product, including the effect on you and your family, your neighborhood, and your individual rights.

Consider some of the other things a few neighbors might do to directly influence other conditions of the society in which their children are growing up. Suppose a few junior high school children are terrorizing their peers or extorting money or property from them, and the school authorities seem unable to do anything about it. A few adults, who want to stop this and are willing to give a little time, can have a tremenduous influence simply by being present at the scene. You might offer your help to the school in this way, and the school may be glad to have it. If not, put yourselves in the vicinity anyway. It is not necessary to intimidate or punish anyone; simply be there. Or suppose you have reason to believe a certain area or establishment is the center of drug activity among young kids. Take a group and go there and simply let your presence serve its natural deterrent effect. If your community has a crime problem, take advantage of the public records of the police and the courts to alert your friends and neighbors as to the nature and extent of criminal activity, the effectiveness of the police in dealing with the crimes, and the attitude of the courts toward the persons convicted.

In another vein, suppose you have in your town a few scurvy examples of the counterculture. It is not unusual for such groups to set about deliberately drawing younger children into the orbit of their activity and influence. They may promise instant gratification in the form of total freedom, uninhibited or orgiastic sex, or the phony philosophy of drugs. They may deliberately encourage further alienation in children who already have problems at home, by offering an underground refuge, subtly condemning the values of the parents, or preaching the glories of the counterculture. Such actions can be dealt with in many direct ways: by a group of parents investigating and publicizing their activities; by youngsters who recognize their depravity starting a truth campaign; and by utilizing the full force of existing law, with such charges as statutory rape, contributing to the delinquency of minors, vagrancy, and even kidnapping. In any case, it is not necessary for responsible citizens to stand helplessly by, while their communities are turned into sewers and their children's lives are ruined.

Or, suppose a local minister is caught up in the romance and excitement of activist involvement in political issues. He may be carrying on these activities out of the persuasion of his conscience, and you cannot, of course, make any judgments about his motives, at least not publicly. But if his political concerns begin to dominate his spiritual ones, he had better run for public office, where the full force of his talents and beliefs can be put to practical use. And you can assist him in this effort by refusing to contribute your money to his personal sinecure, since he should surely have a sufficient degree of courage in his own convictions to suffer a bit of inconvenience on their behalf.

In short, wherever conditions in your community seem to indicate attitudes of decadence and tendencies toward the breakdown of society, direct action can assert both your power as an individual and the influence of small groups in bringing such activities under control. It is not necessary to break the law to do these things. You do not have to pour dirt over welfare records to dramatize the failure of such programs, or burn down public housing units to illustrate the dehumanizing conditions imposed by this operation of the bureaucracy. Within the law, there are opportunities to assert yourself in no uncertain terms against conditions adding to our social decay. It only takes courage, commitment, a bit of imagination, and a willingness to communicate facts to the members of your immediate community.

On the question of facts, another interesting community activity can be developed around an analysis of the information and bias in the public communications media. As an exercise in objectivity, take any issue of current concern, and accumulate as much exposure to it as the media will provide. Look for examples of deliberate or inadvertent selectivity, distortion, or emotional appeal. Compare the examples you find with those uncovered by your neighbors. Then, on your own, put together a brief presentation of the facts and the various interpretations that may be gained from them. A little thought in collaboration with a neighborhood group may enable you to produce a fact sheet or a news analysis of your own, which, if you are really ambitious, you might like to mimeograph and distribute around the community. The analysis should be designed to point out the full implications of each interpretation, the possible bias in the gathering and selection process, and, most importantly, the effect on an orderly, reasoned process of solving problems resulting from the slanted view.

Earlier, I suggested that you do your own cost-benefit analysis of the educational programs to which your children are exposed. By this, I merely mean for you to determine the effects of a program on the goals you have for society, balanced against the immediate and extended costs of the effort. This technique is increasingly used in business and government. However, as now applied, the analysis is largely in terms of short-term goals and such considerations as efficiency, profit, and the effect on the people immediately involved. It makes better sense to test the effects of various programs in regard to long-term considerations and the basic strength of the system. Massive federal programs, for example, may meet the immediate needs of certain groups of people, but at the same time have a destructive effect on the more fundamental matters of individual strength and competence, reasoned solutions, discipline, the balance between freedom and responsibility and between personal satisfaction and the general social interest, and so on. In short, it is time to apply the hard test of results to the hundreds of programs the bureaucracies have devised as "solutions" to our problems. If any of these fail to meet the test of strengthening the individual against the mass society, developing persons with a sense of self-respect and competence, maintaining the internal balance between free-

248

dom and responsibility, or in any other way fail to contribute to the development of traits necessary for effective participation in a free democratic society, they are not worth perpetuating. We must apply the most rigorous possible test to such programs, not merely in terms of their immediate economic effects, but, even more importantly, in terms of their effects on the basic psychology and attitudes of our people. However beneficial or humane such programs may appear on the surface or in the short run, they are ultimately destructive if they take away from us and our children the strength and resolve we must have to cope with the serious challenges of the future.

When faced with the tremendous power of the bureaucracies, the ordinary person may suffer from a quite natural sense of helplessness and inadequacy. However, the ability of determined individuals to recapture greater control over their own affairs is immense. The massive organizations most Americans must deal with are the federal government and the giant corporations, but the same principles apply to all bureaucracies. The basic power of any bureaucracy lies in money, which we, the people, provide. If the flow of support is cut off, the bureaucracy begins to shrink. The cutting off of support to an industrial corporation is relatively easy to accomplish, and the managers of such organizations, recognizing this fact, tend to be responsive to consumer attitudes. They can be made much more so through the freely taken, concerted actions of individuals and small groups. Suppose you are dissatisfied with the response of a corporation to a clear need to cut down on the pollution its factories are contributing to the environment. Or suppose you think a product is overpriced, inferior, or detrimental in some way to the disciplined, principled way of life. There are many things you can do. The most basic is not to buy the product, and to tell the corporation why. The next is to advertise in some way that you are dissatisfied. If an automobile dealer sold you a lemon, park it in the vicinity of his showroom, with a sign on it telling your story. Or if a corporation, through its advertising, is supporting a TV program that subtly tears down the standards of society, let it know that you do not intend to buy its product until the program is stopped or changed. If a newspaper is habitually biased, give its advertisers the same message. The place to attack a corporate industry, or a chain store, or any other private arm of the free enterprise system, is in its pocketbook. And all it takes is a little common sense and imagination, and the ability to discipline yourself not to buy immediately everything you think you want. Fortunately, it is still within our free choice as individuals to apply sanctions to assure that corporations support our efforts to create a better society.

It is not so certain that the bureaucracy of the federal government can be thus influenced. But if we are to salvage the democratic ideal, we must unite to take back to ourselves some of the government's enormous power. For in its present philosophy and operation, the governmental bureaucracy is the principal culprit pushing us toward even greater dependency, social mediocrity, and individual impotence. Governmental programs are only remotely subjected to any tests at all. Efficiency and consumer response are of little consequence. And the vital psychological questions, concerning what its programs do to people's basic attitudes, are never asked. Congress has become so accustomed to increasing the flow of tax monies that it makes few decisions as to whether a program should be continued, but only considers how many millions or billions should be provided to perpetuate it. In the recent history of our government, have we ever closed an agency or terminated a program? If so, the occasions are very rare. It is interesting to speculate about what would happen if we could, by some magic or massive surge of public resistance, force upon the national government the 10 percent or 20 percent budget cut that I advocated for families a few pages above. Perhaps we would then force a reasoned consideration of priorities, and a set of judgments including more than the examination of short-term effects. There is no mystery in the growth of government to the point that it is out of control—we allow it, or even encourage it, by our mistaken belief that it will somehow provide the easy way out of our problems. When the mere existence of massive government contributes to the conditions that rob us of the will to solve problems in any way except by making it more massive and more powerful, it is past time to call a halt.

At levels more immediately responsive to the opinions of individual citizens, there is growing evidence that we have had enough of bureaucratized, mass, collectivized solutions. Cities, school districts, and even states are increasingly meeting resistance to added taxation for programs that have flagrantly failed or are advocated on some flimsy basis. Whether this phenomenon grows out of a reasoned conclusion about the need for the individual to reimpose discipline in our public life, or whether it is merely due to people wanting more affluence for themselves, I cannot say. But whatever the motive, the application of similar resistance to the endless growth of the federal bureaucracy is long overdue. And if we, the citizens, should succeed in caging that mighty monster, what a surge of individual power might appear among us!

The individual or the small group has little hope of obtaining such an impressive reform. It will take a concerted, organized, and persistent effort of great numbers of people to return us to self-determination, self-confidence, and self-respect. Where shall we turn to find the commitment and readiness to sacrifice immediate ease for the future good? Where shall we find the devotion to discipline and decency to arrest our slide to decadence? Where are the men and women of good faith, honesty, and integrity to restore dignity to our human relationships? Who are the custodians of sufficient common sense and mental discipline to return objectivity and reason to our decisions? In what corner of our country dwell the people who are willing to do their productive best and stand to judgment on their merits? Where does the responsible exercise of freedom flourish, and who cares about our future? In short, where can America turn in this hour of her need?

There are some obvious places not to look. The pampered radicals, whose hatred and irrationality are already devoted to vilifying the nation and its symbols, could hardly care less. We can scarcely expect that the dropouts, freaks, and misfits of the counterculture will rouse from their drugged impotence to pursue any noble venture. Only frustration will result from a continued reliance on soft-hearted, softer-headed social theorists whose sense of responsibility to the nation barely goes further than viewing it as a laboratory for experiments in short-term remedies and long-term futility. And we need hardly expect a dramatic turn-about from those timorous compromisers, sitting in positions of supposed responsibility, who systematically give away every principle for the sake of temporary peace.

Yet as one moves across the length and breadth of America, around its cities, into the suburbs, and through the towns and farms, one sees again and again that the people we need are there to be called upon. There is still a vast reservoir of strength and purpose in America—a commitment to decency and discipline, to productivity, to responsibility and reason, and to the value of the individual, pursuing his way to freedom despite the repression of the mass society and the lack of faith of the bureaucrats. Individual competence is found everywhere—among sincere teachers who fight to maintain standards in the face of defiance and permissiveness; among the men of the construction crafts, who still take pride in a job well done; among the teamsters who tough-haul their rigs along the freeways; and among ranchers and farmers, who know that survival is not guaranteed, and that an added personal effort and an inch or two of rainfall can make the difference one way or the other. The devotion to reason, integrity, and intellectual discipline is seen in the engineers and technicians who have given us the means to master the environment and are now working on the means to save it; in the scholar who fights to maintain the value of truth in the face of emotionalism; in the honest newsman who yet believes that Americans have the good sense to make the right decisions if they are provided with the facts; and in the pithy cynicism of the Manhattan cab driver, who can spot a phony four blocks away. The belief in our future is testified to by the mass of students who quietly go about the business of preparing themselves to meet our problems with steadfast purpose and patient effort; by the older citizen who harbors his resources to insure himself a better life than that promised by the pittance of Social Security; by the suburban housewife who knows that the good of her children is best served by maintaining a decent home and community, and not by responding to every self-indulgent whim; and by the businessman who invests and builds, rather than squandering his profits on his immediate personal ease. The value of productivity is well understood by the workers in the nation's industrial plants, who have seen its worth in their own lives, and who properly resent the burden placed on them by the nonproductive, the indolent, and those seeking a society where everything is "free." And the importance of balancing freedom with responsibility is still understood by the mass of citizens, who recognize that the orderly, lawful processes of the American system are the most fundamental basis of a civilized society.

These, then, are the people on whom our future rests. They are the people of Middle America, which is defined not by geography, or race, or socioeconomic status, but by a commitment to the principles on which our nation was founded. Our difficulty is not that the system has failed us, but that too many of us have failed the system. Too many have begun to take it for granted that security is automatic, that ease is guaranteed, and that somebody else will do the job for us. Too many have forgotten that we are merely one nation among many, that there remains in the world a powerful surge to compete and to improve, and that other peoples are making the sacrifices necessary to get where we already are. Too many have assumed that freedom is merely to be enjoyed, and have forgotten that it must be worked at, and defended, if it is not to be lost.

On the actions of the great majority of Middle Americans, then, rests our future. If scores of millions of us continue to close our eyes to what is happening in our midst, and go blithely about our permissive and self-indulgent ways, America will surely fall, and its fall will not be long in coming. If, however, we devote ourselves to the task, we can yet emerge from these troubled moments as a proud, strong, united people, and the idealistic dream which is the American system can perhaps extend its benefits throughout the world. What must we do? Permit me to suggest the following as items of the highest priority:

1) We must restore discipline to our society, beginning in our minds, our personal lives, our families, and our communities, and gradually extend the practices of the disciplined life to every aspect of our national existence. This means that we must insist on accountability, the just and uniform enforcement of the law, and the acceptance of responsibility for actions taken in the name of freedom.

2) We must assert the superiority of reason and considered judgment over emotion and impulse as a means for solv-

ing problems and as a basis for an ordered society of free men. In this connection, we must take into greater account the long-run implications of decisions, rather than merely responding to expediency and the need for immediate relief from pressure.

3) We must reduce self-indulgence, and recognize that material comfort and personal ease are not all there is to life, even in an affluent society. We must be prepared to sacrifice some of our immediate personal satisfaction for the future general good, and to set an example to our children that we care about what kind of world they are left to inhabit. As a corollary, we must recommit ourselves to productivity, and must insist that people who demand an equal share of its benefits participate equally in the effort required to insure it.

4) We must restore the value of the individual in our society, by taking back to ourselves some of the power that has been seized by the bureaucracies. To do this, we must again develop pride in personal competence, quality performance, and individual resourcefulness. Our public educational system must foster the development of such characteristics, rather than a superficial acquaintance with vague general concepts. We may also have to sacrifice some of our commitment to efficiency as an overriding value, and weigh its benefits against the depersonalizing effects and massive bureaucracy it seems to produce.

5) We must recognize that the family is the basic building block of society, and focus more of our efforts on it, no longer viewing home merely as a place to sleep and park the car. Family relationships must provide discipline, but must also offer the deep satisfactions of love, mutual respect, trust, and dignity. Through the family we must communicate to our children that freedom implies responsibility, that pride and self-respect come from competence and achievement, and that the fundamental satisfactions of life are ultimately found in deep, permanent emotional commitments to others.

6) We must vigorously and forcefully attack the signs of decadence wherever they appear, and must stop confusing being human with being destructively permissive. We must quit acting like helpless, frightened, impotent people, and must demand the restoration of quality and decency to every aspect of our national life. The more we are intimidated by

emotionalism, threats, non-negotiable demands, and violence, the more we encourage the irresponsible minority to believe that such tactics are valid. We are faced with some very tough challenges, both internally and externally, and we must be tough and resolute in dealing with them.

In short, let us assert once more our strength as individuals and as a people, and from that base, move forward in unity and determination to attack the pressing problems of our nation and the world. To do otherwise is a betrayal of the faith placed in us as free and responsible citizens by the inspired men who founded our nation.

THE LIBERAL MIDDLE CLASS: MAKER OF RADICALS

Richard L. Cutler

Johnny is a radical. A Maoist. And from the middle class. His liberal parents, with a modest home in the suburbs, loved Johnny, met his every need, sent him to the respected local schools where he got mostly A's and B's, even trotted him off, regularly, to Sunday school and church "because every child needs a little religion." Then, after years of scrimping, they sent him to a proper college.

But somewhere Johnny revolted — against family, school, church, country. It didn't happen overnight. But it happened. Why? How?

This important work is one of the first serious attempts to answer these questions by spotlighting the largely overlooked liberal middle class, spawning ground of the New Left. Few men bring better qualifications to this work than Dr. Richard L. Cutler, himself a former radical and over ten years professor of psychology at the universities of Michigan and California at Berkeley, and now a successful child psychologist and family man.

Before turning from radicalism, Dr. Cutler got to know many of the leading New Leftists, Timothy Leary and Tom Hayden among them. He was their friend, often their counselor. He studied their backgrounds, listened to their frustrations, learned their uncensored views on sex, the family, drugs, education, Marx, Mao, America. Dr. Cutler knows the radical mind from the inside. Now he lays it bare in this thoughtful book.

Dr. Cutler reviews the influences that helped sire these radicals: the glorification of sex, permissiveness in our courts and schools and homes, tolerance of drugs, the welfare mentality, doubleminded politicians—but he digs deeper, too. To the equation he adds Mom's and Dad's nights out and weekend vacations "to get away from the kids"; their easy acceptance of everything the *Times* and TV had to say; their failure ("We're just too busy") to check out Johnny's teachers and textbooks, to attend church with him (where they might have been shocked at the preacher's latest exhortation); the dozens of other "little" things that shape today's radical.

Shunning the conventional remedies that have already shown themselves threadbare, Dr. Cutler revives virtuous—and surprising—solutions that concerned parents, educators and all who work with young people will welcome as a fresh breeze. And none too soon.